Centerville Library
Washington-Centerville Public Library
DISCARD
Centerville, OHIO

Wheels On Fire

My Year of Driving . . .
and Surviving . . .
in Iraq

D1319815

Michelle Zaremba

with Christine Sima

Hellgate Press
Ashland, Oregon

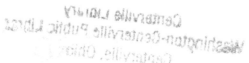

Wheels on Fire

©2008 by Michelle Zaremba & Christine Sima
Published by L&R Publishing/Hellgate Press

All rights reserved. No part of this publication may be reproduced or used in any form or by any means, graphic, electronic or mechanical, including photocopying, recording, taping, or information storage and retrieval systems without written permission of the publisher.

Hellgate Press
An Imprint of L&R Publishing
P.O. Box 3531
Ashland, Oregon 97520

info@hellgatepress.com

Book designed & edited by Harley B. Patrick
Cover design by Lynn Dragonette

Library of Congress Cataloging-in-Publication Data

Zaremba, Michelle, 1976-
Wheels on fire : my year of driving (and surviving) in Iraq / Michelle Zaremba with Christine Sima. -- 1st ed.
    p. cm.
Includes bibliographical references and index.
ISBN 978-1-55571-656-1 (alk. paper)
1. Iraq War, 2003---Personal narratives, American. 2. Zaremba, Michelle, 1976- 3. Truck drivers--Iraq--Biography. 4. Truck drivers--United States--Biography. I. Sima, Christine, 1978- II. Title.
DS79.76Z37 200 2008
956.7044'342092--dc22
[B]

                                   2008034832

Printed and bound in the United States of America
First Edition 10 9 8 7 6 5 4 3 2 1

Dedication

To Mom and Dad, for your love, support and encouragement. I wouldn't be the person I am today without the living examples you've taught me of tireless work ethic, love and compassion. Thank you for loving me that much.

- Michelle Zaremba

To the two veterans in my life:
To my Dad, I am so proud to be your daughter.
And to Matt for believing in me.
I love you both.

- Christine Sima

Contents

Foreword

It is amazing how many times the lives of two people can cross before fate steps in. I first met Michelle Zaremba when we were both working in a steel mill in Cleveland, Ohio. Our fathers had worked there all of our lives, but it wasn't until one summer during college when we were hired to work as laborers there that we met. I never dreamed we would become war correspondents a few years later.

We later worked as nannies together while we both wrapped up our college careers at Kent State University. Michelle graduated a year ahead of me and went to Dayton, Ohio to start her career. I still had another year to complete. We lost touch, as many do after college, but I always wondered what happened to her.

A couple years later, I was killing time in the newsroom where I worked when a co-worker mentioned there was a story in my inbox that I might be interested in covering. Immediately when I saw the signature, I sat upright. The woman's daughter—Michelle Zaremba—was being deployed to Iraq within days and she wanted the paper to do a story about it. After some smooth talking, I convinced my editor to allow me and a photographer to go to the training camp in Indiana where Michelle was stationed.

Just before I left the base, Michelle agreed to send letters home to me that I could publish in the newspaper. Without hesitation, fate took control again. If Michelle had known how many of the letters were going to be printed initially, I don't think she would have agreed. And had I known I would have to later write a news article about my friend who was ambushed in Iraq, I don't think I would have readily jumped at the chance.

As I backed out of the parking spot, Michelle, dressed in fatigues, smiled and waved like she was headed home for Spring Break. She looked so confident, yet I was deflated. I didn't think she would make it home alive.

It might sound outlandish, but it's hard to say what might have happened if we didn't have to work in that steel mill together. But maybe that's the best part. The lesson they preached behind those filthy doors was if we stayed in college, we wouldn't have to work in a place that dirty. Instead, she got to trade it for a mouthful of desert sand drenched in the sweat of knowing people directly around her were trying to kill her. Cheers to our college diplomas.

But as I sit here a few years later, waiting for Michelle to deliver her first child, I know that fate has carried us to a place where our friendship is cemented in the memories of newspaper clippings. We opened the eyes of people who could never have imagined a day in the life of a soldier until we brought it home to their kitchen table while they drank their morning coffee. We put a face on an American soldier who could have perished in an ambush, but instead lived to tell a tale similar to thousands of sons and daughters who have fought for our country. Both proud and humbled by my small role in telling Michelle's story, I will be forever grateful for fate bringing home my brave friend.

- Christine Sima
March 2008

Christine Sima (l) and Michelle Zaremba (r) in the barracks for a quick interview before Michelle leaves for Iraq

Introduction

The dust has settled over the memories of my time overseas, but the throbbing pain in my back from the weight of my flak vest will never let me forget. As a staff sergeant in the Ohio Army National Guard's 1486th Transportation Unit, I crisscrossed Iraq hundreds of times over the course of a year in a convoy of semi trucks delivering supplies to fellow soldiers stationed throughout the country. It amazes me to think I was fighting a war in Iraq, because I joined the Guard when I was a seventeen-year-old kid looking for direction.

It became pretty clear we were going to be sent to Iraq after September 11, 2001. I was working as a mediation specialist in Dayton, Ohio when I was called to active duty. My civilian job revolved around finding peaceful, agreeable solutions to problems, so it was a little disturbing to think I was headed to a place where passion seemed to strangle logic. I didn't go to be a hero. I went to take care of my guys. I was in command of anywhere from twenty to fifty soldiers in my unit and I was responsible for making sure all of us came home together. There were times I thought some of us wouldn't make it and other times when I thought none of us would make it, but my job as a squad leader was to see to it that we protected each other.

Just days before I was scheduled to leave the United States, my mom sent an email to our local newspaper to see if they were interested in writing a story on my departure. That email landed in the mailbox of a friend from college who was working as a reporter for *The Gazette*. I agreed to write letters home to be published in the newspaper while I was away so that I might be able to show people at home what the life of a soldier was like.

After a year of writing letters, I was sick of it. I didn't want to share what was going on anymore for a myriad of reasons. There were times when I called home and asked my family not to ask questions about where I was or what I was doing because I couldn't answer them for security reasons. When I was home on leave, and shortly after I returned home for good, I dreaded the questions because I didn't want to answer them. These days I pray no one asks questions because I don't remember the answers or I'm trying to forget.

There are hundreds of stories like mine, or rather, thousands. Somewhere in Iraq, a soldier is sleeping on top of a trailer dreaming of the innocence he or she will never regain. And for those who will never make it home to tell their story, and others who can't express the details of such a humbling experience, I hope this represents the hardest journey for us all.

This is the most accurate recollection I have of my days in the desert.

– 1 –

Prelude to Deployment: 2003

February 14, 2003

"Staff Sergeant Zaremba," the voice boomed into my ears.

"Yes," I answered back.

"What's going on?" I managed to sputter before my lieutenant cut me off.

"Don't talk," she commanded. "Just listen."

"This is Lt. Garner with the 1486th Transportation Company. Comply with the following instructions: Do not come in to the armory at this time. Standby either your home phone or your work phone listed in the alert notification roster for further instructions. Do not inform anyone except your employer and immediate family of this notification. This is an official order.

"Do you understand?" she asked.

"Yes."

"Do you have any questions?"

OK, I thought, what the hell did that mean? Where are we going? What do they want us to do?

I was exploding. My head was spinning and I could feel the confusion pulsing through my body. How was I going to break this to my mom? What was I supposed to do with my house? How was I supposed to go to war and leave my whole life behind?

I was standing in the middle of my office still holding the phone when my boss appeared in the doorway. I tried to stare through him, but he knew what was up.

"We have a little problem," I said.

"You got the call didn't you?" he said in a more matter-of-fact voice than an actual question.

I knew this day was coming and I had planned to train a part-time employee in my office to take over my duties while I was gone. I handed her a folder with thirty minutes of instructions and wished her luck. I left without so much as a goodbye to most of my co-workers. Not knowing how much time I had, my other job had to take priority over everything else. If we were going to Iraq and my guys were getting that same call, I needed to know what to tell them. The only way to do that was to get answers and pass them along. I needed to be in Ashland, Ohio.

I whizzed through traffic as I made phone calls to my family on the two-hour drive from Dayton to the armory in Ashland. The paragraph my lieutenant read to me over the phone didn't apply to me because I was a staff sergeant and someone in an authoritative position. I was one of the people who needed to come in early to help make phone calls. I was used to being in charge, but I didn't want anything to do with delivering this order. I couldn't believe I was trapped in a horrible fate that I had brought on myself.

I was seventeen years old when I first joined the National Guard because I wanted to give back to my country. I know it sounds cheesy, but I wanted to help disaster victims and other people who needed it. I didn't realize I could volunteer through AmeriCorps or the Peace Corps, but it probably wouldn't have mattered. I was attracted to the military because of the discipline and the opportunity to learn skills I otherwise wouldn't in the civilian world.

When I was a senior in high school I told my parents about my plan, but I don't think they ever thought I would go through with it until we were sitting across from a recruiter at our kitchen table. We talked to the Army Reserves, but the National Guard just seemed like a better fit for me because there were more benefits and more money for school. I sat there daydreaming about different jobs I wanted to do while my dad ironed out the details of the contracts I had to sign. It's a pretty good thing, too, because I wasn't mature enough to the see the big picture. I needed his signature because I was only seventeen, so he said he would do it if I promised to finish college no matter what. I signed my six-year contract and on 19 July 1994, I officially became a soldier in the Ohio Army National Guard.

During my first six-year tour in the Guard, there were several floods in Ohio where we helped haul hay and deliver fresh water. Although I was trained to fire a weapon and engage in combat, I never really thought much of it. It was a good skill to have, but I didn't think I would ever really need it. I never really thought much about being a truck driver either. I picked a transportation unit because it had the shortest school time compared to the other jobs and there was a truck-driving unit forty-five minutes from my house. Looking back, it's ironic that my life was put at risk convoying through the roads of Iraq all because of a decision I made when I was a teenager.

In 1999, I began working for the City of Dayton's Mediation Center and loved every minute of it. With a degree in Applied Conflict Management from Kent State University, I was so thrilled when I found a job in that field. Every day was a learning experience and my co-workers became like family.

In 2000, I re-enlisted in the Guard and so began my moral dilemma. After September 11, 2001, it was pretty much a given that I would be shipped somewhere. There were always rumors that we were going to Iraq, so I tried not to take on anything new. I attempted to go for my Master's degree, but every time I started a program, something would happen with the Guard and I had to change my plans. I stuck close to home, waiting for the military to decide my fate after that first call that said my unit was going to be mobilized.

In the Guard, there are three stages of mobilization for a unit: The sourcing stage, where units are considered; the alert stage, when units are told to prepare to leave; and mobilization. We thought things would happen pretty quickly once we got that first phone call. It was always in the back of my mind. Someone explained it best when they said it was like being pregnant. You know the baby's coming; it's just a matter of when. You only plan enough to take into account that at any moment, you could deliver. The phone call that came that day at work was a year and a half in the making.

As I neared the Ashland exit, I started fidgeting like a sugared-up kid. I knew I had one more call to make and I didn't want to. It was Valentine's Day and I had plans with my boyfriend of six months to go out that night. I only dated him because I knew I was leaving soon enough. I didn't want to deal with the stress of breaking it off, so it was the perfect out. It was just a casual thing for me and I didn't really care that I wouldn't see him that night or probably ever again, but I didn't think it was right to leave without saying goodbye. I got him on the phone and he sounded annoyed when I explained the situation, but said he understood. I didn't really care about his reaction; goodbye was enough.

I met my parents at an Applebee's and downed three beers at the bar before they arrived. As soon as we sat down, I just blurted out that we were alerted, even though they already knew. I had asked my dad to break the news to my mom before they got there because I couldn't. We drank a beer together and I just remember my mom and the strain in her eyes that never really disappeared until I came home from Iraq permanently. My cell phone started ringing off the hook, so I left for the armory.

When I got there, I felt like I had just walked into a bar. People were standing around smoking and there was a cooler of beer in the middle of the room. It was about 5:00 p.m. when I arrived and some people were already making phone calls. We had until midnight to contact everyone, which sounds like a long time, but seven hours didn't give us much wiggle room to track down people. Some had new cell phone numbers, some of the college kids were back at school and all we had was a home phone number, so it took awhile. Phone call after phone call, we broke the news. There weren't many details to pass along, so all the "standard alert" calls did were to rile up everyone.

Some of the members of my unit spent that night drinking together in a nearby hotel. The war hadn't even started so our conversation revolved around what to expect. We wondered if we were going to live in tents or on the ground and whether we would get showers. We talked about what our roles would be and whether our equipment that had gone through Desert Storm would make it through another war. It helped us think about the things we needed to take with us, but we did it more to cope. Some talked about how they were going to survive a year away from their spouses or children.

I couldn't believe the day started out like any other and then changed from my life to war with one phone call. There had been rumors for some time that we were getting called up, but we didn't really believe it until it happened. It was just after President Bush declared the "War on Terror" and several units were alerted. Our unit had some experience because it had been to Desert Storm, but this war was completely different. In Desert Storm, our unit drove in Saudi Arabia and never set foot in Iraq. This time we knew we would be in the middle of it all. The other units from Ohio that had been deployed before us were writing and telling us what it was like in Iraq. It was frightening.

We waited in Ashland until mid-March of 2003, wondering when we would actually head into combat. It was funny because for the first couple of weeks in Ashland at the armory, every sentence from the leadership began with "when you go." Slowly, that changed to "if and when you go," which eventually became "if you go..."

Clueless of what was really going on, our unit continued to prepare to leave for Iraq. We got our shots and physicals, inspected equipment, and waited. The women had to take pregnancy tests. Needless to say, there were a few praying they got pregnant in the month we were there so they wouldn't have to go. (Some actually did get pregnant, but not on purpose. They were accused of trying to snake out of going to war, but it really wasn't the case.) After the shots and pregnancy tests, we filled out mountains of paperwork. Then we were ready to go.

4

It was so intense for a month, getting ready and saying goodbye to family and friends, and then nothing happened. The call then came to stand down. We were told that we were going to be shipped out within ninety days, so we had to be prepared to leave at a moment's notice. It was enormously frustrating that we spent all that time getting ready and then were told to go home and sit by the phone.

Our unit was put on "stop-loss," which meant no one was allowed to retire or transfer out of the unit. The unit was stuck between February and May. In May, they lifted the stop-loss and those able to leave or retire had to decide what to do. Ninety days came and went without another phone call.

I went home to Dayton and tried to settle in, but it was a little difficult. I didn't have any furniture as I had sold it all to my parents because I really had nowhere to store it. I gave away my computer and anything I could think of before I left. I figured I didn't need it if I was going to be gone for a year—or forever if I didn't make it back.

A month later, I was I was back home again. I started unpacking and went back to my job where they didn't know what to do with me. Trisha, the part-timer, almost quit her other job while I was working for the Guard during that month, but decided that she shouldn't until I heard for sure that we were leaving. I made arrangements for friends to move into my house for the year, but fortunately they waited to terminate their lease until they knew for sure I was leaving.

My supervisor and his wife took me to see a woman from Baghdad who had come to the States to speak about how the war was affecting her country and I wanted to hear her story. She was in charge of a museum for children and involved in an organization that helped build schools and hospitals for children. She was also a teacher. She talked of life in Iraq ten years earlier, amid the old regime and Desert Storm, when the literacy rate dropped in half because of all the fighting and chaos. She described how a children's museum was destroyed when a nearby target was bombed. Seeing how the war had affected the youth of her country, she got together with a friend and worked to repair the damage to the school and bring education to the children.

And then here we come again and bomb Iraq, she said. We destroyed the museum they worked to rebuild. She was angry and upset, but I sensed it wasn't just the United States that aggravated her. It was everyone. She made some good points when she said we supported Saddam until we came in to attack him. I mean, you can't really argue with that. The United States also supported Osama Bin Laden years ago. The United States knew Iraq had

5

weapons of mass destruction because we gave them to them. It was ironic to me that we were going to attack them based on what we had done.

Then here comes this woman who speaks of the destruction and how the lives of thousands are affected for political reasons. She didn't care about the politics; she cared about her city, her fellow Iraqis and the children. She told the other side of the story but she was outnumbered. Surrounded by suicide bombers and foreign troops barking orders at her every day, she just wanted to educate anyone who would listen to how this was affecting the everyday people of Iraq. I respected her for coming to our country, the place where she was considered the enemy, to tell her story. Most of what she said about how the war was affecting the Iraqis never really crossed my mind until she delivered that powerful speech.

The war was on television almost daily and all I heard about was the U.S. troops and their battles, but never about the civilians. Some of the Iraqis were there because they didn't have the resources to leave and others were too proud and wanted to protect their property. I could appreciate that. I could respect a man trying to protect his family.

As I approached her after the speech, I felt even worse that I had to go into her country and support something that hurt her so badly. I didn't believe in the invasion. I didn't understand why we were going. Pearl Harbor was bombed and we had a reason to attack, but this one just didn't make sense to me. They kept talking about getting revenge on terrorists and rooting out weapons of mass destruction that nobody seemed to be able to find. Her frustration made sense. Thoughts zipped through my head while I waited in line to apologize to her for everything that she had been through. I wondered if I should talk to her and tell her that I was a U.S. soldier or just let her know that I had empathy for her. Just as I got to her side, I heard another voice behind me.

"She's a soldier and she's going over there," my boss blurted out.

He was like a father to me, my mentor, and he knew how much I had been agonizing over my situation and the decisions I was forced to make. My heart sank. She looked me straight in the eyes with hate and pain. I was humiliated that she just shared her painful story and I was a representative of the military that did this to her. In her mind, my military brothers and sisters had destroyed her country and killed her people. Even if it was done in self-defense, people were dead on both sides.

I felt I needed to take the responsibility for what the group I represented had done to her country. She asked why I would go and asked how as a woman I could be involved in something like war. Women were supposed to be supportive of the loving, compassionate things, like rebuilding and caretaking, like in her country. I tried to explain to her that it was my job and I didn't have a choice, but I could see the fire in her eyes and the hurt on her face. Then in an instant, her hate and rage turned to compassion and sorrow. She understood.

"I'm so sorry you had to make that choice," she whispered.

That was such a defining moment for me. Tears stung my eyes as she pulled me close to her. I told her I was sorry, but it didn't seem like enough. I admired that she could hug me and support my decision through her own anger. That one encounter instantly shaped the way I felt about going there. That experience made me more mindful of the innocent Iraqi people affected by the war. As the months went on, I thought I had forgotten how much of an impact she had on me, but I guess I really hadn't. It was always in the back of my mind over there when I looked at the people who didn't understand why we were there or what was happening. They didn't care about the politics, they were just trying to live their lives.

November 2003

I was on my way out of my office for a conference when the phone rang.

"Staff Sergeant Zaremba," the voice rang out again.

Son of a bitch, I said to myself.

"This is Lt. Garner. The 1486th Transportation Unit has been ordered to active duty in connection with Operation Iraqi Freedom. I say again, the 1486th Transportation Unit has been ordered to active duty. This is an official order. Comply with the following instructions: You are ordered to report to the Ashland Armory on 2 January 2004 at 0800 hours. When you report, bring all government property issued to you and whatever personal articles you will need if we have to stay for several days. Do not inform anyone except your employer and immediate family of this notification at this time.

"Do you understand?"

"Yes," I answered through gritted teeth.

"Do you have any questions?"

I didn't answer.

It was the last thing I needed. I had been working on three major projects since being back at work and the day I got the call to leave was the day of all three events. I was so pissed because I knew what it was this time. I wasn't nervous and confused; I was angry and annoyed that they were going to screw up my life again. On top of that, I had been in charge of planning those events for six months and I didn't think I was going to be able to see them through. I was overseeing an annual volunteer dinner that night and all I could think about was boxing up my life and leaving my co-workers stranded again.

I called my dad to break the news to him and my mom. He was on his cell phone and asked me not to call her because she was still working at the junior high school. He wanted to be home with her when I called. He wanted to protect her, but the reality of it was inevitable.

I made about fifty more phone calls to my troops and all of my family and friends. It was just one phone call after the next with a whole lot of call waiting interruptions.

I was able to finish the other two projects at work and handed my boss the rest of my files. The Mediation Center went ahead and assigned my duties to Trisha, who had been contracted to work with us on another project. I watched everyone fill the gaps of my life that I was leaving behind. My life was going to have to be put on hold until I came back. I had other things to take care of.

I waited and packed and then waited some more. A few days passed and we still weren't given definitive orders. This time I didn't rush to the armory. And my attitude was much like everyone's attitude. This time we all knew our roles and there was no chasing down people and phone numbers. There was no uncertainty in the process. We were prepared. Unfortunately, no one else was prepared for us.

Dates kept changing and the leaders pretended like they were in control and knew what was going on, but no one did. The only thing I had control over was my stuff and myself, so I tried to get as organized as possible. I felt like something was going to happen at any minute and I wanted to be prepared. I arranged my bills in Excel documents on my computer, complete with PIN numbers for accounts and passwords. I left a copy of my will and books of signed checks for my dad. I did everything I could think of to make things efficient. Sure it helped when I was gone, but it kept me sane while I was home.

When I closed my house in Dayton, I didn't have anyone to live there. My friends who originally were going to move in gave up on the idea and signed another lease on their apartment. I was nervous about it sitting empty for a year, so when my sister recommended someone, I jumped on it. She was a single teacher who didn't smoke and went to church every Sunday—a responsible professional who wouldn't destroy my stuff, or at least I hoped. She paid part of the rent, but that didn't matter as much as having her live there. She was doing me a favor. I left my furniture and stowed most of my personal belongings in boxes in my bedroom. I knew I was leaving my house in capable hands. It took such a load off my mind.

We had some time before we were actually set to go anywhere, but we needed to be back in Ashland to start mobilizing our unit. I ended up moving in with my parents around Thanksgiving because it was a lot closer to the armory. I wanted to spend as much time with my family as possible anyway. For God's sake, I could die, I thought. All I did was eat, drink and party because I knew that it would all be over soon. I ate at every restaurant imaginable, drank anything with alcohol and lived in every way I could think of before I left. I was so disgusted with our military because of all the runaround and disruptions in all of our lives, but as much as I resisted, I knew I still had to perform my duty. I volunteered to serve and wasn't going to back out of my commitment.

Camp Atterbury

It was February in Indiana and it was the coldest month ever. The temperature with the wind chill read between minus twenty-five and minus forty-five degrees. We were supposed to be training for the desert but instead we were in an icebox freezing our asses off. We were at Camp Atterbury in Edinburgh, Indiana, an old Army post that was used for training soldiers in World War II. It was just like any other military base, really. There were rows of concrete barracks lining dirt roads narrow enough for one vehicle. There was a PX, a

movie theater, a fitness center and a bar. There was also a federal prison on the base and inmates are still housed there. They were separate from us, but it was encouraging to learn that we were living in the same conditions, or possibly worse. The camp was old and dilapidated, so when all of the troops were activated for the war, they had to kick it into high gear just to make it livable again.

Part of the nuclear, biological and chemical training at Camp Atterbury included learning how to decontaminate oneself

9

Michelle and SSG Chad Schrack discuss plans for the next day at Camp Atterbury

There were four bays that held our beds. There were no walls, just lines of bunk beds. Our barracks had one bathroom with six toilets and six showers. We draped ponchos on the latrines for "doors" until we realized we needed them during the ice storms. They were replaced with extra sheets. I had a twin bed and stowed my duffel bag behind it. The Army gave us what they called "action packers," actually just big Rubbermaid containers in which to put supplies that we would need overseas. They then would ship them over for us. It was the best thing the Army could have done as they came in handy overseas—keeping sand out of stuff, serving as benches and enabling us to store all our belongings in something with a lock on it. We stuffed them to the gills before sending them over.

It was unnerving trying to transition from living in a three-bedroom house to sharing barracks with ninety women. The thirty females in my unit lived together in one building with two other Ohio units. With three females in charge—one from each unit—it became a little problematic. We were forced to deal with personality disputes between our girls, but it was worse when it happened between companies. Everyone was adjusting to the new, tight living conditions and it was frustrating. We were living on top of each other, so squabbles were understandable. Unfortunately, it was my job to deal with the petty, bullshit bickering and I resented that. I couldn't believe I had to waste what precious little down time I had to baby-sit.

In addition to the bickering, we had one company in our barracks that was just a bunch of slobs. We called them the "shitbags." They wouldn't clean the bathrooms and they were very inconsiderate. There were four compartments to a building, one compartment per unit, and overflow was the fourth bay. Anyone from any of the units could use it, but most of the time the girls from one of the other companies hung out there. They stayed up late and left the lights on all the time, so it was fairly impossible for anyone in that bay to sleep. Everyone was on different training schedules so nobody got very much sleep, but they just made it worse. The males lived with people from the same unit and were all on the same schedule. It was just the females who had to combine three different groups to live together. Lucky us.

We decided we were better off only hanging out with the 1487th. We were absolutely thrilled to find out we were going be stationed overseas with the company we liked. It made it even easier knowing we were pretty similar already. They left two weeks before us and we said goodbye with a bottle and a couple of shots. That was our goodbye gift because Iraq was an alcohol-free combat zone and we figured we'd better drink while we could. Sure, there were probably ways to get alcohol over there, but we knew it wasn't exactly going to be clinking around in our trucks with us. We said goodbye and told them to prepare to give us the scoop when we got there. We figured their unit would be veterans by the time we arrived in-country. Once they left, there was a new energy. It was becoming real that we were leaving too. The hell of Atterbury would soon be over. In the meantime, we took over their space and had lots more room!

While we waited around for our orders, the usual suspects pretended to think they were in charge. To make things worse, the males and females had to be separated because the way the buildings were set up. The males in our unit were three buildings away and we weren't allowed in each other's buildings. Males were not permitted anywhere around female barracks and females were allowed in male barracks only until 5:00 p.m. I was a squad leader trying to make decisions, but I was segregated from my platoon. The guys made decisions without me after the "five o'clock deadline," and I had to go along with it because we didn't have time to argue. I felt so isolated. I couldn't talk to the males because they were in another building and I couldn't vent or discuss decisions with the other females because I was in a position of authority. I was by myself in the whole process.

Another problem with the "building rules" was that the females in the other platoons weren't getting information. We would get information from the evening meetings where we would stand outside in the blowing wind after our hot showers with soaking wet hair just to communicate and learn what was going on the next day. We did this all because males were not allowed in female barracks and vice versa. It was becoming impossible for the male leaders to run around and attempt to get information to their soldiers while the females stood outside in the cold. It was decided after a week or so that as the senior female, I would sit in the leader meetings and pass along information to the other women. It saved time and the females were represented in the decision-making process. It took a lot of my personal time, but I figured since I couldn't talk to anyone anyway, it was the perfect place to waste my time. At least I knew what would be going on the next day and so was able to keep the females unified.

Those were the worst forty-five days of my entire life. We went from one building to the next, freezing our asses off, just waiting to go to war. We figured at least time was ticking away on our one-year clock of deployment until we were told there was some "inconsistent information" relayed to us: our deployment was for a year, 365 days, but our time served actually didn't start until we arrived in Iraq. It was called "boots on ground." Now we really wanted to get out of there.

We were waiting for the nod from overseas to come and we were at the mercy of the military planners responsible for calling up the different types of units. We had to sit and wait to find out what types of units they needed, when they needed us, how they needed us, etc. The information was very hush-hush, so we just had to wait until our number was pulled. It became a big joke. We would start rumors that a certain day was *the* day. It was amazing how those rumors would spread like wildfire.

While we waited, I was glad to keep up with life at home. I paid bills online, talked to my dad about my finances and tried to ease my poor mom's worries even though it didn't do much good. I was grateful my parents were taking care of things for me when I knew others weren't so lucky. Some hadn't even left the country and they were dealing with horrific situations. The responsibilities that were entrusted to someone else were falling apart already. One girl who hadn't even been married for a month made her new husband her power of attorney. He sold her car for $50 and a case of beer. It was so awful listening to her on the phone, begging him not to do it, but she belonged to the military and her husband owned her life. He could do anything he wanted. He drained her checking account about two months into the deployment and her grandmother had to transfer the rest of the money into a new account so he couldn't get to it. She spent her leave filing for divorce.

We finally got the call to move forward and I was so excited. It sounds weird, but I couldn't wait to get out of there. One of the last things we did was get uniforms and equipment, which was an absolute joke. They didn't have enough uniforms in the right sizes, so we took whatever would fit us. We had volunteers, mostly the guy's wives and people who lived nearby, in our make-shift sewing room at Atterbury, working day and night sewing the right insignias on the right uniforms.

We had winter and summer uniforms; you were not supposed to mix and match, but because they were so short, we had to. One guy got a used uniform and it said "Lynch," and we busted his balls about it being Jessica Lynch's uniform. Thank God I didn't have to wear it, but it was probably some other

Lynch anyway. It really sucked getting used items. We figured we were going to war and we wanted clothes and equipment that was new. I didn't get the right size flak vest; it was too big. It ended up working out all right when I tightened the straps as much as possible, but I was so pissed that we couldn't even get the right equipment to protect ourselves. I thought I'd hate to be the person to break the news to my parents that I was killed because my equipment didn't fit right.

We were allowed to see our families one last time, so my whole family went to a Holiday Inn for the weekend. We were given forty-eight hours to do whatever we wanted. It was so cold outside, but we were fortunate to find a hotel that had an indoor pool and a restaurant. My parents, nieces and nephews, sister, brothers and their spouses spent most of the time crammed into my room just talking and laughing. I loved having my immediate family so close to me. I knew it was the last time we'd all be together for a long time. We ate and drank and just enjoyed the moment. The hotel bar had a live band and I met up with other soldiers later that night. We danced like idiots without caring what we looked like. We were going to war!

When we said goodbye that Sunday I felt the lump in my throat. It was the same lump I felt when I had to say goodbye in Ashland. My heart was hurting and I couldn't bear to cry anymore. It was so painful. On the ride back to Atterbury my parents sat on either side of me and just held me. "American Soldier," a song by Toby Keith, was playing on the radio and I hurt. I hurt for my parents too. Their baby was going to war.

We left early on a Monday morning. The barracks were cleared and prepared for inspection before boarding the busses bound for the Indianapolis Airport. We didn't have to go through security because it was a military-chartered plane. There was a huge terminal just for soldiers and we all sat around playing cards and talking while we waited for the plane.

I called my mom one more time from a pay phone before boarding and she lost it. I had never heard her cry like that and I hope I never do again. I was happy. I was so excited to go and get the hell out of Atterbury. I thought it was the best thing in the world, but my mom didn't seem to think so. I tried to calm her down, but they started boarding us and I left my mom brokenhearted holding a telephone.

The one thing my mom asked was if I would have my laptop handy, to please keep sending her letters. She said she would feel more comfortable knowing what it was really like. I started writing the letters as soon as I got on the plane.

From left, facing the camera: SGT Jeremy Lauther, SGT Scott Curtis, SSG Bob Carter. Behind them is SGT Nancy Donelson and SGT Mike Shugrue. Facing away from the camera is SPC Ryan "Willy" Gearheart

14

– 2 –

Deployment: February 2004

Killed in Action: 553
Wounded in Action: 2,748

I just wanted to write and say goodbye because I am leaving shortly for the Middle East. The flight is roughly 22 hours and we will have to stay on the plane the entire time due to security reasons. One good thing about the flight is that I get to sit in first class! They went by date of rank and I made the list! I am going to share my seat with some of the taller guys so they won't be scrunched all 22 hours. I hope they have plenty of movies to help pass the time away!

All the troops are packed and ready to roll. Our one-year deployment doesn't start until we hit ground "in country," so we are ready to start our year and get home. Spirits are high because it feels like we are not in this holding pattern anymore and we can actually do our job soon.

We are also ready for some of the 70-degree weather instead of the zero-degree weather in Indiana! We are all just lying around, watching movies and catching last-minute naps and packing. This could be the last time we get to be lazy for a while, so we are taking advantage of it.

I am actually excited to go to the Middle East and so are many of our troops. This will be a first for many of our young troops. Some haven't ever flown before and many haven't left the United States before and they are so excited to see how other cultures live. They have a very open mind and have respect for the people of the country, as long as they aren't trying to harm us.

We have trained hours and hours on how to stay safe, detect things that will harm us and been through so many drills that I feel confident we are ready for our mission.

15

Camp Atterbury trains in a unique way. They talk to the soldiers that come home from Iraq to find out what is actually going on in the country and Camp Atterbury adjusts its training to what the soldiers tell them we should know. This gives us the most up-to-date, realistic training that we could have. I've thought that everything we've trained on has been beneficial and worthwhile.

I miss you all and can't wait to see you all again. Wish me luck on my flight and I will write when I can. – MZ, February 17, 2004

I watched our younger soldiers board the plane, terrified and excited. Some of them had never been on a plane or even out of the state, let alone away from their families. They were so much younger and they were heading into the same combat zone as I was.

We were in the air for fifteen hours before a layover in Rome. We couldn't stop fidgeting, but they wouldn't let us get off the plane in Rome because Italy did not want to appear as though they were supporting the United States and the war. There was an actual regulation against us stopping there. We had to get special permission to allow the crews to refuel the plane while we were still on it, but they did so no problem. We weren't allowed to touch our feet to the ground so most of us stayed in our seats. Smokers piled to the steps outside the plane where they were allowed to smoke, but there were armed guards standing by just in case anyone decided to test the system. The guards who came on the plane were eye candy enough for us to forget our differences

From left: Michelle, SGT Tara Sauer, SGT Andrea Motley, SGT Nancy Donelson, SGT Leo Prince and SPC Ryan "Willy" Gearheart

for a minute, though. They were perfect Italian sculptures and all of the females grinned ear to ear as they swept the plane. The guards said, "Bonjour" and we giggled, "Bonjour" back. They were the first non-military guys we had seen in forty-five days. We wondered why our guys didn't look like them. The males shot us jealous "I-look-as-good-as-he-does" looks and we just rolled our eyes and returned to staring at the Italian hotties.

The 1486th Transportation Company boards the plane to go to Kuwait

Our payback came when the Italian women came on the plane to restock the supplies. The guys drooled and then everyone was happy.

We headed straight into Kuwait from Rome and had no idea if the area was secure or not. No one really told us. I sat there wondering if we were going to run out off the plane shooting or what. The mindless chatter dissipated as we collectively held our breath, praying for a miracle to send us home.

We left on February 17 and we are halfway through the flight. They tell us we will be stopping in Rome for our layover, but we will not get off the plane.

Before we took off, the pilots picked five soldiers to sit in the cockpit while the plane was taking off. One of my soldiers took my camera and got some pictures of the takeoff and he said it was a once-in-a-lifetime experience. How many times can you sit in the cockpit of a 767 and watch the takeoff?

When I went up there to give him the camera, the pilot let me sit in the captain's seat and wear his hat. Security isn't really high since it's a private military flight and everyone is allowed to look at the cockpit and chat with the pilots. We are all just walking around, talking to each other and trying to keep busy on this 22-hour flight.

It really didn't feel any different this past week when we were packing, getting new uniforms or clearing our barracks. It felt like a normal Army day, not like we were going to a foreign country and leaving our families for a year. But this morning it finally hit that I was actually leaving for the Middle East. It took seeing the buses that were taking us to the airport to believe that we were actually going somewhere.

17

It also didn't hit that my family was very sad that I was leaving. Since I didn't get to talk to them that much, I just thought they understood I was leaving and felt the same way I did. Boy, was I wrong!

I called my mom not thinking anything of it and we were talking and she started crying. It hit me that this is probably harder on my family and friends that I am leaving since they didn't have a choice. I understood that by enlisting in the Army there was a chance I may go somewhere and I was willing to make that sacrifice. My poor mom and dad just had to live with my decision and they have no say in this whatsoever.

So, Mom, please understand I know how difficult this is for you and I'm sorry. I hope you can find peace that I am OK with this deployment and I am with my Army family that is going to take care of me. We are all here and are going to look out for each other 100 percent.

I do promise that I will take pictures of all my journeys and write as much as possible so you all can see it isn't as bad as the news makes it out to be. So far, we've had a memorable time and I expect it will continue in the desert. This is a once-in-a-lifetime opportunity and I get a chance to learn so much from this experience about myself, about the Middle East, and about the Army. I am excited to start my journey!

Take care of my mom and dad. I know I'm putting them through hell – again. (We had rough teenage years when I was growing up.) I think they'd agree that deployment is easier than raising me as a teenager! Ha! I love you all! – MZ, February 18, 2004

Michelle shortly after landing in Kuwait and arriving at Camp Wolverine

When I got my first glimpse of Kuwait, I was sick to my stomach. It wasn't the sand and the hollow scenery that deflated me; it was the yellow, eerie sky. Jumbled thoughts raced through my head. Would I ever see lush, green landscapes again? Am I going to live through this? What's going to happen to me? I wondered if I had made a mistake, but knew it was a little late for that. The most important thing was to get off that plane and get our military card scanned and start the 365 days. One day down.

The plane landed just after a sandstorm at Camp Wolverine at Kuwait International Airport. The camp doesn't exist anymore, but it used to be a staging area for soldiers being processed in and out of country.

I missed the briefings when we landed because I was helping with baggage detail. Being on a military plane, there were no baggage handlers to gather all of our duffel bags and set them in neat piles. While we heaped gear together, there were more U.S. military soldiers guarding us. I kept wondering if we were going to get shot. They were just a few feet away decorated in flak jackets and rifles and we're standing there in T-shirts. It was eighty-five degrees. It's funny when I think about it now, because Kuwait was like our resort. It wasn't necessary to wear flak jackets in Kuwait and convoys only needed a few weapons to travel there. It was that safe. And there we were, shaking out of our boots.

We loaded up and headed for Camp Arifjan armed with guards and Humvees, unsure of what to expect at our temporary base camp.

I just wanted to let you all know that we've reached our temporary base camp and I've seen our permanent camp and they are both really nice. It is much better than expected. No really, it is so much better than Camp Atterbury it isn't even funny.

We have brand new showers, running water, great food and brand new laundry facilities. There is a Subway and Pizza Inn that we can go to anytime. We live in tents that have wood floors and fluorescent lighting and bunk beds. There are fewer people in the temporary tents than at Atterbury.

Oh, did I mention that everything is air-conditioned?

There are volleyball and basketball courts and a workout facility too. Troops have been here a while so they have built up the camp as much as possible to make it more comfortable. It seriously looks like a nicer "M*A*S*H."

The weather has been around 70-80 degrees and it's been sunny every day. They say in a few months it will get really hot. Soldiers were saying it got up to 140 degrees last summer. I hope it stays nice like it has been for a while because it feels like Florida. There aren't any bugs yet. I guess that is something that we'll get to experience during the summer months.

There were about 15 soldiers, including me, that got to go on a mission yesterday. We went to our permanent station and picked up some of our vehicles that we will be driving the next year. I got to see our base camp and got to see the people we are replacing. They have been very helpful about what to expect and they have been sharing stories and advice on how to do our job safely.

It is nice to have them here still to talk to about everything. We will be riding with them for about two weeks or until we feel comfortable with our mission.

19

On our mission we got to see Kuwait. The roads look like roads in Ohio and they have the same vehicles we do. There were so many BMW's and Chevy's on the road. The only difference was that there was sand everywhere and camels ... and sheep. The sheep are shaggier than our sheep and look like half goat-half sheep. They have long hair and look very different than Ohio sheep.

Some parts of Kuwait are very clean and other parts are dirty; for example, trash on the sides of the roads. They also have tents set up in the middle of nowhere off the highway in the desert. I think it's housing for the sheep and camel herders.

All the street signs are in English and Arabic, which is nice because there is no way I'd be able to figure out what they were talking about.

The people in Kuwait don't seem to mind the U.S. presence. The children wave and the parents smile at us. The one major difference I've seen is that the men wear the long dresses with the headdress. Some women wear the full coverage burqua but most wear the headdress that covers only the top of their head like the guys.

They will also stop on the side of the road to pray at sunup and down. I haven't gotten a chance to see too many Kuwait people since we were driving. I guess we'll get a better idea of how the people and culture are once we are here longer.

It is time for bed so I'll tell you more later. – MZ, February 20, 2004

Camp Arifjan

Camp Arifjan, our temporary base camp, was like its own city. The soldiers there were in a huge rotation, which meant about 130,000 troops came in and another 150,000 left while we were there. There were people coming in who had to get up north and others leaving from the south. It was insane.

There was a huge difference between the soldiers leaving the country compared to those arriving. We were decked out in fresh uniforms with enough nervous energy to make us dead-giveaways as the newbies. We were in a whole new environment in a different time zone and I just wanted to soak up as much knowledge as possible. The veterans' dirty, faded uniforms looked as tired and worn as the eyes of the soldiers wearing them. They didn't much care for our excitement. They were fed up and ready to go. I remember talking to a soldier who had been traveling in convoys and he tried to offer me some advice, but I told him that what he was telling me contradicted what we were taught at Atterbury. He laughed at me and assured me that there were plenty of things they didn't teach us at the mobilization site where we were trained. I was so naïve. His eyes told me he had seen a lot. It was the same look that every soldier had once they'd been there a while. It's unexplainable but it's there. Now that I'm home I can see that look in the eyes of every veteran who has ever served in a war.

From left: Ed Zaremba (Dad), Michelle, Marie (sister), Mary Ellen (Mom) and Mark (brother). Not pictured: Mike (brother). This was taken in Mansfield the day Michelle left for Camp Atterbury, Indiana

I tried to call my parents when I got to camp to let them know I was in-country, but it took a few tries because the satellites kept going down. We had AT&T phones that cost 50 cents a minute and were basically worthless, but they were our lifelines and all we had. We couldn't just pick up a cell phone and dial out.

We stayed in Camp Arlington, which was like a suburb of Arifjan. Arifjan was the hub that connected about five camps. It was about two miles to walk to anything there, which meant that if you got to where you needed to go and forgot something, you had to hoof it back to your tent.

I tried to convince myself it wouldn't be as bad as I thought. The soldiers who were there when the war began didn't have any of the amenities that we had when we arrived during the second rotation.

But because the size of the place was so overwhelming and packed with people, so were the lines for the laundry, showers and chow hall. We spent half our time waiting in lines. It was so frustrating trying to get anything accomplished.

Soldiers were given one to two weeks to adjust to their new environment before any missions started. We played volleyball and football to pass the time. I kept telling my mom how much fun I was having so she would stop worrying. The temperature was only about seventy degrees, so we walked to the PX and took our time getting places. We practiced convoying around

Kuwait, trying to familiarize ourselves with the vehicles and the country. A guide went with us on those missions so nobody would get lost.

It got warm quickly at Arifjan. When we first landed, I wore my Gortex jacket because it felt so cold. I couldn't believe it was the desert. It would start out bitterly cold, then all of a sudden, there would be a vicious sand storm and then holy mother heat. I figured I needed to suck it up and adjust because it was just one of many things that was about to change for me.

We couldn't wait to get on the road and actually drive in Kuwait. It was a rule that Kevlars, body armor, were to be worn while driving and that included Kuwait. When we first arrived, I was so afraid that it was dangerous to drive without it or that we were going to get in trouble if anyone saw us on our first drive not wearing it. We didn't wear it much in Kuwait as the year went on. In fact, we rarely wore it at all. But I did that first day we were allowed out on the road.

Even though we didn't head into Iraq for a few weeks, we were given our first mission in Kuwait almost immediately. We were introduced to the members of the 720th Transportation Unit from New Mexico. They were the unit we were going to be replacing and they were assigned to train us. We were to drive with them in a five-ton truck, with about twenty of us crammed in it, to Camp Navistar, the northern-most point in Kuwait near the border with Iraq. There, we would pick up our trucks and come back. The smartest thing the Army did was having the New Mexico unit train us.

That first trip made my head spin just trying to take it all in. The guide from the 720th drove us in a deuce-and-a-half, a two-and-a-half-ton truck lined with benches on either side used for transporting people and equipment, on the short mission to see our new home. We had a few hours to check out the camp and pick up the trucks so we could start training.

When we got our first look at our vehicles, though, we were appalled. We thought the New Mexican unit wasn't keeping up on the maintenance, but it was the wear and tear of the desert that made them look so miserable. The unit we trained probably felt the same way, but those trucks were a frightening reality of what we were doing there. Mine had a bullet hole above the exhaust, which was right above my head. I winced just thinking about the person who escaped death by an inch.

The first thing they taught us was what the desert does to a truck. It was a sobering lesson. Brand-new trucks appeared to age quickly as the mud, dirt and sand caked all over them made them look older than their years. The roads were so beat-up that the shocks were quickly destroyed. Side windows and windshields were cracked and broken from flying rocks kicked up as we bumped along. Yet, if a window was cracked, it would not be replaced due to a lack of supplies. We took what we could get, and as long as a truck lasted, we took it.

I sat shotgun on that first drive and stared out the window trying to take the whole country in at once. One of the first things that intrigued me about Kuwait was the people. There was a noticeable difference in the civilians who appeared "modern" versus those who were "old-school." For instance, some of the women wore traditional burquas that hid their bodies and faces, while others wore contemporary clothes. I saw women who were forced to sit in the back seat of a car, forbidden to even speak, while other women drove BMWs and Porsches. But the thing that really amazed me was seeing men in dresses. There they would be, walking or standing along the side of the road and upon seeing them, I would giggle like a teenager.

I was surprised to see camels running in the road and these weird-looking, shaggy sheep. Perhaps even more surprising, were these tents set up in the middle of nowhere that appeared to be for the sheep and camel herders. I later found out they were actually "summer homes" for people who lived in the city and herded sheep and camels for a living.

So far our stay in Kuwait has been pretty uneventful. We are at Camp Arlington, which is a hub for soldiers that are coming into and leaving out of Kuwait. That means that there are twice as many soldiers here than should be and it is an incredibly huge camp. I can't even guess how many troops are here with us, but it has to be in the thousands.

There are lines for everything!

There are lines for the phone, if you can get them to work; there are lines for the Internet, which you have to pay for; and there are lines for Baskin-Robbins, and that line is worth it.

It feels like most of our free time is standing in some kind of line. It is frustrating because there isn't much free time and we are wasting it in lines.

Another frustration is the phones are really inconsistent. They haven't worked for three days and I finally got to call home and they disconnected me! They seem to be working today, but it's a crap shoot whether they will work.

The Internet, phones, etc., are about two miles away. We usually walk to them because the shuttle that takes us there is never there when you need it to be. Sometimes we will go there twice in one day, so we are walking about eight miles just to use a phone and go to the PX.

We do lots of walking and are barely in vehicles right now. It is pretty ironic that the truck drivers have to walk everywhere because they don't have vehicles.

We've talked to the soldiers we are replacing and they say our permanent camp is very small. I am very happy about that because they say there aren't any lines for anything. They have the same amenities as Camp Arlington, but we will share with fewer soldiers. The tents are also bigger than our temporary camp.

We will hopefully have fewer people in bigger tents. Right now we are packed in like sardines and will welcome the space.

Some of us are heading up to our new camp (Navistar) to replace the soldiers who have been there for a year. We will take half our unit and move them to our permanent camp and take half the unit we are replacing and move them to Camp Arlington. So the two units will be split up and work with each other until we have learned their jobs and feel confident we can do it as well as they have. Once we feel confident, the second half of our unit will meet us at the permanent camp.

I am so glad we will be working with people who have been doing this for a year instead of just getting thrown into it with no on-the-job training.

Yesterday was our first sandstorm. It was cold and windy and sand was everywhere. I had sand in my hair, ears, eyes, eyelashes, boots, socks–you get the idea. The sand is very powdery and isn't like sand in Florida. It coats your clothes and skin so you feel grimy all day long, but it's great for exfoliating your skin!

We've been working to pass the time. We have a group that works out together and everybody pushes everybody. Every other day we do eight-minute abs and play sand volleyball. The other days we're doing some kind of cardio. We ran around the camp two days ago and it was two and a half miles in the sand. Running in sand is harder than on pavement, I'm beginning to see.

It is nice that we have time to work out and work off all this food we have been eating.

We are all ready to get our mission started. We've been in a holding pattern since we got here and we want to actually do something. It seems like we are in limbo until we get to our permanent station. It is frustrating for everyone to have to sit and wait.

The unit has set up some training for us and we are all looking forward to that. The only training we've been doing is going out in convoys to different camps around Kuwait. It is great training, but the number of people who can go is limited. We all have to take turns using the trucks and the military guide who travels with us. Go figure: More waiting in line for our turn!

We did get to do one really cool thing on a convoy training. We had to check out one of the camps in Kuwait and we found out one of our female soldiers' husbands was sent to that camp.

She was able to go on the convoy and find her husband. It was the first time they had talked since he left for Kuwait a week before us.

She was glad to see him and it was a surprise for her husband. For 10 minutes, they were the happiest, most relieved soldiers, and we were able to make that happen.
– MZ, February 24, 2004

About a week after we met the New Mexican unit, ten of us had to move to Camp Navistar before the rest of the troops to prepare our new home. I had to go, not only because I was a squad leader, but also a female. I had dual roles again.

It was a miserable two-hour drive to Navistar. About fifteen of us piled into the back of

This was during the first mission. This soldier is removing a poisonous lizard found sitting on the truck

a deuce-and-a-half truck and bounced all the way to camp. We always joked about how a crappy start to a mission turned out to be a good one and vice versa. I went on a mission once in the States where we stayed the first night in this classy hotel with hot tubs and pools. It turned out to be one of the worst missions because they forgot to feed us by the end and we had to scrounge for things we needed. On the way over to Kuwait we laughed about sitting in first class because it meant things were going to go downhill. I hoped the shitty, uncomfortable drive in that truck was going to deliver us to a halfway decent camp to call home for the next year, but I wasn't going to get my hopes up.

Just as we got on the road to Camp Navistar, our guides stopped off at one of the shacks that we eventually termed "Haji marts." They were like little convenience stores on the side of the road. We were stunned to see the labels on everything in Arabic. At least most of the road signs are in Arabic and English, or I'd have been screwed, I thought to myself as I let out a nervous giggle. I tried to ignore the stares from the men who had all stopped to watch me shop. I gripped the strap of my rifle and hung in the shadow of my guide in one of the narrow aisles. I always stood close to my guys in those places because I didn't want to be taken, but I was scared that day. My stark white complexion, rosy cheeks and blue eyes made me a hot commodity over there. Men would stare at me and make me so uneasy. I wore my sunglasses everywhere and as soon as I

One of the tents at Camp Navistar

took them off, they would fall all over themselves trying to help me. On a few occasions, I was almost sold. My guys would negotiate prices with the locals for the females in the unit. The guys were joking but the Middle Eastern men were not! I thought the uneasy feeling would pass the more I went in the Haji-marts, but it never did. The one thing it did teach me was to start using my "charms" to my advantage over there because I figured they sure weren't going to do a damn bit of good back in the States.

Right outside the Haji-mart, a man approached us. At first I didn't know if he was a friend or a foe. I clutched the weapon slung on my back, not knowing what to expect. That was so unlike me, but it was nice to have that rifle. I didn't really care what he had to say until he thanked us for taking care of Saddam. He said we opened the country back up to him. He was exiled from his country and he wasn't able to see his family and he just wanted to thank us. It made my day taking a picture with him. It's weird looking at that picture now because I was still smiling. It's obvious when I look at it that was still in the beginning of my journey.

It was also one of the first times I experienced how women were treated in that part of the world. The man's Iraqi wife stayed in the background with her children. She wouldn't talk to us or even look at the male soldiers. I tried to connect with her but she refused. As I walked away, I felt confused by my heart-warming yet frustrating experience. I wanted to hug the man for sharing his story and knock him over at the same time. He treated his wife as horribly as Saddam had treated the people of his country, but he couldn't see that.

Camp Navistar

I stood on the tips of my boots, trying to look past the mounds of dirt that towered over my head. There was barbed wire and then another layer of barbed wire. There were observation decks all around the camp that a unit of lower enlistees guarded twenty-four hours a day.

This camp was tiny compared to Arifjan, only big enough for a battalion, or about 1,000 people, compared to the more than 50,000 at Arifjan. I couldn't wait to stretch out in a camp with no line for the chow hall, tents right next to the showers and an area to work in our own motor pool. There were fewer amenities, but less brass or bigwigs. The

Michelle's "space" in the tent at Camp Navistar

one thing that took some getting used to, however, was the PX. It was just a trailer without the kind of variety we were used to at Camp Arifjan. I didn't want to complain, but it was a huge adjustment because it was something we weren't expecting. The little choices would have to do until we got our "action packers" and care packages from family and friends.

I moved from tent to tent three or four times that first week. The ten of us planned to keep the males and females together since we were the only ones from our unit at Camp Navistar, but as soon as we got there, one guy threw a fit about letting me stay with my unit because I was the only female. I was pissed that he was going to make me stay by myself with another unit so his wife wouldn't get pissed off about me staying in a tent full of all of us. I didn't think there was going to be any hanky panky when we were living on top of each other. I ended up having to move three times in one day to please that bastard.

My job was to make sure there was the right number of cots in each tent and there were no holes or leaks in the tents. I needed to familiarize myself with the camp so I could show the other soldiers around. The rest of the company made their way to Navistar and the ten of us were there to direct all the soldiers. We had to move for the fifth time when the 720th moved out. Navistar was home, but we weren't settled.

Our living quarters were canvas tents dipped in kerosene to keep the bugs away. We didn't even care how shitty they were because we finally had a home. We measured the tent and spaced ourselves out accordingly. Some people built walls. Others hung up sheets as the year went on. There was air-conditioning, heat and electricity. Some people got extravagant and got satel-

Michelle awaiting her first mission at Camp Navistar

lite cable hook-ups, but nobody in our tent even had a TV because we were always on the road, so it was pointless to pay the $30 a month. We lived in primitive tents that had satellite capabilities. It was unreal.

Our platoon decided to make the tents co-ed with curtains down the middle. We figured if we were going to be on the road and fighting together, we were going to live together. There were about ten guys at one end of the tent and Nancy and I at the other. She and I blocked off an area with a curtain and it was never a problem.

My one luxury item, courtesy of the military, was a field desk—a basic desk with drawers. A girl from the New Mexican unit acquired a bed sometime during her rotation that was made of wood with shelves and storage. She gave it to me just before she left. I bought a Haji mattress to put on it. Haji mattresses were very long and thin and it usually took about two of them to make a comfortable bed. It was nothing compared to home, but it sure beat sleeping on a cot. When we had parties, everyone gathered around my bed. That way everyone could have a seat and watch movies or do whatever we did to waste time. Slowly everyone started making beds or getting them from other people.

We had our first sandstorm at Navistar right around that time. In southern Kuwait, the sand is extremely fine and when the wind started blowing it around, it could get quite annoying. But what was worse was when the wind would really pick up and start throwing small, angry rocks that hurt when they hit us. I remember thinking, dear God, is it going to be like this all of the time?

On the Home Front

Around the same time at home, my parents were doing a little role reversal. Where normally I would confide in my mother, I found myself telling my father things I didn't want my mother to know because I didn't want her to worry. He just seemed easier to talk to at the time.

My dad was a hard-working electrician at a local steel mill. He's a gruff man with broad shoulders, a deep voice and a heart of gold. My dad taught me how to work hard, play hard and do my very best at everything I try. Whenever I have difficult decisions or large purchases, I go to him for support. He's great with decisions, common sense and nobody can take advantage of him. My dad is great to have on your side.

But I never thought I would go to my father over my mother when it came to my love life. I went to my dad because he had been so chummy with my boyfriend for only a few weeks before we left for Atterbury. He and I had gone to the same high school and met up again when I was staying with my parents before leaving for Iraq. He had grown to be quite handsome, a Marine in fact, home on leave. He was so helpful with my deployment because he knew how to prepare and what I should expect because he'd been deployed so many times since becoming a Marine.

I started going to my dad with my problems and he would help me work through them. It made us so much closer, but it was so uncomfortable in the beginning. It turns out my dad gives pretty good advice about men!

My dad was also my power of attorney. I had to completely rely on him to take care of all of my finances and make sure my bills were paid. I will never be able to thank him enough for all of the extra work he took on just for me. Five months after I left, he got a letter from the insurance company saying that the mortgage company would not release funds because I hadn't paid my mortgage. I had direct deposit, but they stopped taking money out of my account after three months because my interest rate dropped due to the "Soldiers and Sailors Civil Relief Act," a law enacted by Congress during the Civil War to ensure soldiers are able to fulfill their financial obligations while they are on active duty. Part of the law caps interest rates at six percent for financial obligations, such as credit cards, loans, mortgages, etc. for the duration of a service member's military obligation. The same law covers a multitude of other issues, from addressing court appearances to ensuring a soldier is not fired from their place of employment due to being called to active military duty.

For some reason, it took three months before my direct deposit stopped. My dad just sort of disregarded checking on it after awhile because he figured it was fine for five months. I didn't catch the mistake either because the military would deposit, deduct and deposit more money. We had three different checks per month that the military would deposit so it was very confusing and impossible to keep up on. They were getting ready to repossess my house and my dad had to straighten it all out for me.

My dad would also get on me if I would shop online. I was trying to save as much money as possible because I was unsure if my civilian job would be around when I got home. My civilian job was funded mainly by federal grants. Because of the economy and the war, the funding situation was looking grave for any grant programs. I found it ironic that one of my jobs, my military one, was taking away funding from my civilian job.

On top of that, he still always found the time to take care of the really important things—like liquor. That was dad's job too. He found creative ways to ship bottles to me, like any good parent did or is doing for some soldier right now. It was just a part of life.

Meanwhile, my mom became everyone's military mom in my unit. She wrote letters to every solider over there for their birthday. Some of the guys' wives had babies so she would send the guys cards. Everybody got something. She kept a log of everyone in the unit and what she sent to them and when she sent it to make sure everyone got a letter. She mothered us to death, but it was comforting. She started making cookies when we were at Atterbury and everyone loved them. I would get a package and the guys would hover around to see if there were any cookies in it. When we got overseas, she found a way to ship cookies in airtight containers. We still think about those cookies to this day!

My mom works at our local junior high school as a secretary. She's a loving, caring person. A beautiful woman, everyone thinks she's my sister and not old enough to be a mom. Mom is such a determined woman and when she gets something in her head, she won't stop until she accomplishes her goal.

I grew up in a very tight-knit family and my friends always seemed to flock to my parents. They became the neighborhood parents when I was a kid and everyone called them Mom and Dad. My parents have been married for thirty years and they are the sweetest people. They are so in love and are together all the time.

My sister, Marie, had duties of her own while I was away, like birth control. I wasn't sure I could get the patch over there to regulate my cycle while on the road, so I called my doctor and she gave Marie a year's worth of patches. She was in charge of running around and getting anything in Dayton together for me. She took care of a lot of work-related things, too, because she was right there in Dayton. She kept in touch with my boss and kept me as up-to-date as I needed to be while on the other side of the world.

Mark, my baby brother, lived at home and passed along messages to Mom and Dad for me. He dealt with them stressing out all the time, which of course, stressed Mark out.

Mike, my other brother, sent care packages. His wife's brother had just returned from Iraq doing the same job as me, so they were used to the military family roles.

My old roommate, Julie, sent me a package a month. I liked a certain brand of tampons that I could not get in-country, so her job was to get me a package a month and send them.

My aunts and uncles sent me cards and letters to keep my spirits up. One uncle took lots of pictures of the family and had my cousins color pictures for me.

I was so blessed to have supportive people behind me. It made being away just a little easier. Others didn't have it so lucky. Some soldiers' spouses took all of their money and spent it. Other people had their parents taking care of their money while they were gone and they spent it. Some parents drank it all away. One guy's wife moved another man into their home and he didn't find out about it until he went home on leave. These soldiers were so stressed over there just thinking about how their lives were being ruined at home while they were away at war. Thank you; thank you, to my wonderful family.

Finally it was time to start working on some of our trucks and setting up our motor pool. We were still there with the New Mexican unit, the 720th, so the trucks were really still theirs. While we wrestled with chains and binders and tried to figure out where to put everything, they were signing all of their equipment over to us.

We had to take all of our trucks to maintenance so they could assess the tractors and make sure they were safe to drive. Between March and April when we took them in to fix or replace certain components, it always seemed like such a fiasco because we had a lot to do in a little bit of time. We always tried to instill in our young soldiers the importance of preventative maintenance checks and services because we didn't want them to get caught in a bad situation where they could get killed because their truck wasn't running right. Everyone thought the college kids were going to be bad and they wouldn't take things seriously, but all of their trucks were always running. We had two, twenty-two year olds in the truck together by the end and they kicked ass! They were always on time, they never cut corners to rush through a job and we could trust them to soldier a truck alone without any supervision from those of us who were more experienced.

Our platoon decided to use part of our motor pool as a "common area." We aligned two trailers together with a built-up sidewall and took another truck with a big box on top for storage and parked it perpendicular to the trailers. Sitting on top of those trailers was like our home away from our war home. We nicknamed it "The L" and that was where the Third Platoon hung out. We had our Christmas and Halloween parties there just because it was our space away from everyone else at camp. The other platoons followed suit, but we just wanted to be away from our battalion. It was a nice idea until our leadership got involved and tried to tell us what could and couldn't be there. Then it became more of a pain in the ass. It took away the whole essence of what we were trying to do, which was to get away from it all and relax.

Leadership was always a pain in the ass. The first thing they told us was to fill our trailers and make sure we had the right equipment according to our list. Then the next day, they would decide we were going to do it differently and we would have to take everything out. We were trying to figure out what equipment was supposed to go where and it was like a circus. We would fill our trailer and have to secure it so no one could steal anything, which happened a lot because no one had enough of the right supplies. We eventually learned to do what we were told at camp and to save what really worked for when we were on the road and there was no one watching. We had certain places and ways to park the trucks but it became a war among us just on where to park because there were too many vehicles fighting for cramped parking places.

It was getting hotter by that point; around ninety degrees. To pass the time, we would practice backing up the trucks, fixing flat tires and plotting how we would recover a broken down vehicle on the road.

There were times at Guard back home at the armory in Ashland that we couldn't do our job at drill, where we trained once a month, because our fuel budget ran out for the year. So, the trucks just sat there. We would just roll our eyes and shrug. But when it came to life and death, where the leaders were responsible for people's lives, we knew we had to fight for what our people needed. Training was even more critical now. We weren't about to sit around and wait to go on the road without properly training some of the soldiers who never got a chance to train at home.

The younger kids weren't the only ones who needed the practice, though. It had been awhile since I had been in the trucks, so I was a little rusty using reverse. I was relieved to find out I wasn't the only one having problems getting the feel of things. Some of the other girls admitted they had forgotten some things, too, so we got a group of females together so nobody would feel uncomfortable about doing the maneuvers. Just doing that drill together gave us the confidence we needed to assert ourselves so we wouldn't get pushed aside or undervalued. Even the little things, like getting a few females together to lift the heavy things, gave us more confidence knowing that we were capable of getting the job done. It kicked in pretty quickly for the guys that we were soldiers, too, and we could do what was needed.

That's not to say there weren't lazy people who hung back and tried to get out of working, but I tried to keep on the girls. Sometimes the girls worked even harder to prove themselves and some of the lazy guys took advantage of the fact, but they were stupid to think no one noticed. Everyone's true colors came out during the deployment. But females-versus-the-males really wasn't an issue among our platoon. We played sports together and everyone was treated equally. It wasn't about guys and girls to us; we did our best to remain equal.

But the people above us constantly tried to remind us that we were different. For example, females had to take a "buddy" to the bathroom or anywhere in the camp. Males didn't have to. Our tents were about fifty feet from the bathroom and it didn't make sense. It just widened the gap between males and females by constantly pointing out that we were different. The females didn't need "special rules." We knew when to buddy up and when to not go somewhere alone. They're the same rules a woman in the States would follow to take precautions and stay safe.

Needless to say, some of these rules were abandoned once common sense took over.

Crossing the Border

One day I was just sitting around when I was told I was going into Iraq for the first time the following day. I had to load the truck with MRE's (Meals Ready to Eat), water, supplies, flak jackets, Kevlar, nuclear and biological training gear, gas masks and rounds. It was incredibly disorganized because it was our first mission and we didn't know what the hell we were doing. I was so pissed because it took half the night to find my truck, get my equipment in the vehicle, check out the truck and then recheck everything.

The first obstacle of each mission was trying to get any kind of equipment. My first truck didn't even have armor. I'm not even sure the New Mexican unit had flak jackets the whole time. They had it the worst out of all of us because they started with nothing and left with little more. They were the first ones in-country when the war started. To put it in perspective, the New Mexican unit was told that if there was a roadside bomb and an explosion incapacitated a truck, the rest of the convoy was to continue driving and the last truck would pick up the stranded soldiers. They didn't have any kind of communication, so trying to formulate a plan on the road that they could adhere

Michelle in front of Saddam's palace in Tikrit. This was during the first mission with the New Mexican unit

to was not an option. They had to rely on the fact everyone would remember the drill in a situation of actual panic and chaos.

We even had to buy our own two-way radios, so we'd be able to do quick assessments. We bought them at Wal-Mart. They were able to transmit between a truck or two in the convoy, so it was better than nothing, but not much better.

We had a terrible supply sergeant who was known for always saying, "Well, I really can't do anything, my hands are tied." It would be 1:00 in the afternoon and she'd be running on the track or doing everything else but working on getting us the right supplies. One of my soldiers, SPC Plummer, was very petite—barley five feet tall with blazing red hair you could spot from across camp—and had very small feet. She was unable to get desert boots before we headed overseas and wound up the only solider with black boots and a desert camouflage uniform. That supply sergeant took forever to replace her boots. It could have been because there really were no boots her size available, but it took a lot of nagging before they finally arrived.

Additional equipment we were assigned before going into Iraq for protection were "sappy plates" for our flak jackets. These provided extra protection to repel bullets and scraps of metal or flying debris. The New Mexican unit used one of the vests for target practice one day when they were bored and discovered the plates actually worked. They got into big trouble and had to pay for the vest and the plates, but we were just amazed it worked.

When I went to get my plates, they didn't have any small sizes. They WILL find them, I thought, because I was not going to have to stay off the road the first mission because they did not have the proper supplies. I was the squad leader and I had to go out before my troops. I didn't want them to do something without the leadership doing it first. Somehow before the first mission, I got my sappy plates and calmed down a little. I shouldn't have been upset because some soldiers didn't even have flak vests yet. There were only so many extra-large vests in Atterbury, so the rest of the extra-large vest-wearers had to wait until they arrived in Iraq to get theirs. Before we left the States we were guaranteed that "nobody would get off the plane without a flak vest." But the guys waiting for the extra-large vests didn't see theirs until the day before we crossed the border into Iraq.

We were taught to take only the necessities when we went out on the road into Iraq, so I tried to pack light when it came to my personal belongings. I took clothes, ammo, toiletries, medical supplies, bug spray, a sleeping bag, water and food. I was proud of the way I prepared for missions because it was very methodical. By planning what to take, I had more control over the situation—and my life—in a place where things were generally out of control. It turns out I didn't need half the shit I brought, but it did the trick.

I called my mom before I left for that first mission and she just started bawling. My dad gave me the speech about how he wanted to protect his daughter and couldn't. They were such a handful and I had a hard time dealing with the guilt I felt by putting them through this. I secretly just wanted to start moving already and check the place out.

Our final assignment before we headed out was picking up our civilian truck drivers. The funny thing was we didn't speak a lick of Arabic and they didn't speak any English, so we had a hell of a time in the beginning. We were trying to communicate with them because they had been driving throughout Iraq for a year and they knew more than we did about routes and locations of camps, but we couldn't understand them.

I was a little nervous about our mission until I was assigned to a truck with a Native American named Jerry Hood. Jerry was a member of the New Mexican Unit. He was about 5'9" with black hair and olive skin. The months in the desert kept him lean. By looking at him, you wouldn't think a forty-year-old man would be able to climb and maneuver around a truck the way he did, but he was as agile as they come, carrying chains and binders around his arms and snaking in and out of tight spaces. I could tell he was a hard worker and he knew a lot about the trucks and how to keep them running in the desert. I respected him instantly. He was a quiet, insightful and caring man and we got along very well. He explained the different kinds of terrain, what to look for and what was normal around there. He taught me how to stay safe.

I actually drove three times with him. The first mission, he made me drive without observing him. Then I had a right-seat drive where I sat shotgun and tried to absorb every last detail of his routine. I couldn't understand why he wanted me to drive first when I had no idea where I was going or what to look for, but now I know what he did made sense. It was better the inexperienced, nervous person drove first because southern Iraq is less populated, an open desert, and less dangerous. It was the safer leg of our journey.

My hands trembled the first time we crossed into Iraq and I gripped the wheel as we approached traffic. But Jerry assured me it was no sweat. Cars ran next to us like a regular, two-lane highway in the beginning, and I didn't like it. It turned out to be a pretty good instinct because it got too dangerous to trust cars around us because of the suicide bombers in the vehicles. By the end of our time in Iraq, we tried to keep the traffic away to keep moving. If we were running northbound, we had to push cars into the southbound lanes. It was safer having civilian traffic closest to our convoy travel in the opposite direction. That way, the amount of time a civilian vehicle had contact with a military vehicle was significantly less than if we traveled in the same direction. But if another convoy passed in the opposite direction, we shared the road with them.

I tried to watch the road, but I spent more time scanning my surroundings. I expected Iraq to be war-torn from watching the news, but it was beautiful. I remember the first couple of missions remarking about the pretty landscape. Southern Iraq was flat and sandy, but the region near Baghdad was lush and green. The Euphrates and Tigris rivers running through the background made for some good scenery. But it didn't take my mind off why we were there.

The soldiers from my platoon were so excited with so much energy. We talked about everything from our personal lives to the military and whatever chatter we could think up. We didn't have anything to do but talk and drive. It is amazing how positive and naïve we all were. One of the guys in my platoon said he was driving with his New Mexican partner and they were entering into a pretty dangerous area. As my guy drove along nervously, he looked over to ask his partner if he was doing okay and he was fast asleep. All of us new soldiers vowed we'd never get that complacent.

Our first mission lasted six days. We got to go to a camp in Tikrit and see Saddam's palace. Actually, I should say palaces. We arrived late at night, so it wasn't until the next day, after we downloaded the equipment, that we were able to explore the camp and see those beautiful buildings. I just couldn't believe I was standing in the middle of history, staring at the famous building that was blown up at the beginning of the war, the one where Saddam fired his shotgun off the balcony. There was marble and gold everywhere, beautiful staircases and ornate chandeliers dangling from the ceilings. Some soldiers got to stay in the palaces or they had workspaces there. Our energy level was high and we couldn't understand why the New Mexican unit was laughing at us and didn't want to go sightseeing. Finally it dawned on me that they had seen all of these places for the past year and the novelty had worn off. They were exhausted and war-torn.

Policy in the camp at Tikrit said we had to wear our flak jackets because it was dangerous. At first we didn't take the threat seriously, but when we heard mortars going off around us, we quickly changed our minds. What really clicked for us was when we learned that a mortar had blown up the chow hall the previous night. The enemy usually tried to target the most populated areas, like chow halls, to kill the largest number of people. Everyone was in gear that first night!

From left: SPC Andrea Brooks, SSG Robert Hupp, Michelle and SFC Richard Bartlett; behind them is SGT Andrea Motley

We were pretty creative about making our own rules when it came to driving and staying safe. One guy, Staff Sergeant Bartlett, was always in the lead of our convoy and he was great at getting us through certain points. He had a lot of military experience and was very much an alpha male. A highway patrol sergeant in his civilian life and towering well over six feet tall, his broad shoulders, barrel chest and booming voice commanded respect when he was looking to finish a job. He always spoke articulately, but he used military lingo all the time. Sometimes, it was a bit over the top the way he was always throwing out phrases like, "We're gonna push off at oh-six-hundred."

We never worried about passing cars. They were directed off the road and if they wouldn't move they were pushed. There were too many stories of car bombs blowing up convoys for us to be polite. At the end of our tour, we would tell the Iraqi vehicles to scoot over and they were fine with it. Most civilians didn't understand what we were doing because every convoy probably did it differently, so they took cues from us.

Our military dummy-proofed our routes by spray-painting signs that directed us to different routes and camps. Often, the most recent number for the emergency channel would be painted across a bridge. You could tell how long you had been in-country by how many different numbers were scrolled. There was a lot of spray paint everywhere.

But that practice seemed to stop by the time I left Iraq. I don't know if it was because those in charge decided we shouldn't be broadcasting our safety net across bridges for the enemy to read or if it was more because the Iraqis

A soldier catches a nap on top of his truck

were trying to clean up the country a little after the government was turned back over to them. They seemed to be letting us know they wanted to take their country back.

Everything about Iraq surprised me in the beginning. In some cities, I could see the destruction of war and remnants of car bombs, constant reminders that this was no joy ride. Most of the people were poverty stricken. Children walked around barefoot wearing torn, ratty clothes. Women worked without shoes. Food and water were scarce.

We would throw food to children when we could, but even that was risky because it put the kids in danger of being run over if they ran into the streets in front of the convoy. One time when we were stopped on the road, we handed MREs out to a group of children. We couldn't get over how skinny and malnourished they looked. I hoped someone would take care of them. Children didn't get routine showers or even have toothbrushes. Sometimes we'd put packages together for them when we had extras in our own care packages. We'd give them soap, water, candy, anything they might want or need. I told my family and friends about it and they sent over toys. I tried to give the girls purses and the boys balls and trucks.

Iraqi kids love soccer. Once we saw a group of children playing with a deflated ball. Someone donated a bunch of balls to us, so we were able to throw them to the kids and they were ecstatic.

Staff Sergeant Chad Schrack was a thirty-six-year-old soldier in my platoon. At 6'2" and 200 pounds, he was the poster child for fitness. With blonde-peppered hair, he was friendly, but always demanded a good work ethic from everyone. However, he always took the time to look for personal details that would help him understand where each person was coming from. Although it was business, he relied on finding out about our personalities to give him more information on where each person was coming from. It was never manipulative; he wanted to get to know each soldier on a human level. Although his baby blue eyes may have deceived those who didn't know him, they held the knowledge of a man who had lived a hard life (but you could never tell.) Schrack was one of my team leaders and an all-around great guy. He had a commanding yet charismatic presence and worked as hard as he could. Anything we wanted to give to the locals, we gave to Schrack's truck crew, because he was in a gun truck and he could maneuver more easily. He would zoom up, stop, hand a box to a child and go. And we could still roll at a constant speed, which was safer because nothing had to be thrown from the vehicle, reducing the chance of anyone getting hurt.

I know our government frowns on soldiers doing the kinds of things Schrack and our other crews did—worried that kids might get hurt or even killed in the process—but we did it safely. Taking care of Iraqi children was one of our top priorities, personally if not officially.

Girls had it rougher than the boys in Iraq. The boys would often shove the girls away and take their packages because that's the way of their society. Women are not equal, they're considered property. That's why whenever we were low on supplies for the kids, I'd make sure to throw whatever we had—food, candy, etc.—to the girls first. It seemed like things were changing by the time I left—I remember seeing little girls going to school.

I remember Jerry Hood telling me that someone gave a woman M&M's. She started eating them and refused to give them to this man. He started beating the hell out of her and our soldiers couldn't do anything but watch.

If women were working in salt fields, which is a very common job for them, I'd give them water and other things and attempt to tell them not to give them to the men. Looking back I guess I really wasn't all that surprised at what I saw. My first impression of Iraq was different than I thought it would be because the landscape was so amazing. Yet much of it was also just as I pictured it might be: depressing with lots of destruction, inequality and poverty.

Since most of the country was impoverished and had so little, Iraqis always kept even the most ancient trucks rolling down the road. One time, there was a guy driving with the hood up and his buddy was sitting inside with his feet dangling near the engine holding onto something to keep the truck running. Another time, we watched a guy with cattle crammed in the backseat. He stopped and let five of them out onto the road. We'd see thirteen-year-old kids driving trucks as big as ours. They drove in the wrong lanes or wherever they could. The lines on the road and north and southbound lanes meant nothing.

Kids would be on the side of the road selling just about anything you could imagine: old Saddam currency, scarves, jewelry, liquor, Viagra, hash, bayonets, porn, God knows what kind of pills and Marlboros. I don't think they were really Marlboros, though, more like second-hand cigarettes that didn't quite taste right, but people paid $5.00 a pack for them.

Some of the guys bought the porn even though they weren't supposed to have it. Much of it turned out to be gay porn or 1970's porn with women with hairy crotches. Poor guys were so bummed.

These child entrepreneurs gathered at places where they knew we regularly stopped our convoys. A little girl named Sara used to find me at one of our stops and I'd buy scarves from her. Even under all the dirt and ratty clothes, she was so beautiful. I loved to see her smile.

Iraqi men were interesting to watch. American women intrigued them, but they were more social with the men. From what I was told, women are for babies and men are for pleasure. It seemed to me like there was an underground homosexual community because it wasn't uncommon to see men holding hands and kissing. Men embracing men was more accepted over there and our guys would be so sick when they saw it. We couldn't understand why they were so obsessed with us then. It must have been our independence and light skin. Little kids would come up to me and touch my arm and tell me how white I was. At least, that's what I assumed they were saying. Another female soldier had red hair and she had to take her picture with everyone. The blondes were wooed. We didn't understand how they could be so pleasant to us and treat their own women like worthless property.

When we would finish for the night, we'd stop at military camps to shower, eat and sleep. We had gotten used to sleeping under, above or around our trucks out on the road. If we slept below our trucks, the New Mexican unit told us to put up chem lights so people knew we were there. It was rumored that this was because they had a situation where someone was actually run over while sleeping under their truck. Having the chemical light on would let people know someone was underneath the truck. We slept on cots on the ground or under the trailer of our trucks. Others slept on the hoods of their trucks. When it was cool, we'd sleep on the ground with a poncho

SSG Chad Schrack (l) and Michelle (r) pose with two Hajis during a mission

around the trailer to block the wind. When it was hot, we'd sleep on top of the trucks to keep the bugs away. In the beginning, it was pretty cold at night. We'd wake up to frost on the windows, which wasn't that bad because we'd just left Atterbury where we were living in igloos.

Al Asad: First Attack

We returned from that first mission crossing the border into Iraq a little exhausted, but got a second mission as soon as we walked through the gate. We had just enough time to get our trucks ready to go and we were out on the road again. Things were so fast-paced we wondered when we were going to get to rest. It was nice staying busy because time went so fast and we didn't want to stay off the road. All of the units that were in-country for the beginning of the war were being rotated out just as the new units were coming in, so there were tons of equipment to move in and out of Iraq. It was called a "surge."

We were attacked on our second mission into Iraq. An IED (Improvised Explosive Device) went off in the middle of the convoy. We didn't have radio communications to tell the front of the convoy the middle was hit. I watched the thick, black cloud of smoke mushroom into the air while I attempted to call the front of the convoy. My co-driver, Mullen, and I were trying to determine if it was really an IED that just exploded since we'd never seen one before, but it was too far away—about a quarter of a mile, near the front. It took about five minutes to get the front of the convoy to stop. Then it felt like it took another five years until I heard everyone was okay. Luckily, the IED blew in between two vehicles and everyone got away unscathed.

Later on that same mission, on the way to Al Asad, we saw a civilian bus explode from a roadside bomb. A Marine convoy was stopped in front of us because there was an IED buried on the side of the road in the town. The Marines called the EOD (Explosive Ordinance Device) team, the soldiers who take care of the IEDs. We were a little concerned about getting attacked because we were trapped between the roadside bombs in front of us and 200 civilian cars behind us, so we made sure we had full security. I remember seeing kids playing soccer nearby when the bus ran over one of the IEDs and hearing the deafening noise of the explosion followed by a huge black cloud of smoke that filled the air. It seemed so surreal. It wasn't like what I'd seen in the movies; this was the real deal and people actually were killed by the bomb. The kids playing soccer didn't even flinch. When I think about their lives, I think about how lucky we are here and that we don't have to worry if someone is going to live or die when they go to work that day.

Michelle and SGT Mike Mullen pose for a shot in the cab of the truck

We finally arrived at Al Asad, a Marine camp, six hours late because of the six IEDs that were found that day on the one-mile stretch of road.

On the way out of Al Asad, Mullen and I were in the lead truck. Sergeant Mike Mullen was a soldier who transferred into our company right before we were deployed. He was my age, tall and thin, and very laid back. He had every piece of electronic equipment, from MP3 players to computers and cameras. Whenever I wanted to purchase something electronic, Mullen was the man to find it at the best deal.

As I was driving out of Al Asad, Mullen was looking out for IEDs on the side of the road because it was inevitable that there were more. We were about five miles outside of the military camp when he started yelling, "Oh shit, oh shit!" Mullen was usually so unexpressive, that an "oh shit" would be like someone else yelling "murder" at the top of their lungs. He told me there were four holes next to each other and he thought he saw wires coming from the holes. That was a tell-tale sign that the holes were one big daisy-chained IED that would make one hell of an explosion. It was frustrating knowing there was danger and we weren't able to relay the information to the rest of our convoy because we had poor communication. We finally got hold of another vehicle in the convoy and they stopped before passing the IED. The convoy commander sent a message to let the people in charge of the roads know about the IED, figuring they would take care of it before it killed someone. We were part of the convoy that had made it past the IED and we were stopped a mile up the road, waiting on the trucks that were behind the IED. Mullen and I had stopped a whole line of civilian vehicles that were traveling the opposite way on the road until the rest of the convoy caught up. Those civilian vehicles were headed right for the IED but had no idea.

The first civilian vehicle had a man and woman in it and they looked pretty frustrated. I walked over to the man and said hello and communicated to him through hand gestures and "boom" noises that there was a roadside bomb up ahead. He immediately understood the delay and relayed it to the rest of the civilian traffic. After I told him, he headed to the trunk of his car. Oh Lordy, I thought, he's going to kill us. Mullen and I stood there gripping our rifles, ready for the worst, when the man pulled a box of chocolates out of his truck. He thanked us for warning him and gave each of us a piece of chocolate. That became the tone for the year. Interacting with civilians that seemed nice enough but always being cautious because at any moment they could try to kill us. We kept our weapons slung on our backs with one hand on the trigger and the other hand waving at the civilians. We never turned our backs on them either.

After waiting around for the IED to be cleared, the convoy commander decided to chance it and drive past it so we could get moving. It wasn't safe to drive by it, but the alternative was to sit on the side of the road and wait for the enemy to attack us. We weren't in a very good area. Once the IED was reported and the convoy was back together, we took off. Nothing happened to us, but I later found out two soldiers were killed by an IED on the same day in the same area. I couldn't help but wonder if word ever got back to the right people to remove the IED we thought we saw. I wondered if those guys would still be alive if we would have waited for someone to clear the bomb. It may have been a completely different part of the road, but I still wondered if it was the same road we were on earlier that day.

St. Michael's

St Michael's was a tiny camp in the run-down town if Iskandariyh. There was no running water and every Port-o-Potty truck driver got killed on the way to the camp, so they were always overflowing. The mailman was shot while trying to deliver the mail. The camp was so primitive that soldiers would make the food and put it in big, green containers that they used every day. They put on rubber gloves and used their hands to slop it on our plates. We just smiled and went with the flow because we only had to deal with it for a meal. Those guys lived like that every single day.

The camp was in a heavy combat zone, so there were no military women with the exception of maybe two medical personnel. On one day in particular, I remember our truck pulling into the camp with a huge communication antenna on top. We pulled to the gate for directions on where to park, but the guard said I had to climb on top and hold the antenna down while my co-driver maneuvered us through the overhead wires. I jumped up on top of the truck, pulled the antenna down and we were on our way. Then I noticed everyone around me had stopped working. They were all staring at me. It finally dawned on me that it was a camp full of Marines who were transitioning into that area and the 82nd Airborne, who were finally leaving country, was giving the reigns to the Marines in this little camp in a combat area. Some of them hadn't seen women in several months and there I was on top of a truck. I stayed close to my guys that night. It's not like I thought any of them would hurt me, they were just gawking and probably didn't even realize it, but it felt creepy. Yet, I sympathized with them. I felt like I was on a big, green platter for the guys to look at. I didn't like the attention.

For the first couple of missions, we were going to camps that had only been around for about nine months, so some of them were pretty rustic. Some didn't even have showers. It sure wasn't the Navistar that we were used to and I felt sorry for the soldiers who had to live like that for a year. We had to wear our flak vests everywhere we went at those camps. It was sweltering hot and the vests weighed about twenty to twenty-five pounds, but we did as we were told. It was a lot of weight for me in the beginning. I remember once I jumped into my truck to grab extra ammo for another soldier while we waited for the IEDs to get cleared on the way to Al Asad and the shifting weight from the flak vest threw me off balance and to the ground. I landed on my ass and immediately looked around. When I was sure no one saw me, I jumped to my feet. That was when I realized what a problem all of the extra weight was going to pose until I got used to it. The vest was about twenty percent of my body weight. Eventually, it just became a part of my body, but it took some getting used to.

I saw a lot of hearses on the road around that time. Iraqi hearses are basically cars with wooden boxes strapped to the roof. The dead are wrapped up in blankets and placed in the box. When a big attack happened and a lot of people died, we'd see these cars traveling with the boxes strapped to the top and wonder what happened the day before. Four days later, we'd find out about a battle with U.S. forces or insurgents launching an attack in a certain town.

Then—and even now—Al Asad was hell on earth. Tragically, the imminent dangers in Al Asad really hit home when fourteen Marines from the Third Battalion, 25th Marine Regiment were killed in a roadside bombing. The regiment was based in Brook Park, Ohio, which is only a stone's throw from my hometown. That attack came only days after six other Marines from the same regiment were killed in an ambush along the same stretch of road. We were already home when those Marines were killed, but it was enough to make our skin crawl to think that could have been us on any one of our missions through that same area.

We were having a hard time with directions out on the road. We didn't know where we were going, and when we got to a camp, whom to deliver to. By the end, we knew the roads and their signs to point us in the right direction. The New Mexican unit made us makeshift maps of some of the routes, but it was written on the back of cardboard and not very accurate. It was better than nothing, but getting lost in a combat zone was not something that any of us wanted to do. The first rotation, like the New Mexican unit, had to navigate with little to no directions. We had makeshift directions and by the time we left, there were maps from computers that were extremely accurate. Stories were always flying around about convoys getting lost for hours in downtown Baghdad. Soldiers were said to have paid taxi drivers $50 to get them to where they needed to be. Other stories told of the commercial Haji drivers attached to U.S. convoys who had driven longer on the roads than the soldiers leading convoys to where they needed to go. Our platoon had several people who were fantastic with directions and had GPS's with our routes entered in. Of course, Mullen was one of them.

Camp Scania

Camp Scania was the camp in between northern and southern Iraq. It was the place that took one day to get to from Navistar so we stayed there at least once a week. Scania was the last safe place before heading to the northern camps and a good resting place after returning from the more dangerous camps in the north.

There wasn't much there. It was a convoy support camp so the majority of it consisted of a huge parking lot for trucks to stage. The convoys would pull in for the night into the long rows of parking. There were barriers that separated the lanes that held around twenty trucks per row. There were tents for the soldiers stationed at the camp, a chow hall, showers, a PX and a gym. That was about it. Scania was in the middle of a farm so there was nothing around the area. No lights from towns, no noise, nothing. It was very peaceful. Since its whole purpose was to support convoys, it was the place where we were guaranteed a shower!

There wasn't any place for us to sleep inside the camp, so we stayed on our trucks and stared at the stars. There was no light pollution and all we could see were these brilliant, bright stars everywhere. It was like sitting in a planetarium. It was so peaceful at night when there was nothing but those quiet, beautiful stars for company. Schrack and I would sit and talk up on the top of loads on our trucks for hours, probably because we were so sick of talking to our co-drivers. I loved stopping on the road during night missions. I couldn't comprehend how some place so beautiful could be in the midst of something

45

so ugly with all of the violence and destruction. It was hard for me to grasp the beauty at first and the lives of the families who lived there. I couldn't imagine growing up in a country constantly in a state of conflict.

There was a little Haji-mart outside the gates of Scania. The Iraqis in the area had a great relationship with the military camp so they were able to set up a little shop outside the gates where soldiers could buy genuine Iraqi stuff. They sold old Saddam money, bootleg movies, jewelry, homemade purses, clothes, scarves, head wraps that all the Iraqi men wore and Iraqi flags. There was also a pet camel in this area and for five bucks, soldiers could sit on it and take a ride. The camp also had a golf driving range for soldiers to relax and actually do something fun. It was my favorite camp.

Camp Scania. This was behind the camp near one of the Haji marts where you could ride a camel for $5

The thing that sucked most about not having a place to stay while on the road was the dust and dirt. With no showers, no sinks and no toilets, we resorted to baby wipe baths. The first month we didn't bring stuff like that because we didn't really know what we needed. The New Mexican unit gave us a huge box of supplies to tide us over until care packages arrived with the necessities. We shared things so we would be comfortable. I would do a baby wipe down and then a bug spray bath. We would stink and be like that for about four days before we'd get a shower. We didn't want to change clothes because we were still dirty. Sometimes I would bring an extra uniform on the road and change into the clean one halfway through the mission. When I got back to my camp and opened the bag, I could smell just how bad I stank and then would rush that uniform right to the laundry. I've never smelled anything like it in my life. We would go to the chow halls at other camps and not realize we smelled so bad. The soldiers living at the camp who got showers regularly would either stare at us or get up and leave. There was no makeup, no looking pretty, no trying to do my hair. I would pull my hair back in a bun and leave it. My first shower after five days was absolutely amazing. I swear I never felt so fortunate to be clean in all my life. I didn't care if it was hot or cold water, it was a shower and I would thank my lucky stars for those days. I felt like I was going to Cinderella's Ball on the days I was able to shower.

The guys would call the females in the platoon "beautiful" just to make us feel like girls for a little bit. We would call them "handsome." It was the littlest things that made us feel halfway human and happy. They were our brothers. We teased each other like crazy, but every now and again they'd try to make us feel good, just like my real brothers would.

After a couple of missions, I had it down pat. I had a bag I took on every mission and had it packed as soon as we got back to camp. I had a whole routine with packing. I'm a hell of a packer these days because I know exactly how much soap, shampoo, lotion and toothpaste will get me through a week. I always had two bags—one on the road with me and one at camp, ready to go.

But all the control in the world over my things didn't always make me feel better. Some days were just bad. It might have been the heat or doing physical work that we weren't used to that made us edgy. For me, it was the most dangerous situation I'd ever been in and I was trying to deal with that stress on top of trying to do my job well. It was hard to keep it together sometimes. I was frustrated from the physical demands and weather and having to deal with making decisions, lack of resources, being hungry and dirty and dealing with the limitations the military put on us. It was tough not yelling at the people in charge who told me "no" or not going off on someone for something stupid. There were many times I just wanted to take my M-16 and beat it on my trailer just to get out some frustration. Every now and again when I'd reached my limit, I would let out a scream or throw something in the truck.

My friend, Elaine, would take our radio and beat it against the dashboard while yelling about how stupid people were. One day I got really fed up about something and took my Kevlar off and just threw it on the dashboard and the window shattered.

"Do you feel better now?" Mullen asked.

"Fuck you."

SSG Aaron Brown (bottom) and Lt. Bruce Neighbor

Around this time was when I realized my letters were being published in the paper back home. It took awhile to get the first copy from my Aunt Sandy, but when I saw it, I was shocked. I thought there would be a couple of sentences in there. I didn't know they were going to publish the whole letter. My stomach dropped when I saw it because I was writing from my heart to my family and just saying whatever came to my head. Everyone is going to think I'm an idiot, I thought. By the time I realized it, we were getting busy and I couldn't write or concentrate, so I would just write about whatever came to mind. The whole reason for writing was for my mom. I tried to write at least once a week, but it was probably less. When I realized everything was in the paper, I started to be a little bit more cautious writing about where we were and where we were going.

My mom said people were really responding to them and enjoyed hearing my side instead of the media. I liked showing the daily side of the life of a soldier instead of the media showing the deaths of the day.

Now that I'm home safe, I can say that I was fortunate enough to be in a transportation unit because I got to see the whole country. Some arrived and never saw much beyond their own camp. We got to interact with people more and drive through some amazing cities and see historic landmarks. My perspective might be different than others, but it was an awesome experience when we weren't in danger.

– 3 –

March

Killed in Action: 605
Wounded in Action: 3,071

I just wanted to say hello and let you all know that I'm still safe and sound.

I am very happy tonight because I finally got a shower with real running water! It has been five days since I've taken one and let me tell you how nice it is to be clean for the moment.

I see a sandstorm coming in, so I'll be sandy any minute now. Baby wipe showers just don't cut it after five days.

I finally had a decent meal. I ate breakfast the other day and the scrambled eggs didn't taste like eggs at all. I was so hungry and I took a bite and was disgusted with how bad they were. Then I took another bite and complained to another soldier about how bad they were. I thought to myself, if I wasn't starving these eggs would be uneatable. Yes, I finished it all even though it was terrible. Hey, food is food at this point.

After actually serving in a combat zone, I can really appreciate what my fellow brother and sister veterans went through. If you see a veteran today, thank him or her for their service and I bet they'll appreciate it.

We are all gearing up for St. Patrick's Day. Some of the soldiers are getting together and having a celebration of our own. Iraq and Kuwait do not allow alcohol, so we got nonalcoholic beer and we're using the green Gatorade packets to mix in the water for our beverages.

We are wearing our "desert" uniforms, but one of my soldiers brought one green "woodland" uniform and he's going to wear it for St. Paddy's Day. It's going to be funny because we'll all be in sand uniforms and there will be one guy in green!

49

We'll make the most if even though we can't celebrate as well as you all will back home. So have a beer for me!

There is not much to report back right now about Iraq. The only new thing I've learned is that northern Iraq is very cold. It drops to the 40s at night. It is not fun sleeping outside under your truck in 40-degree weather and having to wake up and get ready in the cold.

I was talking to soldiers who have been here for six months and they say it is always that cold at night.

We had our first mission where the Middle Eastern truck drivers convoyed with us. There are civilians that convoy with military vehicles to drop off supplies. It takes some of the load off the military truck drivers and supports the Iraqi economy.

That was an experience! We had to get all our soldiers on the same page and non-military, non-English-speaking people ready for our mission. It was funny watching everyone communicate with hand signals and sounds, and frustrating to find out the signals didn't work that well. After a while, everything worked out and everyone fell into a routine.

The Iraqi truck drivers were very friendly and polite. Every morning they would offer me tea and cookies. If any of the trucks broke down, even military vehicles, they would jump up and help us out. It was like we were one big team that couldn't communicate with words, but only by our experience together. They would talk in Arabic and we would talk in English and we'd all know what we were talking about. It was wild!

Now that I've been on the road for a while, I'm beginning to understand how important the truck drivers are to the military. The camps we pull into are so helpful and polite to us because they are so grateful to finally get their equipment.

I was in charge of this one mission and the captain was so thankful he gave all the drivers in the convoy these really nice Wiley-X goggles for the sandstorms. I thought to myself, we are just doing our job, but thanks!

Then on our next mission, we got a huge box of goodies from the Marines because we did them a favor by hauling their equipment.

I am beginning to see that I'm in a great position and my occupation is in high demand!

Well, I have to go to bed now. I need my sleep so I can be ready to drive tomorrow. It is pretty intense driving down the Iraqi roads and so I better rest while I can!

— MZ, March 15, 2004

S t. Patrick's Day was the first major holiday we were going to miss. We really had no concept of time. Monday or Friday didn't matter because it

50

was all mashed together. We never knew what day it was, but we realized St. Patrick's Day was coming up. We couldn't have alcohol in Iraq and Kuwait and we were bummed. The guy in the woodland uniform made us smile every time we saw him that day, but that was about it. We got some non-alcoholic beer that Budweiser sent us and took Gatorade packets and dyed them green. It tasted awful. We tried to celebrate by taking pictures, but most of them were posed. I knew my parents wanted to see us all at camp celebrating, so we would make up a scene and take Gatorade bottles and dye them green and then take pictures and say alright, let's go on with our day.

Holidays didn't seem all that important over there. For one soldier's birthday, his mom sent cookies, candles and party hats. He invited us all over for the cake, but more for the pictures he was going to send to his mom to show her that he celebrated his birthday. Some of the younger guys took it pretty hard on holidays. I think it was especially difficult for them because most of them had never been away from their families. It was a struggle for all of us to be away from home during the holidays and to be in a war zone, but they had it the worst. We tried to make it better by celebrating and making it at least a little special, but it never really did the trick.

We celebrated every kind of anniversary, like weddings and contracts, and births of new babies. Nancy's time in the Guard was up about three months into deployment and of course, she was at war and couldn't leave, so when she ETS'd (estimated time of separation or in laymen's terms, when she was supposed to get out of the military) we put balloons on her bed and made it a big deal. She was extra bitter for being in Iraq because she should have been out of the military and with her four-year-old son.

Regardless of whether it was a holiday or not, our platoon would all converge and talk. We were so close because of it. I noticed when I ran with another platoon, they didn't do that. They all went to their trucks or small groups. They didn't watch movies together and joke around. It was so depressing. Some of the guys in our platoon were just as emotional as women. If they went to breakfast and didn't invite each other, they got bitchy about it. If they didn't get enough attention, they threw temper tantrums.

A down side to being on the road was that we did miss out on what they call MWR, or morale, welfare and recreation. Toby Keith toured the country and we were a day behind him at every camp. The Baltimore Raven cheerleaders came to our camp and we missed it. Of course, all of the guys were hard up and totally bummed.

We had to find our own ways to have a good time and take our minds off things. We were stopped on the side of the road in a semi-safe area and the stop was taking so long so we passed time by dancing with the locals. It was entertaining for my co-driver, but I was still cautious not to turn my back on them and my weapon was slung across my back just in case. I hated being so suspicious, but that was the way it had to be because we didn't know who the enemy was. If the locals had jewelry or things they made, they gave them to me as gifts, but I always felt bad so I would have to trade them for a bottle of water or whatever I had on me. They treated American women with such respect it was a shame to see they couldn't do the same with their own women. We'd see the little girls and they would be amazed when they saw a female driver. I wanted to tell all of them they could do the same things and they didn't have to live in a country where they are shunned, but I didn't for obvious reasons. I wanted to tell them things could be different. You could see in the eyes of women who couldn't respond or show any emotion that it gave them hope. I just wanted to connect with them so badly.

Today we had to say goodbye to our new friends from the New Mexico 720th Transportation Company. We are now out on our own and they are finally going home to see their families.

It was amazing how close we got to them in such a short amount of time. Both of our platoons had the same personality, so it was easy to work and joke around with them.

Before they left, the 720th gave us all kinds of supplies that made their life easier while they were stationed here. It was stuff we probably wouldn't have thought of until halfway through the deployment. Jerry, my co-driver from the 720th, gave me a bag of tools. I really appreciated all the help they gave us and all that we've learned from them. I hope we will be able to pass on knowledge and some comfort to the people who will be our replacements like the 720th did for us. – MZ, March 20, 2004

The 720th was kicked out of the nest and we were on our own. Jerry, the guy who trained me, gave me a huge bag of tools that he knew would come in handy. I was even more grateful that they were practical. Some platoons were so into playing war they had knives strapped across their chests. We just kind of shook our heads at them because we weren't fighting the kind of war that we'd ever get close enough to need a knife as a weapon.

Sometimes it was frightening to watch how other platoons operated. One platoon had a young guy in charge because their platoon sergeant was injured and sent home. The next guy in charge was a lot younger and tried to follow all of the rules. They were happy just to be making it.

My platoon was a lot more creative and our leadership supported our creativity. Our commander called the other groups the "Yes Men" and we were always the ones questioning the authority. See, we all had civilian jobs and the leaders in our platoon were compensated for the difference between our military and civilian pay for the year we were there. So we were able to be a little bit more vocal about others making decisions for us when we knew they were wrong. We had people too far removed from what was really going on in the war making decisions for us and we were just trying to use common sense and make practical decisions. We didn't care if we got demoted because we'd still make the same amount of pay. Safety and keeping our soldiers alive were more important than following some nonsense decision.

Now that we were on our own we had to be even sharper. When we first took over the missions, things didn't go well at all. We were all frustrated with each other and we couldn't figure out why things weren't running smoothly. The New Mexican unit just sat back and let us figure it out. We got into a huge argument with a platoon sergeant one evening while we were trying to figure out a better system than we used for the convoy that day. We started having AARs (After Action Reviews) after every mission, to figure out how to make things work and create a routine for ourselves. By the end, convoy operations were a fine-oiled machine. We knew our roles and what needed to be done. It was entertaining training our replacements because it was comforting to watch them go through the same trials. I'm sure they didn't feel that way at the time, but I'm sure they understand now. We just had to realize our place in the cycle. The growing pains of the convoy have now become a fond memory.

It seems like we are getting into a routine now with our missions. We go out on the road for five to ten days, return home for one day of maintenance, and go back on the road. It doesn't give us much downtime, so we have to be organized in order to get everything accomplished before our next mission.

Mullen and I have to inspect our truck, fix anything that is broken, get our laundry service, buy snacks and baby wipes for the road, clean our weapons, and try to rest with the little downtime we have.

We look forward to the maintenance day because it is the one or two nights that we can sleep at our camp, in our own cot and collect our mail that you all send us! It is also the time that we get good chow. Camp Navistar, my home, has the best food anywhere around Iraq!

Mullen and I will start talking about our "plan of attack" when we are about 30 miles from camp of how we will get stuff done.

This last mission was pretty uneventful. The only excitement we had was when we were traveling down this bumpy, dirt road and Mullen and I noticed this crazy rat-

tling sound. Neither one of us could figure out what it was, but everything seemed to be intact. I finally figured it out once we got to our rest point for the evening.

We parked our truck and it was dark and all I wanted to do was get our cots set up so we could go to sleep. I climbed onto our truck and noticed that one of the cots was not where it was supposed to be. We keep our cots bungee-corded to the outside top of the cab and one of the cots was standing on end on the back of the catwalk.

I thought to myself, aaahhh! We almost lost one of our beds! That would have been tragic! I quickly pulled it down to make sure nothing was wrong with it. As I pulled it off the catwalk, I noticed it was singed.

Apparently it got loose from the top of the cab and as it was falling, it melted to the exhaust because then it didn't fall off the truck. As I opened it to make sure it was still usable, I said to Mullen, "Mullen, YOUR cot is melted."

He looked at me and said, "I am pretty sure that was YOUR cot."

We both looked at each other like, hmmm, what are we going to do now that there is only one cot? I opened it up and it sounded like burnt plastic ripping away from itself and it looked really charred on the ends. Fortunately it was OK.

We've learned our lesson and we make sure our cots are extra secure before we go anywhere now.

There were more civilian truck drivers in our convoy again. It was not as difficult the second time to work with the non-English-speaking civilians. I think we all realized it takes patience and good visuals to get everyone on the same page and for things to run smoothly.

The civilians were from Pakistan and Saudi Arabia. Most of the soldiers would trade food and tea with them for candy and cigars. They'd set up rugs and sit beside their truck and eat meals, play cards and drink tea. There are little kitchens set up on their trailers with an ice cooler and a mini stove.

When we stop for the evening, they make gourmet dinners. We are eating an MRE, and they are making homemade rice and chicken! Every time we stop, the civilians will offer us food and drink and love to try to talk to the soldiers. Nobody knows what each other is saying, but it's fun to just laugh and try to figure out what is being said.

By the way, the tea is awesome! It is sweet and great to drink first thing in the morning.

The civilians have different cultures than us westerners do. For example, the men wear dresses or flowing clothes, they embrace when they greet each other and give kisses to other males and they will hold hands while talking to one another. It is great because sometimes they will talk to soldiers and hold their hands. The guys are getting used to it and are not as freaked out by a male grabbing their hand like they were in the beginning.

One of the civilians asked if I was married and if I wanted to be his third wife. I said no thank you. They are not used to working with females, especially light skin, blue-eyed females. They are cautious talking to the females unless we approach them. They will stare and wave when they see me.

The male soldiers keep pretty good tabs on the female soldiers to make sure there are not any problems. I feel like I have 30 big brothers that look over my shoulder to keep me safe. It is annoying at times but when I think about it, I appreciate it.

We got to see more camps this trip. We had to go to two Marine camps and it was very interesting. The first was really nice and had lots of amenities and the second was a hole in the wall. The second camp didn't even have a kitchen to cook food. They had been eating MRE's for the past year and barely had running water! I don't understand why because 30 miles down the road was the really nice Marine camp that had it all.

I haven't figured out why some camps have it all and others don't. The only thing I do know is my camp looks better and better after every mission. I am really fortunate to stay somewhere so nice. Now if I could just spend some time there! – MZ, March 26, 2004

We were starting to get into the swing of things and become familiar with some of the camps we were stopping at regularly. In the beginning, we were happy just to find our way to a camp. Then we had the movement control center scheduling when we were leaving. Each camp had a movement control center, similar to an air traffic control center, responsible for convoys moving in and out of the camp. They scheduled times for convoys to leave so the roads were secured. Convoys coming into the camp were told where to park, where to stay, and whether room was available to sleep, or if soldiers would have to sleep in their trucks. After that, we had to figure out where the chow hall was and other places we might need while we were there. And every camp had its own set of rules. At this camp we had to salute, but at that one we didn't. At this camp we had to carry weapons, but at that camp we stored them somewhere. We were like abused children and got yelled at a lot because the rules changed everywhere. Once we got to a camp and inside the wire, as it was called, we were able to settle down for a while and regroup. We couldn't just stop and pitch tents on the side of the road because we'd be killed.

By the end of our tour, we had our camp stops mapped out. We stopped at this one because they made omelets for breakfast and that one because there was a movie theater. One camp had killer milkshakes and another had an amazing PX where we could stock up. One had cheaper phones. We planned our routes around food and entertainment. Whether it was the computers, showers or a place to eat, it was worth the push to make it there. It gave us a routine. We had it down to the point where we were able to eat two meals a day, which was huge to us because we were lucky to make it to the right place on time in the beginning.

We started to prefer being on the road. It probably sounds weird because that's where the danger was, but there was less stress and we were in charge. When I told my mom I'd rather be getting shot at than in my camp she told me she'd rather I was miserable and safe at camp. But from our perspective, we wanted the control to make our own decisions rather than letting a few idiots make them for us and change everything around. It seemed like they didn't understand what we were going through and didn't really care. On the road, at least I could rely on the people around me to work toward the same goal of staying alive and getting to the next camp.

It got to the point where we told our truck master not to give us any off days because we didn't want to be at camp. They put so many demands on us it was ridiculous. In between missions, we had to go to an equal opportunity class or a sexual harassment class although it wasn't even close to what we needed at that time. We didn't want to deal with paperwork and all of the bullshit that happened there. Every time we went home, tents changed or the truck parking rules changed. When we finally got radios, we would call ahead to Camp Navistar and find out what had changed so we could prepare ourselves to be pissed off. We would be so relaxed on the road and then get about two hours outside of camp and just start snapping at each other and tensing up. It took a couple missions to figure out why we were fighting so much right before the end of a mission. Sometimes we weren't even unpacked and they were already throwing new rules at us. At one point, they decided we weren't allowed to keep any personal belongings in the trucks in between missions, which became a real pain in the ass. We'd be dead tired and dirty and have to clean out our trucks, the same trucks we'd been in for months, and put everything away just to turn around and get back on the road in a day or two. That was where we lived. We had a radio, food, books, paperwork, coats, blankets and it all had to be cleaned out after every mission. If they had just kept it consistent, it would have made things that much easier on the soldiers.

Living on the road had drawbacks, but they didn't compare to the hair-pulling days at Navistar. Sure, we had to learn to deal with the extreme temperatures changes, but we would have done the same thing at camp. It was pretty cold on our missions during the first few months. Up in northern Iraq, it dropped into the forties at night. I thought the cool nights and warm days would last forever, but it was just hot by Easter. The one thing the military did provide us with was wonderful sleeping bags. They were Gortex with three layers and stayed cozy on the inside. We wore stocking caps on our heads and it felt good until the middle of the night when we realized how cold it was. It was so cold, in fact, that we just couldn't jump out of our sleeping bag and throw on freezing clothes. So, I learned to sleep in boxers and a T-shirt and keep my clothes nearby. In the morning, I'd put my uniform inside my sleeping bag before putting it on. I did the same with my shirt.

We had a lot of little tricks like that. We learned not to put our boots on the ground when we slept under the trucks because there were wild dogs running around that would take them. We learned to prop them on the truck so they wouldn't be on the ground because we never knew what was wandering around. Bartlett had a hard time sleeping one night because he felt like someone was staring at him. When he woke up, there was a dog sitting right in front of him staring at his face. He just propped himself up, started laughing and watched it until it wandered away.

As difficult as the cold was, it was better than the heat. We contemplated that question a lot, by the way: Which was worse, heat or cold? When we were on the road, and for ninety percent of the time over there, we were always outside either driving, sleeping or working. The heat was miserable to drive through, but the chill was impossible to shake. We called the guys in the gun trucks the "Teenage Mutant Ninja Turtles" because they wore their Gortex and it was all emerald green. They were just trying to stay warm on top of their trucks with the wind whipping at them. They had nothing to protect them from the weather, explosions and dirt. We called them our little "heroes in a half-shell."

The bugs out on the road were pretty unbearable in the spring and summer months. My neck was always covered with mosquito bites and the sand fleas took care of my forearms. My shoulders, elbows, hands—everything was covered in bug bites. A friend rubbed Cortisone all over my arms to stop the sting, but it just made them itch more. Most of us scratched until we bled and it happened every mission. For some reason Motley and I got bitten more than everyone else. SPC Andrea Motley was a young college student. She was average height but very lean and all muscle. Motley exercised all the time and participated in several decathlons in the States. When we were out on the road, Motley was down to business. She had her truck organized and ready to go every mission.

It didn't matter how much bug spray I used; I itched the bloody scabs until we got back to camp and they had a chance to heal. As soon as they started to, we were already back on the road. Every night, before I went to bed, I sprayed my sleeping bag down before spraying my arms, legs, face and hair.

Then I'd repeat as necessary. It was like that all summer. We all smelled like bug spray, sweat and the stink of the day. If we didn't shower, at least we still had the bug spray so they weren't as attracted to us. Eventually, I had five different kinds of bug spray. My parents got me this deep forest bug spray and it turned out to be the only thing that worked. I always had a bottle of that stuff with me.

Another thing I couldn't stomach while on the road was eating MRE's, so my family and friends sent gobs of food. I ate a breakfast bar and water in the morning. The food in the chow halls was barely edible, but we ate every bite because we never knew when we were going to get a chance to eat again. I remember eating eggs that weren't even the right color, but I didn't care. Now that I'm back home, it took months before I could eat an egg and I still can't eat a breakfast bar because I ate so many overseas.

The one thing I'll probably never get over is how incredibly hot it was there. Temperatures reached 150 degrees Fahrenheit and although most of us had air-conditioned cabs, it didn't matter because we had to have the windows down to stick our weapons out. It just kept getting hotter and hotter and hotter. Just when we thought it couldn't possibly get any worse, the mercury would shoot off the charts. It was so hot we could make Ramen noodles in our trucks. All we had to do was cut off the top of a water bottle and pour in the noodles because the water was already plenty hot enough. If I poured water on the ground, it would evaporate immediately. If I laid down to change a tire and my skin touched the ground, it burned.

We didn't waste water on the road. JD and I knew exactly how much we drank and took extras just in case. JD was another one of our bright college students. He had dark hair and brown eyes and at 5'10," his black hair framed a little boy face with a smile women noticed. Everybody thought he was cute, but he was never confident enough to pursue women. He was one of the few people everybody got along with. We rode together for much of the deployment. We probably each drank about a case of twelve-liter bottles per day. Everyone had a cooler in the back of their truck just for water. There came a point in the summer when we were rationed a bag of ice per person. Every night someone was in charge of getting ice for the convoy. That was an actual task. Another one was to make sure the trucks had coolant. We were constantly reminded of the blazing heat and believe me, it didn't matter that there was no humidity, it was still hot. I was wearing my PT (physical training) shorts one day at camp and the wind blew and burned my legs. The only way to describe that kind of heat is like taking a blow dryer on the hottest setting and blowing it on yourself outside in the middle of summer. It was asphyxiating, but it was amazing how our bodies adapted to the climate. It cooled down tremendously one night and I was shivering so hard I could barely stand when a soldier walked up to me and pointed out it was seventy-nine degrees. I still couldn't stop shivering.

All of the chow halls had air conditioning, but because of the incredible heat, they overheated all the time. We'd be in a camp and all of a sudden we'd hear the slow motion of everything shutting down. There were many days when the generators would overheat and shut down. When it happened, Nancy and I would strip down to boxers and sports bras while the guys sat there in their shorts and we all just dripped with sweat. Nancy was another female in our platoon and we were the same age. She was a strong-willed, intelligent single mother and although she was only five-foot-three, Nancy was strong as an ox with broad shoulders and blonde hair. Having worked on a farm as a kid, Nancy understood the meaning of a hard day's work and could do what a lot of others couldn't physically. Although she was capable of hard work, she was easily agitated, which made her somewhat intimidating. She ran a tight ship and could snap in an instant. She had problems with her blood pressure and would not tell someone immediately if she was upset, but she would make them pay later.

We dealt with the heat like any adults by hurling water balloons and dousing each other with water guns that we got from care packages. We had a big water balloon fight one day while some Italian guys were stationed at our camp and they accidentally got involved. Water balloons were flying and they thought we had lost our minds. I ducked for cover behind one of the Italians and egged them on to hit me with a balloon. The Italian guy eventually figured out what was going on and then all of a sudden moved and they all drenched me. Then we went after the Italian guy. He didn't speak any English and we didn't speak Italian, but we all laughed and chased each other with water balloons. It was little things like that that kept our sanity.

Showers were a gamble depending on the weather. They didn't always have cool water and sometimes it was just burn-your-ass hot. We had to get clean and get out. There was no such thing as a shower just to cool down.

Showering in general was a unique experience anyway. In another military camp, Baghdad International Airport, or BIAP, the showers were outside and constructed of two pieces of wood that formed a cross to divide it into four showering areas with wooden doors. There was a tank above the wooden "shower" so gravity forced the water down the pipes into the shower. It looked like the showers used in M*A*S*H. The nice thing about an outdoor shower was the cool breeze. It was weird showering outside, but I kind of liked it. I loved standing in that little wooden box completely naked, covered

The showers at Baghdad International Airport

only from my knees to my neck. When the wind blew, it was wonderful. There were no boots or flak jackets. It was just me completely naked getting clean.

One time Elaine was showering in those wooden showers and there had been a larger number of troops than usual that day and she ran out of water in the middle of her shower. We happened to be on the same mission that time and she came walking towards me in a towel and her hair looked strange. The closer she got I realized that her hair looked funny because it still had shampoo in it. She begged me to dump bottles of water over her head to get the shampoo out. After I doubled over from laughing at her, I cut a hole in a bottle of water and it trickled out until she was shampoo-free.

The Hajis

Along with shitty food and curious showers, the Hajis became another part of life on the road in Iraq. Haji was a term used by the military to describe an Iraqi person, or any person from the Middle East. It was quicker than saying "Iraqi person" or "Middle Eastern person," so pretty much anyone was called Haji if they we not us. In the beginning I questioned whether that was a derogatory term until I saw one of our contractors with a nametag on that said Haji. I realized Haji was a common Middle Eastern name, like John is for us. That was good enough for me. The term Haji got hyphenated and came to mean anything that was indigenous to that area. There were Haji-tents, Haji-food, Haji-marts, etc.

The civilian truck drivers who escorted us were supposed to cut down on the number of soldiers that had to be on the road, but realistically there weren't enough military trucks or drivers to handle all the work. It was the luck of the draw on which civilian truck drivers went with us on missions, but after sixth months we generally had the same civilian drivers over and over again and we got to know each other.

One thing about the Hajis, they made the best chai tea with sweet milk. The Middle Eastern culture is all about sharing, so if they have food they're going to offer it no matter how little it might be. We always gave them food back, like an apple or something to drink. Sometimes we would eat what they gave us and sometimes we wouldn't. It all depended on how daring we felt, but we always took whatever they gave us. One guy always had pistachios, which I love, so we shared back and forth. My favorite driver gave JD and me a

Michelle with two Hajis

non-alcoholic beer every day. We didn't even like it but it was insulting not to take it. His nickname became beer-Haji.

One time in an early mission, I noticed a Haji in one of the military trucks backing up while the soldier who was supposed to be driving it just stood there looking confused. "I don't know, he's trying to tell me something and I don't understand so he just jumped in the truck and did it his way," he said. It was so entertaining when we finally figured out these guys knew more than we did. We were brand new and this civilian had been driving for at least a year in-country.

Another time I came outside and there were five Hajis standing on the back of my truck and when I asked what they were doing they told me, "This no good." They were fixing a load they didn't think was secured well enough.

One of my favorite Haji stories was when we were in a parking lot draining our cooler. Suddenly, this Turkish guy started bathing in our dirty, old cooler water. We kind of ignored him and just let him do his thing. Because security was so tight, they couldn't go into chow halls and they couldn't bathe. They would sometimes be on the road for two weeks with no shower or they showered right out in the open. Some did their laundry on the road. By the end, they started getting showers at the camps for the commercial drivers and some places had snack areas where they could eat, but it took a lot of time.

Because Hajis weren't allowed in the chow hall unless we escorted them, Schrack and I did so every night. We just wanted to make sure they got at least one hot meal a day if we got one. We would eat first and then return to the vehicles to round up the civilian drivers. They were allowed in the chow hall only fifteen minutes before it closed. Some of the military guys didn't think they were worthy of sharing their food with them and they didn't take care of the civilian drivers. They argued that the company they worked for gave them food. But I argued that the Army gave us food and MREs and I knew how much I hated eating them. These poor guys were driving by themselves through a combat zone with no body armor, no armor on their vehicles, nothing. The military always rode two in a truck so we drove half as long as these poor civilians. They were tired, dirty and hungry.

But Schrack and I always went out of our way to treat the Haji truck drivers like human beings instead of dirty foreign people and they appreciated it. In return, they looked out for us and helped us out when they could. They would help me strap down a load if I needed it because they understood it was a give-and-take relationship. We were all on the same team there, but a lot of the military guys couldn't understand that. It was fun having broken conversations and trying to understand each other. We had a good time with them. They would always ask, "Where's your boyfriend, Superman?" He was another one of the military guys that felt the same way as I did and helped out taking care of the civilians. They called me "the little girl" or "blue eyes."

These people who traveled with us risked their lives as well. If we got stopped, they were screwed, too, because they didn't have any protection. At least we had armor on our doors, but they had nothing. The enemy targeted their trucks because they were "soft," easy targets. Little kids threw rocks through the windshields because they felt betrayed that these men were helping American troops. The kids knew we wouldn't shoot at them and the Hajis got hurt for us. There were many missions where a civilian truck driver sought aid from U.S. soldiers because rocks or bricks had been thrown through the windows of the commercial trucks.

Michelle (second from left) and SPC Joanna Kim (fourth from left) pose with Hajis

In the military's defense, any civilian could be a threat and we were trained not to trust the civilians or the Iraqi National Guard, but we also realized which civilian truck drivers we could trust and which ones to look out for. We wanted to give people the benefit of the doubt because we were sick of being suspicious of people, but we really couldn't afford to let down our guard. At the beginning of missions, the convoy commander would collect all the Hajis' cell phones because there had been situations where information about convoys leaving and their locations was getting back to the enemy. Also, cell phones were used to set off IEDs, so we didn't take any chances. In another incident, a Haji in Mosul walked into a chow hall wearing a bomb that killed several soldiers. We knew we had to be cautious of our foreign friends, but there were several levels of trust.

For some reason, their companies barely gave them enough water and really didn't care if they ate so they were constantly begging us for food. It got to the point where the Hajis from other convoys started stealing things off of our trucks. I yelled at one of the guys when he tried to nonchalantly grab a bottle of water off my truck. I found out they had been there for days with no water and they were being treated terribly.

The two companies owned by Halliburton, KBR and Al Hamada, made a killing on these "third country nationals," or TCNs, that traveled with us. A U.S. soldier responsible for being the liaison between our military and Al Hamada told me the Al Hamada group got $250,000 a day to send their truck drivers out no matter what. All they had to do was get their drivers out by the time we needed them and the money was theirs. The drivers were paid pennies for what they did. One company hadn't paid their contractors in months, so the drivers were basically working for free.

The money that certain corporations are making over there is ridiculous. We as soldiers aren't making nearly enough for the amount of danger we're put in. You see, Kellogg, Brown and Root and KBR are connected to Halliburton, a company whose board Dick Cheney used to sit on. And KBR was making a fortune and pushing it in our faces. We know these big companies are in bed with the government and they're getting paid a shitload of money. The American contractors who worked for KBR would laugh in our faces because they would get more protection, tons of tax-free money, free vacations all over the world and their jobs weren't that difficult. The KBR people had two-person trailers and we lived in fifteen-person tents. Camped out in front of the trailers that the KBR employees lived in at Navistar was a huge satellite with the Halliburton logo branded across it, so we were pretty sure they were connected. We lived in the same camp, so it wasn't like they couldn't get the stuff there. We weren't allowed near their trailers. We were sleeping in tents that leaked and they just laughed at us.

The money for soldiers versus contractors was disproportionate. At one point, Halliburton couldn't account for six billion dollars and the government just dismissed it. It was front-page news in the *Stars and Stripes*.

Our country is struggling as it is; we can't afford to pay teachers what they deserve or grant-fund many important non-profit positions. Yet the Halliburton scandal was explained to us as an "accounting error." It's ironic that the civilian job I am currently working at is funded through grants and yet the job that I did over there still can't save my job here at home. Once again, they're taking away something I'm passionate about.

It was strange that all this was going on and the Hajis couldn't even communicate with us to tell us how corrupt the company was that employed them. There wasn't much we could do, but right around when we found out they weren't getting paid, a soldier in a leadership position contacted their company and they suddenly got paid. We all volunteered to go to war but these guys didn't. They were told this was their job and ordered to do it. Their contracts lasted about two years and they were bound to them. It was all about big business. The war had nothing to do with civil rights.

– 4 –

April

Killed in Action: 740
Wounded in Action: 4,283

Guess what, I'm back on the road – surprise, surprise! Our mission this time is different because we are supporting another truck company and providing security for them.

I am sad because I'm not in my semi, but a Humvee. One of the nice things about driving in a Hummer is that I can take it to more places than I can the semi. For example, I can drive to chow instead of walking. I can go to the PX if it's far away.

I can't complain too much about this mission. Look, I'm typing right now instead of unloading a semi. This really isn't too bad! I just miss having my semi as my little "home away from home." I also like sitting up much higher in the semi than the Humvee.

This has been an interesting mission so far. We had a vehicle get stuck in the sand and I had to call for support from the "military sheriff." The "sheriff" is this mysterious radio frequency that you see written all over Iraq on bridges and passed out at safety briefings.

I'll pass a bridge and spray-painted on it will say, "emergency sheriff freq is . . ."

I never thought it worked until I had to use it to get the vehicle recovered. The sheriff called a company to provide security for us and they called a unit to bring a vehicle to pull out the stuck vehicle.

It is amazing how the whole U.S. military works together to support each other. We haul stuff for companies, like the engineers. The engineers use their equipment that we hauled to build us stuff and the MPs provide security for both of us while the cooks feed us. I am beginning to see how we are all interconnected.

I miss my friend Elaine (Coleman). She is the girl who went to Buckeye High School with me and then joined the unit I was in. We are in different platoons, so we hardly get to see each other. She is usually on missions with her platoon while I'm on missions with mine.

I think we got to see each other one time last month because we both happened to stay at Camp Navistar at the same time. When we saw each other, it was like a reunion! We ran and hugged each other like it had been years! I think we had a total of 10 minutes to talk before we both had to drive away.

Even though we don't get to see each other that much, we found a way to keep in touch. We have a notepad that we write on when one of us is back at Camp Navistar. We write about our missions, what is going on at home and things like that. We also can ask each other for favors, like turn in each other's laundry if there is time.

If I write in the notebook, I'll put it on Elaine's bed and she can read it and write back while she is at Navistar. That was our creative way to keep up without seeing each other.

All the soldiers have to rely on each other to get anything done at Camp Navistar. Since we've been so busy and we are out on the road so much, it is difficult to get personal stuff done in such a short amount of time.

There is usually one person, though, who is staying back who can help us out. Usually someone has an appointment, has to go somewhere in a few days, or his or her truck is being worked on. This stay-back person is treated like gold because he or she can get valuable tasks accomplished for us.

The types of things that have to get done that we don't have time for is dropping and picking up laundry and mail.

My friend Dawn drives for the commander and he isn't always on the road, so she may be back at Camp Navistar and can help me out. She will drop my laundry off and mail things for me. In return, I will buy her a carton of cigarettes in Iraq as payment or buy her some gift from out on the road.

Turning in laundry is quite the experience. There is a trailer set up for it.

You walk into the trailer up to one of the workers who is sitting at a cubicle with a pad of paper. You have to dump all of your dirty laundry out into the cubicle and hold up each item for the person to document on the paper.

There are four cubicles, but there is usually a line to drop off laundry, so everyone in line gets to see what you are turning in.

They write down what the item is and the color. It is an embarrassing experience to hold up your underwear and try to decipher what color it is based on the little flower pattern. It is even worse if it's someone else's underwear!

We pulled into a camp yesterday and since we weren't unloading, we had some down time.

SGT Hicks saw a puppy wandering around, so he had to go play with it. Hicks is such a tough guy until he sees the Iraqi children and puppies. His heart just melts and he has to take care of them.

He fed the puppy three MRE's and the puppy's brothers and sisters came over and wanted food. The puppies surrounded Hicks and they all were trying to get food from him.

By the end of the day, Hicks decided he wanted to take one of the puppies back to Navistar to have as a pet. We talked him out of it.

At the end of the evening, we set up our cots and got ready for bed. I told the guys to make sure they put their shoes on the truck so the puppies didn't take them. I told the guys three times to put their shoes up before we went to bed. We woke up in the morning and SPC Hawk asks, "Where is my shower shoe? I'm missing one."

It turns out Hawk forgot to put his shower shoes up and the puppy took it. We found it about 200 feet away and it was all bitten up.

I couldn't help but laugh and I though to myself, "Didn't I say put your shoes up?" I didn't say anything because I didn't want to sound like his mom.

Well, it is about time for us to leave camp and return to Navistar. Home sweet home, here I come. – MZ, April 2, 2004

About three hours outside camp, we always stopped in a camp called Cedar to check out our trucks. Cedar was in Southeastern Iraq, only miles from the city of Ur, the oldest city in the world. We checked the tires, greased up everything, cleaned the truck out and wrote out maintenance slips. When I got to Camp Navistar, I packed more food and baby wipes and prepared the truck. When it was my turn to be in charge, there wasn't much time to worry about too many personal things because mission tasks took precedence. I had to think about whether we had a soldier from maintenance and a truck, who was in which truck, what weapon serial numbers everything had, who our combat lifesaver was, who was going to pick up this and that, who was going to run south and whether we had enough gun trucks before I could think about myself. We assigned a person as the non-commissioned officer-in-charge and another the convoy commander, and they worked on the issues. It was a lot of hard work running a convoy because of all that was involved preparing for movement, but we always managed to get it all done.

From left: SSG Bob Carter, Michelle, SPC Elaine Knopf and SPC Ryan "Willy" Gearheart

Staying at Camp Navistar became a usual routine of cramming laundry, letter writing, maintenance and inspections into our down time. Nothing ever seemed to change at camp, including the faces of those who somehow managed to dodge every mission. We had only minor contact with the enemy during a mission by that point and that was when the roadside bomb exploded in our convoy. Most of our experience was just being dirty and not getting time off, but when we started telling brass that we needed more support and they weren't helping us, we also started noticing the same soldiers hanging out at camp when we returned from every mission.

There was a distinct tension between the soldiers who mainly stayed back at camp and those who actually went out on the road—and so the struggle began. Those of us who went on convoys felt that those who stayed back didn't understand what we were going through. Those who stayed behind felt like they were busting their asses at camp. People were starting to take sick leave for minor injuries and illnesses, and some soldiers began taking advantage of it. They would go to TMC (Troop Medical Center) and whine about some kind of pain so they didn't have to go on the road. We started seeing the potential problems of those who would abuse the system and they started to emerge. The soldiers who were always figuring out how to get out of work only made us have to work harder and we resented them for it. Some people had legitimate reasons for using sick call and missing a mission or two, but those who abused the system will have to live the rest of their lives knowing their laziness and selfishness put other soldiers in danger. Since we were always busy and on different missions, it was difficult to notice who was on sick call until someone pointed it out to us. If anyone stayed at the camp for more than a few missions, they became different than those on the road because they were considered lazy. It's hard to explain, but the tension developed. The leaders knew who they could count on and who was unreliable, and I wished they would have been treated worse than the Hajis.

When all the work was done for the next mission, we had a little time to ourselves. I tried to spend as much time with Elaine as I could. Elaine was my best friend from high school and she joined my unit back in 1996. She's 5'6" and very thin. Elaine is a very picky vegetarian and the chow halls didn't have much of a selection for her so she lost twenty pounds in the first six months. It was so great having her in the unit. She had finished her contract in 2002 and reenlisted when she found out we were going to war. It was comforting having someone there who had known me since the eighth grade. Elaine is very organized and

Michelle and SPC Elaine Knopf on the side of the road

detailed and she can get stubborn if she thinks no one is listening to her. She knew what I was thinking or feeling just by looking at me and I could do the same with her.

One of the drawbacks of being at war together was some of the conversations with those at home. Elaine's sister worked at the same junior high school as my mom and we learned early on that we had to get our stories straight before we called home. If one of us told too much information to our families about how our deployment was going, the other family would find out. So, part of the notepad was also to put what we could and could not tell our families. For example, if one of us got attacked or found out about getting extended, we had to confirm with each other that it was time to break the news to our families at the same time.

When the work was done and we conspired enough to keep our families sane, we used our computers and laptops to play DVDs. Mr. Humphrey, a friend of my mom's, sent me the first six seasons of "M*A*S*H." My sister sent me "The Simpson's," which I absolutely love, so we started watching them when we were stressed out.

We'd get together and do yoga from a DVD. One day, a group of us were right in the middle of chanting "aum" when Schrack came in and said we had a mission. We looked at him like, "We're in the middle of yoga, can't we at least finish?" Some of the guys were even open enough to at least try yoga and it was great. One day SGT Boron even tried doing yoga with us. He was a bit

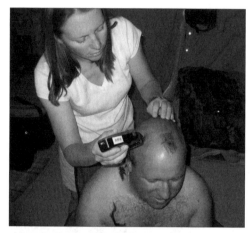
Michelle cutting SGT David Boron's hair

overweight and almost looked like he was pregnant. He was bending, stretching and sweating, trying to keep up with us. Then the panting and grunting started, but he never gave up.

Being so close to the border, we sometimes wondered if we were safe. For the most part, we were, but there was a nearby town called Safwan where things occasionally got pretty dangerous. I was sitting in my tent with a soldier and we heard a huge BOOM and told ourselves it was just a storage box that fell off the back of a truck. We knew what it was, but denial felt better. It was freaky when things like that happened. In the beginning, we were allowed to keep our weapons in our tents, which made sense to us because Camp Navistar was an eighth of a mile from Iraq's border. In fact, there were times when I wondered if the enemy would cross the border and overrun the camp. By the end of my tour, our battalion wanted everyone to keep weapons secured in a connex, which is like a storage box that we used to haul equipment on the trucks. If anything would have happened, we would have been sitting ducks because there was no way we could have defended the camp in a timely manner.

The mayor of Safwan kept in touch with our Battalion Commander and they had a good enough relationship to let us know if there was some special occasion in the town. That way if there were guns being fired out of celebration, the military wouldn't overreact. Part of the culture in Iraq included shooting guns off for holidays and weddings. We'd hear pow-pow-pow and wonder what was happening, so it was reassuring that the mayor kept us in the loop. We heard a story about some celebration going on with gunfire and a helicopter flew in and started firing, not realizing they just killed a wedding party. Again, it could have been rumors or maybe I read it in *Stars and Stripes,* but it was enough to make me jumpy occasionally. It became background noise to us eventually and we relied on an alarm to sound if we were really in danger. Plus we had Intel reports coming in that told us when things were bad in Safwan.

As time went on, we could tell a lot from the sound of a mortar or gunfire. In Anaconda, a camp in northern Iraq, mortars went off daily, so we learned

70

to judge whether they actually hit something or disappeared into the desert. We could tell approximately how far away they were too. When it was gunfire, a clack-clack-clack was bad because it was an AK-47. On the other hand, a doot-doot-doot was comforting because we knew it was one of our M-16s. Sometimes we could hear gunfire and see what was happening, but most of the time we had no idea.

Although we mastered some key skills to stay safe and tried to run with as much integrity as possible, some things were just out of our hands.

We had just returned from a mission and were trying to run in the same squads, which was about twenty people, when we started having missions where only three trucks or ten people were needed. Then a big mission would come down and it seemed like my squad was always getting separated. SSG Brown, the Third Platoon's other squad leader, and I were trying to keep our people together because it was safer to keep our routines, but we weren't always able to do that. We were forced to split up and ride with other companies in convoys, which only made us homesick for the people we arrived in Iraq with—those who we assumed would be there until we left.

In the beginning of April, our squad was attached to a Puerto Rican unit that had been in-country for about twelve months and they were an absolute joke. They asked for security from our battalion and our squad was given the order. Our squad was broken down between two different convoys, but we were all still on the same mission. There was also another brand-new unit that was going to ride with us because we were considered "old war vets" by then. We had been in-country about two months and we were soldiering gun trucks. Nobody had a clue what we were supposed to do and we had no radio communication again. My Humvee didn't have armor let alone a door. We took two bobtails, semi trucks without trailers, and two Humvees. Bobtails could maneuver better without a trailer. We put the younger, lower-ranking people in trucks because they were easier to maneuver and put the higher ranking in the Humvees because we didn't want to put them in the more dangerous vehicles. It was more convenient to drive around the post instead of having to worry about a semi, but that was about the only nice part. The "gun" on the truck was a joke as well. The largest weapon we had was a "saw," or machine gun, which was nothing compared to the equipment the gun trucks had by the end of the tour. It was pure luck that nobody got hurt with the limited amount of firepower and armor. I swear it was more luck than skill that determined whether a unit got attacked or blown up.

So in the middle of this mission, we realized that the Puerto Rican unit we were supporting was so unorganized that we were amazed they survived the whole year. They were nothing like the New Mexican unit and we were nervous. My squad met up when we stopped for a quick break on the side of the road and we just rambled about how dangerous these guys were. There was one convoy on one side of the road and the other convoy was across the street when all of a sudden, both convoys took off down the road and the two convoys got mixed together. All the commercial drivers were confused and wondering what was going on. The convoy I was on took off and one of my gun trucks was not with them and they didn't want to stop, but I refused to leave any of my guys behind. It made me nervous that they had no idea how many trucks or soldiers they had with them and I refused to move until I saw our guys. It was decided since everything was such a mess that both convoys would just travel to our overnight spot together.

Up the road a few miles traffic was stopped for a car bomb. We were about twenty minutes from Baghdad and the airport where we were going to stay. One of the MPs who was securing the car bomb found an alternate route through a field to a dirt road where one of the Puerto Rican guys flipped his tractor in a ditch. He and his co-driver bailed and hitched a ride with another truck, but we were stuck securing the vehicle since we were in the gun trucks. The people from my squad and the even newer soldiers had to wait at that spot until it was towed. So there we were with two months under our belt, sitting by ourselves. Then all of these locals came running out and they were getting ready to loot everything and we were pissed. We weren't in-country two months and we were stuck on the side of the road with a broken truck that didn't even belong to us. We called "sheriff," which was like 9-1-1, for help and they said they would try to get there as soon as possible, but they were dealing with the car bomb. All we had were our three gun trucks, machine guns and M16s, which was nothing. Hours went by as we sat on the side of the road just outside of Baghdad. We tried to make light of the situation by convincing ourselves we were going to be attacked, which might sound sick, but it was more like reverse psychology. It turned pitch black while we sat with the disabled vehicle and without a convoy.

Finally, they detonated the car bomb. The explosion was fierce and we were close enough to feel the heat. Sheriff contacted a security crew and a wrecker to tow the flipped truck out of the ditch. They met us once the car bomb was detonated and shot off a star cluster, which is a pyrotechnic launched into the sky that for about thirty seconds made it look like the middle of the day. The wrecker had the vehicle towed out within a half hour. I felt better having extra security that most likely had been in-country longer than us.

At this point we found out that a few trucks were up the road, waiting for us. I had to ride with one of the new guys from North Carolina since his co-

72

driver jumped into the abandoned truck. It was dark and we were trying to find the airport. I went the only way I knew at the time and unfortunately it was the really dangerous way. Only one other truck followed and I realized we were screwed and had to turn around. Luckily we didn't go too far and caught up with everyone quickly. I got teased for that all year.

Schrack led the way in a flatbed and we made it to the airport safely. When we finally delivered the truck, we realized the Puerto Rican unit had no idea we were even out there. Thank you for deserting us on the side of the road. Not only were they at the camp, they were sleeping and we had to wake them to give them back their keys to the truck. When Schrack threw the keys at the convoy commander, he said he didn't even know he was missing a truck. It was pathetic.

The one thing that was reassuring in the whole experience was knowing that sheriff actually worked. Once we called, we had security and support from the engineers who towed the truck out. It was my first experience with the whole process, but I learned early on how the military supported each other and how to use it to my advantage.

The two convoys were split up the next morning and we finished our mission. Our group had to go to Taji to deliver some equipment and we were stuck there for several days. Taji was a camp nestled inside the Sunni triangle between Baghdad and Tikrit. While we were stuck there, Mullen, Dominguez and I explored the camp. There were local vendors selling rugs, artwork and knickknacks. Mullen bought an area rug for $120 and I got a framed pictured for $25! Everything was so cheap and could be mailed home from their post office at the camp.

There was heavy fighting going on all around us, but it just didn't seem real at the time. SGT Hicks was with me that day in my gun truck. He was such a tough guy, but any time he saw animals or kids, he'd say, "Gimme food," and give it to them. He found a puppy that day and fed it three MREs. He wanted to take it back to Camp Navistar, but decided to let it go because we couldn't have animals. We sat in the middle of the gunfight with mortars pelting the earth fawning over a puppy. Our life was so surreal at that point. We slept out on a runway under the stars that night. When we finally returned to Camp Navistar, we vowed never to go out with that unit again.

SPC John "JD" Delaney on his gun truck with no armor. This was during the Easter attack

We thought we were getting a reprieve from the grim reaper when our company was told around the first or second week of April that we were going to be taken off the road for a while to pull security around Camp Navistar. By that point I already realized it was like *Alice in Wonderland* where nothing was ever as it seemed, so I tried not to get my hopes up. I didn't want to cling to any sort of consistency because it was useless.

Some of the soldiers in the company in charge of securing our camp were starting to go home, so we were told we would be taking turns staying at Navistar. It didn't seem like it would be too bad because we thought there would be a consistent schedule for a couple of months and we would be out of danger so our families could relax a little. After consulting Elaine, I called home to tell my parents I had one more mission before I got to sit in a secure camp for three months.

Just one more mission. It was only supposed to take two, three days tops. All we had to do was deliver flak vests to the Polish army in Hillah.

Sorry it's been a while since I've written, but as you all know, Mullen and I had some Easter excitement.

Everyone has been asking what really happened with the ambush. Since this is the first e-mail since the "incident," I am going to give everyone the real story of what happened that day.

About a week before Easter, we were informed we would most likely be off the road and pulling security for our camp for the next two months. It was a rotation all companies would sooner or later have to do and it was just my company's turn.

A few days after hearing the news, I called my parents and told them they could stop worrying about me being on the road. The very next day, my squad got a mission. It was our last mission before the security detail.

I was told it would be a two-to-three-day mission, tops.

Once we were out on the road in Iraq, word came down that things were heating up with the insurgents.

Our convoy was delayed a few days and we were stuck at a military base just sitting around, waiting for road conditions to change. It seemed like each hour we were waiting to leave, reports of new terrorist attacks were being reported–especially bridges being blown on our supply route, making it impassable.

Our convoy was finally allowed to leave on an alternate route with additional security. The drive was going fine until we turned onto the alternative route that went through this town.

Military police gave us the heads up there was enemy in the area before we made the turn. Once we all turned onto the road, all hell broke loose.

There were mortars and rocket-propelled grenades (RPGs) flying in front of us.

Mullen and I heard on the radio the rear of the convoy was being attacked as well, so we had to drive into the smoke-filled attack zone because there was nowhere else to go. As we were driving, a mortar hit on the driver's side right by my vehicle and an RPG hit the front passenger's side.

While all this was going on, Mullen and I were receiving small arms fire from the front, left and right sides.

I was driving and I drove until the vehicle could not go any farther. Unfortunately, it stopped in the middle of the attack zone, where most of the fire was coming from.

Mullen and I returned suppressive fire until we were almost out of ammo. (Suppressive fire is just firing so the enemy isn't firing at you.)

I saw out of my mirror that a military vehicle was pulling up next to us. Mullen and I jumped out of our bullet-riddled vehicle and into SGT Hupp and SPC Hawk's vehicle. These soldiers got us out of the kill zone and into safety.

Their vehicle took several bullets to the frame, which blocked those shots from hitting us.

Unfortunately, our vehicle was unable to be recovered, and Mullen and I were told it burned to the core.

Our convoy regrouped a few miles up the road and while we were getting accountability, the enemy was following us in a dump truck and began firing mortars at us.

We quickly drove out of danger again and headed toward the Marine camp that was down the street. We regrouped there, but the fighting was still going on outside the camp, so the Marines sent out soldiers to secure the area.

The Marines informed us the next day there were around 400 to 500 enemy forces in the ambush. The ambush was also spread out for three miles. They found a cache of weapons in the area spread throughout the town that next day.

The Marines also let us know we did an excellent job of defending ourselves. They were impressed with how well a transportation company from the National Guard could take care of themselves during the attack.

Mullen and I were happy to be alive, but we lost everything – personal and military. (Not to mention that Easter will never be the same for either of us!)

We relied on people from our unit to clothe us and give us personal hygiene stuff so we could make it until we got back to our base camp.

Since there were so many attacks around Baghdad that week, it took twice as long to drop off our loads and return to Kuwait.

Our two-to-three-day mission turned into 12 days. Once we got back to the unit and filled out the endless paperwork about the incident, I was told the truck, trailer, radio and personal stuff that was lost amounted to $250,000!

I learned three very important lessons from the attack.

Life is more important than material stuff.

The repetitive Army training really does work. Mullen and I were able to react without thinking. The training we'd received was drilled so deep into our memory that we could react properly without having to think.

Never get your truck blown up in front of all your Army friends. The teasing will go on forever.

Thank you all for your continued support. I really appreciate all the e-mails, letters, care packages and prayers. I truly have the best family and friends in the whole world. I love you all very much and I'll write more now that The Gazette sent me a computer.

I found out one of my soldiers, SGT Dave Boron, has a wife who is reading The Gazette articles I've been writing. He asked me to pass on a message for his wife through the paper:

"Ali, thanks for your support (and the cigars). I could not do my job if you weren't in my life. You are a great wife and mother! Your work in the USCG is just as important as what I am doing. We are all a cog in this great big machine. Each part must do its thing if we are to be successful in this war.

"Let the kids know I love them and am proud of them. Ali, I love you very much. I miss being with you. Life is tough without you by my side and to hold me and tell me everything is going to be all right. I can't wait to hold you when I come home on leave.

"Love, David." — MZ, April 24, 2004

There were only eight of us in four flatbed trucks when we were sent to Hillah to deliver flak vests to the Polish army. They didn't have any body armor and were in a very dangerous place, so the eight of us headed out into what was supposed to be pretty dangerous territory. At the same time, Brown, my counterpart, had a mission and tried to take all of the gun trucks and anything with communication. Needless to say, things got pretty ugly. I told him he might as well go ahead and take our M16s, too, and take away any hope of survival. It was extreme but I got my point across. I wanted all the equipment and so did Brown. We sorted out our limited resources by borrowing the communication and gun trucks from the Second Platoon, which offered to escort us. Brown's group got our gun trucks and was sent with an eighty-seven-truck convoy with three different units running together. The size of the convoy was unbelievably huge and unmanageable.

Our convoy met up with the Second Platoon where they were stationed at Camp Cedar. Their sole mission was to escort KBR convoys, with the exception of this mission. We were to stay at Cedar the first night of our mission and then deliver the flak vests on the second night. As soon as we got to their camp, the Second Platoon let us know that three soldiers from our company had been shot: SGT Dyer, SPC Coe and SPC Miller. We were even more shocked to hear it was close to the same place where we were stuck for hours on the previous mission. It was unreal. The violence of the war suddenly became more real and so did the enemy because we now had casualties from our own company. Our convoy took six gun trucks, the most we ever had, rushed into the Polish camp, dropped off their supplies and got the hell out of there. It was a smooth run with no enemy activity, but it was enough to scare the shit out of us.

We took a deep breath and headed to Scania for the second leg of the trip. It was a good stopping point because it was almost dark and we had been on the road all day. But after we left Hillah, the enemy blew up several bridges leading into Baghdad and we had no idea what was happening. Nobody could believe that the insurgents had the potential to do that. They had really underestimated the enemy. We were surprised that it got as bad as it did because the New Mexican unit told us that the country had been very low-key lately. There were rumors that all movement was shut down and no one was allowed up north because of all the violence. Having convoys all over the roads interfered with the Marine and Army infantry ground operations in situations like that and nobody knew what was going to happen next, so Scania sounded like an even better stopping point. When we got there, we saw SGT Brown's convoy and decided we should help him out by including our four trucks in his convoy of eighty-seven trucks, which had only a few radios for communication. All of our trucks were empty, having dumped our loads at the Polish camp, so the convoy commander of our group told our unit back in Kuwait that we were going to go with Brown's group. Our secret agenda, of course, was to make sure that our platoon all got back on the same mission. Our unit was telling us not to go with Brown and go further south,

Michelle changes a tire during another "typical day on the road"

but we told them we were going to stay with the convoy for communication purposes and they finally agreed.

Scania was packed with convoys that night so we slept outside the camp, listening to gunfire, patrols—and our own minds. We were in one of the camps we considered to be safe. The one-day trip from Kuwait to Scania was always the easiest day of our mission because there was never any enemy activity and it was mainly open desert. The worst part of the trip was the eighty-seven-mile stretch of dirt road that beat us up in the truck, but we suddenly doubted every instinct we had been relying on.

The next morning Mullen and I awoke to a flat tire. It was not a good way to start off the morning. The roads were still shut down and no convoys were allowed to leave unless they were high priority, like ammo or combat equipment, but somehow our convoy magically became a priority. Someone had convinced a major that we could take an alternate route to get around the blown bridges. The major told them this decision was going to make or break his career and we promised we would take extra security.

The captain in charge of Brown's convoy had never been in charge of a mission before and we soon found out why. Their convoy consisted of troops from the 1486th Transportation Unit, the 172nd Transportation Unit, some First Cavalry Division guys who were riding in armored personnel carriers (APCs) that we were hauling and lots of civilian truck drivers. Nobody knew exactly how many Hajis we had with us and it was a confusing mess. The First Cavalry's tanks were loaded onto flatbeds in the convoy and the guys rode inside of them to lend some extra firepower. Shortly after we pulled out of Scania we were stopped for about twenty minutes but nobody knew why. We were getting restless because the enemy knew we were leaving and we didn't want them to have time to prepare. There was some confusion with the number of trucks in the convoy and we later found out some of the delay was waiting for extra security. But the captain was actually the one who had us stopped for so long. She was so disorganized that she made us stop in enemy territory because she couldn't figure out where the four extra trucks in her convoy came from. Mine was one of the trucks she had forgotten. Brown, who was just in disbelief and frustrated with her, said to me (loud enough for her to hear), "She's an idiot and it's been like this since we started." We were supposed to be relying on her to take care of us and she didn't even know we were there. Brown had reached his breaking point trying to work with her and it was showing. It's difficult to be

Humvees hauled back to Navistar from Iraq. Sights like this brought home the reality of war and stressed the need for body armor

respectful when your life and the lives of your fellow soldiers are at the mercy of incompetence.

We took an alternate supply route called Cleveland to get around the bridges. We were heading to MSR (main supply route) Jackson when we were stopped by military police (MPs) pulling security in the area. They warned us the enemy was in the area because there had been activity all day long, so we proceeded with our weapons out the windows. Mullen turned on "Tiny Dancer" by Elton John on the MP3 player. It was one of the "relaxation mantras" we listened to when things stressed us out.

We got about 500 yards down the road and had just turned right onto Jackson when I saw an explosion on my left and one on my right. As soon as I heard the gunfire I flashed back to all of our training simulations and mock ambushes. I told Mullen we should turn around because we were always taught not to head into an ambush. I felt nauseous from the pit of my stomach down to my toes. It was like I had just walked into a class and found out about a pop quiz.

"There's an ambush up ahead, we're getting fucking ambushed. Oh my God!" someone shrieked into the radio. "We're getting shot at!"

As we listened to it, we realized the back of the convoy was getting ambushed too. It was a gut wrenching decision to go forward, but we didn't have a choice. Just as we started moving, our truck was hit on the driver's side by a mortar. That day, it was my side. As I ducked down, I felt the whole left side of the truck shake before an RPG hit the front of the truck on Mullen's side and we were both thrown to the left. We saw smoke billowing from the front of the truck as the left side shook again. I looked down and realized Mullen and I were both bleeding.

"I think I got hit," I said.

"I think I got hit, too," he answered back.

We fell silent, paralyzed by shock and confusion. We saw blood, but neither of us was seriously injured. Mullen re-positioned himself and started to fire his weapon out the window. We couldn't see anyone, but we knew they were lurking. We were still driving and trying to go as fast as we could, but couldn't go any faster than twenty miles per hour. Our truck slowly died and ground to a halt.

"Go, go!" Mullen roared.

"I'm going as fast as I can!" I shrieked.

"Go!" he commanded again.

"I am fucking going," I screeched back.

I couldn't even hear myself and I was sure he never heard a word I said anyway. I was standing on the accelerator, praying my truck would just go. The whole time, I was thinking Oh my God, we're getting attacked. Oh my God, I'm shooting out the window.

As soon as I realized we were getting attacked, I fired. I fired at the woods where the mortars came from. I was constantly thinking, damn. I didn't want to ever have to fire my weapon. Mullen aimed at a nearby building. We could tell the gunfire was coming from overhead. Just then I heard the clink of a bullet hit the windshield and Mullen slumped over. The bullet actually hit eight inches from my head, but I thought it hit Mullen and he was dead. He wasn't responding, wasn't moving and I didn't want to know whether he was dead or alive. A second later his weapon started firing.

"Mullen, Mullen, are you alright?" I yelled at him. I couldn't deal with him being shot or dead. We were passing the skeletons of burning trucks when ours stalled. We heard a jumble of radio communication before it went dead.

"Mullen and Zaremba have been hit. We're stopped and we need to be recovered," I called into the radio. No one answered. Our antenna was destroyed so our only means of communication was worthless.

Smoke funneled through the air behind the truck like a fog. My mouth never stopped while Mullen sat silently.

"Good God, we are so screwed," I kept repeating, almost laughing.

The thump-thump-thump of bullets piercing the sides of the truck didn't compare to my pounding heart. It was almost amusing that we were getting shot at and stranded because I knew it was coming. I have the worst luck.

Then I saw a civilian truck pass and spotted Hupp and Hawk. I've never been so happy to see those two guys. I told Mullen to get ready to bail from the truck. I was worried they were going to miss us and fled with my weapon and nothing else. An even darker, black cloud of smoke bellowed from our truck.

"I'm not going to miss them," I chanted, afraid they would miss me.

I was in the middle of the road and I could hear bullets whizzing past when we just looked at each other and ran toward their truck. Hawk laid down suppressive fire as I dove into the truck, breaking their radio in the process. Mullen and I both ended up practically sitting on Hawk's lap and the whole time I kept rambling, thanking them over and over for stopping. Mullen told me to shut up.

Fortunately for Mullen and me, Hupp's truck shielded most of the bullets. But, unfortunately for the truck, it was getting ready to die. I told Hupp we should drop the trailer and get the hell out of there because the lines from the air brakes were leaking badly, but he told me to be patient and continued on to catch up with everyone else.

Once we caught up with part of the group, Sauer, one of the combat life-savers, cleaned our wounds and I got more ammo. The trucks were set up in a defensive position, forming a perimeter with them and putting our Hajis in the middle while we sat on the side of the road waiting for the rest of the convoy to catch up. One by one, the convoy's trucks emerged. But not before we started getting mortared again. I never thought that day would end. I was sick of being attacked.

As I was checking Mullen's wounds, Willy walked up to another female and asked if she wanted to make out. She gave him a look like, "Have you lost your mind?" I know he was just trying to lighten the mood. Either that or he wanted to die happy.

We couldn't really fire back during the mortaring because any weapons we had with more power or a longer firing range took more than one person to operate, so we jumped back in the trucks. I rode with Bartlett and Sallee. I was trying to operate the radio and call for help, but it was dead. We drove about three miles down the road with the expectation of getting attacked again, but we found a town instead. People were outside and kids were waving at us with no clue that we had just been in a big ambush. It baffled me that things could be so different just three miles down the road.

We remembered St. Michael's was nearby so we pulled in there to re-group. We needed more ammo and medical attention. Some of our soldiers were wounded and three of our civilians were bleeding badly. The Marines were impressed that we all lived and reminded us that others weren't so lucky. I immediately went to the phones.

"Mom?"

"Happy Easter," she chirped.

I didn't want her to know we had been attacked. As long as I talked to her for Easter, she didn't need to know. I tried to make the conversation quick because my mom and dad are very perceptive and I tried to sound like it was just another routine phone call.

I wish I could tell you what I just went through, but I can't, I thought to myself as I choked down the softball forming in my throat. "If anyone from the family support calls you," I said, "don't pay attention, you know how rumors spread."

When she said she wouldn't, I was stunned. She started casual conversation about the Easter eggs and the family gossip of the moment. I didn't care about any of that. I just wanted to tell her how much I loved her and how precious life was. I talked to my dad briefly before he went back to the Easter celebration and I went back to reality. I knew if my mom knew what just had happened, the conversation wouldn't have been so casual. It was like a dream. Actually, it was more like a nightmare.

We were directed to a concrete building that looked like a shack with beds that was supposed to be our sleeping quarters for the night. There wasn't nearly enough room for all of us, so some crammed into a hallway. We were just starting to wind down when they told us they expected the camp to get attacked that night and we had to help them defend it. It was never ending.

We were all assigned various jobs. I was a combat lifesaver, which meant assisting the injured. Others were on perimeter guard. The Marines had to give us more ammo because we were tapped out. Mullen and I were told to go seek medical attention before duty because we had cuts and tiny pieces of shrapnel in our arms.

On our way back from the infirmary we stopped to assess the damage on our trucks. Hupp's was destroyed. We ended up leaving it there because it couldn't be hauled to the next camp. Other trucks had blown out tires. Bartlett and Sallee's truck had an RPG go clear through the load. They were hauling explosive materials and it missed within inches. We lost three Army trucks, three commercial trucks and two Egyptian men. It was so chaotic we didn't even realize the Egyptian men were missing until a day later.

We were worn out emotionally and physically. All of our personal belongings that we treasured over there were gone. We had no clothes, no food, no toothbrushes, nothing. Part of our procedure was if we were hit, we were to leave the truck, get in another one and the rear of the convoy would cover us. When I started asking who had my truck, I was in denial. I didn't want to believe it was gone. I realized they were only material things, but they were mine. Someone told me when they drove by my truck it was a glowing, green flame.

There were a couple of Navy girls at the camp and they gave me a sports bra, new underwear, a toothbrush and anything else they could spare. I only had the clothes on my back until they took care of me. I got their address and later sent them a thank you care package with whatever goodies I could scrape together.

The next day was the Monday after Easter. We sat in disbelief in our agonizing thoughts, but we were numb to them. We were crushed. It was our first time in a firefight. We wondered if we were going to make it, but at that point, we had tuned out reason. Then like a little ripple, we could sense the determination in everyone to see this mission through and live to talk about it.

I didn't have to fire my weapon except that one time. I was in a place where I didn't want to be and I fired my weapon when I didn't want to, but it wasn't just my life at stake. I fired into the woods just to make noise out of our truck so they would stop mortaring us. I didn't have to physically look at someone and kill them, thank God. There was a lot of distance and I never came in direct contact, but I was shooting to kill. It made me realize what I was capable of in a time of survival. I didn't know that side of me existed. I didn't feel bad about it, although I was shocked by my actions. It took a long time for me to get over the fact that I could fire a weapon in that situation. But it was fight or flight. If it were just me, maybe I wouldn't have done it. It even ran through my head not to shoot, but in a situation like that where all you have is trust, I needed Mullen to know that he could trust me. I had to fire and suppress the activity on my side of the truck. It wasn't fair to poor Mullen that I wanted to take a moral stand and not fire my weapon, but I didn't have a choice. We saw a lot that day, but the one thing that still gets me is that I had to do that. Through the whole war it was the one thing I prayed I wouldn't have to do. A lot of people back home were really impressed that I survived a firefight while others heard rumors that I killed a bunch of people. The story was so exaggerated that I used my Easter letter to set the record straight. I didn't want to be seen as this great hero because I wasn't. I did something that was more difficult on a moral level than a physical one.

We sat around in what was their chow hall on a makeshift picnic table and waited for word on our next move. I still couldn't get over how these guys lived. It was so primitive and depressing. This time they started putting tape on the port-o-potties so people would know when they were overflowing and not use them. They started digging holes in the ground like pipes for guys to pee. The camp was located in the Anwar Province, a rough battleground known for casualties.

We were in the chow hall line awaiting K-rations, watching the Marines slop bacon and eggs on plates, again thinking about how we had our asses handed to us. We had to eat this shitty food and sit on a shitty wannabe picnic table, but we were relieved to be alive. I sat there a shell of a person and didn't like the fact that I had to rely on everyone to take care of me until we got back to camp. I was losing control, but I was still in charge in my head. I continuously reminded myself that I had to keep it together, but I was crumbling and terrified to look at the other somber faces around the table.

No one was talking when Schrack sat down.

"Don't you just hate Mondays?" he said. "It's just so hard to get started again."

We just busted out laughing, paying no attention to the Marines staring at us who had been living like this for months. They couldn't believe we could laugh at a time like that, but it was all we had. We needed the release, but the Marines just stared at us, emotionless. They were hollow and our sick sense of humor was lost on them. They had seen too much to even think about letting loose and laughing.

"Hey, how's you're hearing?" one of the guys asked me after we had settled down from our giggle fit.

"Surprisingly very good considering all the explosions," I replied.

He just looked at me in disbelief and said, "I asked how your gear was, not how your hearing was." Again, the table exploded into laughter.

Unfortunately, our Hajis weren't able to relax quite the same. While we were trying to get supplies, we kept them near their vehicles because the Marines told them they would shoot them if they made a wrong move. We gave them specific instructions to stay by their trucks and to not make any sudden moves or they could be killed. Again, nobody knew who could be trusted, not even our own Hajis. By that point, they would do whatever they were told because they had to rely on us as their security for the rest of the trip. The small camp was overcrowded with personnel and eighty-four extra vehicles; fuses were short.

Suddenly, a Marine one-star general appeared at camp. He was stationed there and had been there all along, but it was the first time I had seen him. It was pathetic that they needed a general at that sorry place, but he was put there for the sole purpose of having some pull when it came to getting what was needed. It was a dangerous, miserable place and anyone other than a one-star general wouldn't have been able to convince those behind the lines to send the proper supplies and equipment.

As he surveyed the situation and sized us up, I respected him instantly. I could tell he didn't take any shit. This guy was a bad ass. When he asked if we were ready to move, we weren't sure. We didn't want to go anywhere because the instructions the general was giving us conflicted with our truck master in Kuwait on where to go from there. The general said we were a liability and we had to move on. We sent an MTS, like an instant message, back to our company telling them we had to move and received more conflicting messages in return. The Marines told us they would escort us to Baghdad because that was where all the convoys were meeting up and getting extra security.

We were just getting ready to move when we were delayed. We were told to stay another night because it was too dangerous. The next day we were trying to coordinate how we were going to move, but conflicting information about what we should do continued to be thrown at us. We were trying to get everything in order when we received another MTS telling us we couldn't get to where we wanted to go. Meanwhile, the general was telling us what to do and it was getting extremely frustrating, so I showed him the email and told him to make the call. His information was much more accurate than what we were getting from the people in Kuwait as far as what roads were opened and which were closed. The general decided it was time for us to move. We were a huge liability at his camp.

As I didn't have a truck anymore, and because I was the smallest, I was crammed into a tiny spot in a gun truck. I was grateful that it had protective armor on the doors, but a bullet had gone through the handle and through a water cooler, so we knew our protection was shit. And because the bullet went through the door handle, the door wouldn't open and that was where I had to sit. I had never been claustrophobic, but after getting blown up I was a little skittish and sure as hell wasn't ready to go on the road in a vehicle that I couldn't easily get out of. I knew if I didn't get back on the road, though, I would never want to go again. I climbed in there feeling pissed off, suffocated and helpless. I made them clear a space for an escape route. I didn't care if they put their stuff on top of the truck or left it behind; I was going to have an escape route. I was trembling with fear, but I didn't want anyone else to know so I pretended to be angry instead of nervous.

We were forced to travel the route where the ambush occurred and made it to Baghdad without any trouble. All over the route there were shells of tanker trucks that had been attacked and burned up and we pretended like they weren't even there.

We made it inside the line at BIAP and collapsed like we had just crossed the finish line of a marathon. But because we lost three civilians and still had vehicles that needed to be recovered from St. Michaels, the gun truck's mission was not over. Unfortunately, I was in the gun truck. We didn't even get out before we were told to turn around. As the trucks pulled into BIAP, we waited outside the gate until all the vehicles were safe and the gun trucks were ready to go. As we sat waiting to return to St. Michaels, I noticed another gun truck with only two people in it.

Hmmm, I thought to myself. There is much more room in there and the doors work!

I got the hell out of my death trap of a seat and rode in that vehicle. I could have just bailed and got into one of the trucks that was heading into BIAP, but I wanted to go back out and overcome my fear and nervousness.

Just as we approached St. Michael's, we were told to turn the convoy around without much of a reason. We were within arm's reach and had to turn around. It was the third time we had to drive down the road where we had just been attacked and this trip was in vain. We headed back to Baghdad to meet up with the rest of the convoy, which was trip four on the same road.

When we got to BIAP, Mullen and I were able to buy clothes but I didn't have an ID or even a wallet. All I had were dog tags. Schrack gave me his credit card and I promised to pay him back but he told me not to worry about it. I bought underwear, a toothbrush and a blanket. It was April and it was still pretty cold out at night, so I spent a few nights freezing my ass off before I bought the blanket.

We met up with Elaine's convoy in Baghdad and spent our time there trying to figure out who had the best war stories. Both of our convoys had just been attacked and half of us didn't want to talk about it. Mullen and I had gotten separated because we were riding in different trucks, so we didn't utter a word to each other about what had happened until about a week later. Finally, one day we were getting ready to go to bed and we starting talking about the attack, piecing it together, playing off of each other's memories. We processed it and let it go, unsure of whether it would happen again.

We didn't know how long we were going to be stuck at BIAP and didn't think much of it until we started running out of water. We had plenty when we got there and we were doing normal things, like brushing our teeth, when it dawned on us our supply was getting low. We went to the water supply point to get more and learned they were almost out, so we had to start rationing. We were cautious about how much we drank and how much we used. After that mission, our platoon filled an extra connex with tires, maintenance supplies, water and food—just in case. We called it the "Mother Ship."

After about twenty days, they started to let convoys leave BIAP. It became a running joke that we had another twenty-one-day mission on our hands anytime things started to go wrong.

We weren't far from the Green Zone and still hadn't made it to where Brown's convoy was supposed to deliver its load, so that was our next stop once we were given the okay to leave BIAP. Just as we were getting ready to go drop off the loads, all of our commercial truck drivers went on strike. They decided it was too dangerous and said they weren't going any further. SGT Brown had all these guys backed up against a trailer practically at gunpoint when I walked into the situation. They refused to move. We were heading to a camp in "the Green Zone," which is code for "you're fucked," and I really didn't want to stand there and have a debate. We were supposed to drop our loads so we could head back to Kuwait. Three drivers agreed to go, but the other thirty guys wouldn't budge. We couldn't understand it and didn't really care because we just wanted to be done with it. Now our Army drivers would have to make several trips to get all of the loads delivered and we knew we'd be the ones to make those trips. I felt like they were trying to sabotage what we were trying to do, but that was when we found out about their pay and how they were being treated.

There was that one truck still stuck at St. Michael's, so I volunteered to get it. I knew I needed to stay on the road and actually drive or I would never want to do it again. I had to get back into a truck as soon as possible and that was my chance. I borrowed someone's truck and Schrack and I headed out. Fortunately the trip was uneventful and I felt more confident about driving again. Finally, all of our equipment was out of St. Michael's. In all, we drove the road where we were attacked six times in one week.

Once we returned to Camp Navistar, the combat stress team was there to greet us. Anyone involved in Easter action had to meet and talk to them, which was fine because we got an extra day off. It was more of a formality and nobody really said anything, but we knew they were there if we needed them.

I felt sorry for myself for about a week after my truck blew up. I caught a lot of flak and got teased for the fact that it was my truck that was destroyed, but anyone who was involved was teased mercilessly. One of our guys was shot several times and was sent home where he had to have several surgeries, but it was all a joke to us later on. We didn't really think about our sick sense of humor because our way of making it through the day was laughing about getting blown up. I think nurses and paramedics do a lot of the same thing.

We were laughing about people getting shot when we could have been killed. We heard that one of the guys who got shot during the convoy attack screamed when he was hit and that was a big joke the rest of the time we were over there. Even if someone got shot and had to go home and come back, we still made fun of them.

"Knock, knock," someone would yell.

"Who's there?" we'd all chime in.

"James screaming like a bitch."

Anything associated with that day became fodder for torturing one another. "Tiny Dancer," the Elton John song that was once my soothing lullaby through dangerous areas, became a demonic song. Whenever we were driving through danger, I always told Mullen to put on something soothing to keep us calm. Whenever Elton John came on after that, I made him change it because I associated that song with getting ambushed. Mullen kept making me listen to it though, so I wouldn't have post-traumatic stress over Elton John. We laugh now about how the world was blowing up around us and "Tiny Dancer" was playing.

I didn't want to tell anyone at home that we had been attacked, so I called my dad when I got a chance and told him I needed a new computer. I lied and said it was because my truck was in an accident and my computer was destroyed. When he told me to send it back so he could fix it, I tried to tell him it caught on fire. I've never been able to lie to my dad and he immediately saw right through my pathetic story. He started freaking out and I decided the truth was better because I felt like he was going to beat my ass or have a heart attack. Once he found out, he called everyone he knew. Mom said the story got bigger and better with every beer he drank. I decided the email to everyone better have the real version of what happened.

From the time my parents found out about the ambush, I had to call them every day to assure them I was safe. My mom wanted details about what happened. My dad didn't really care about the details; he just wanted to know I was alive. I didn't have a calling card since it was blown up in the truck, but I remembered the numbers of my credit card. I didn't realize how expensive it was to place calls overseas using a credit card and I ended up spending a couple hundred dollars on phone calls that month.

When I called my parents, I tried to sound casual. I let them know that I only got scratches on the Easter attack and told them not to worry. They finally started to believe what I told them until they got a phone call from the Army's casualty hotline. Pandemonium broke out in the Zaremba house. My parents missed the phone call so the voice on the answering machine said I had been injured and they needed to call right away. They called back but not before my mom hit the floor sobbing while my dad held her. My brother, Mark, told me he thought I was dead or hurt really bad. They knew things were heating up and since I'd already been attacked once it was believable I got injured again. After calling the number, getting redirected to several different departments and sitting on hold for what seemed to be a lifetime, they finally talked to someone. The Army causality hotline told my parents I had been injured. My dad was yelling at the person asking if it was from the Easter attack or another one. My parents couldn't understand why they would wait a month to call them about my small injury. It turned out they had the wrong information and the call was regarding the Easter attack.

The same hotline put Mullen's mother on hold for ten minutes without telling her what was wrong with her son. They told her to hold for the casualty department. They also told her the injury occurred on a different day than when it really happened, so she wasn't sure if it was the same incident or different. Both my parents and Mullen's mom couldn't wait until we called just to make sure we were okay. I was so upset that our families had to go through that horrible experience. That's when I started to realize how incompetent the Army really was and that we were going to have to take care of ourselves and rely only on each other or we weren't going to make it. This image of the United States having the best Army in the world scares me because of all of the problems we had. After that, my brother Mark packed up and moved to California for a month because he just couldn't take it anymore.

I feel awful that I disrupted my entire family's lives for a year. Every time I called they had to drop everything and talk to me. I know they wanted to, but that wasn't the point. I would call and ask for a special favor and they would do it for me within a week. I hated that they all had to worry as much as they did. After that ordeal, my parents put me on a calling schedule. I was bound to it and if I didn't call on time, they thought the worst.

We started wondering who the enemy really was, not in a conspiracy way, but more like who was trying to kill us quicker, the enemy or our military by not giving us the proper supplies? It was more in the way that they didn't sympathize enough with us to keep us safe. There were several times when we went to Camp Arifjan in southern Kuwait and saw hundreds and hundreds of brand-new, up-armored Humvees sitting there for weeks and weeks, but we didn't qualify for them because we were stationed in Kuwait. It didn't matter that we were the targets driving through Iraq. Our address was Kuwait. I invite any higher-ranking official to travel in those vehicles. We cannibalized other trucks all the time to keep them running.

Then we heard they were trying to cut our hazard pay. Now we have no supplies and they're going to cut our pay? Gee, is there anything else we can do for you? In the end, they never did cut our pay, but it was a slap in the face that they even considered it.

We would see soldiers sitting in Kuwait complaining that they didn't have a mission, blaming it on poor management, and we were on the road constantly. There were people sitting at the pool every day with nothing to do and we were living in our trucks with a day here and there at camp to regroup. Granted, sometimes that stuff happens, but the bottom line is the way they managed the war didn't impress me one bit.

After watching it for some time, I asked, "Are you sure we've ever won a war? Because they way you're running things makes me think we couldn't possibly win one."

By that point, I didn't have much tolerance for people, but especially those who could make things harder on me. After being away from camp for twenty days, I figured the clothes and equipment that Mullen and I lost in the truck had already been ordered. I expected uniforms, nuclear and biological chemical gear and all kinds of other things to be waiting for me. But the sergeant who ordered our supplies hadn't done anything because she had a few questions about what we wanted and never thought to ask them over phone during one of the million calls I made from BIAP to the unit. Therefore, our supply order was on hold until we got back. I was sick of it, so I took it out on the people back at camp. When they tried to explain the process, I didn't give a shit. I wanted my shit. I was so cold at that point. I was irate that nothing was ordered and became a pain in the ass until Mullen and I had enough supplies to go back out on the road. I wasn't about to miss a mission waiting for supplies and getting off the rotation with our platoon that we had worked so hard for. I also had heard of people having post-traumatic stress and struggling with getting back on the road and I didn't want that to happen to me. I wasn't trying to be a demanding, pain in the ass over there, but we did tell them twenty days prior and something could have been waiting for us.

Between my temper tantrums and the supply sergeant, we were able to piece together enough supplies so we could go back on the road. We were satisfied with almost everything until we were given truck #312. Mullen and I instantly took note of it because our truck that was blown up was #321. I felt a little sick.

We weren't the only ones with horror stories, though. It seemed like every story we heard made the experience even more unbearable and unbelievable. The Second Artillery Division was sent home and already on a plane headed to Germany when the military decided to keep them longer. They just turned the plane around and brought them back. All of their equipment that we had hauled to Kuwait to ship home for them had to go back to Iraq, so we spent what was supposed to be our time pulling security back at Camp Navistar hauling that stuff from Kuwait to Iraq. Those people got pulled back for about six more months and lost several soldiers along the way. When we saw them on the road they looked beat down, depressed and defeated. They had no soul left. Their energy was gone and only a look of disgust remained on their faces. At the same time, the 720th was sitting in Arifjan waiting for a plane to take them home when they were extended for a fourth time.

I would pass my New Mexican buddy once in a while. They had given us all of their equipment and supplies they had invented to make life easier on the road. One of their inventions was a gadget to blow sand out of small spaces. They gave us everything and they were back on the road like they were just starting out. It would have sucked to have to ride in someone else's equipment after spending a year getting my truck prepared. Each solider knew exactly what to expect from their truck; they knew all of the quirky little things that happened only to that vehicle. It must have been unnerving to be mentally prepared to be sent home only to be sent back into danger in unfamiliar equipment. It was a double-whammy.

There were also other tragedies for our New Mexican buddies. The wife and child of one of the guys got in a car accident and died while they were on their extension. He could have been home with his family if they would have been sent home when they were supposed to. Another guy found out he had intestinal cancer while overseas on that last extension and was in the last stages. He is probably dead by now. He had held off on getting it looked at because he didn't want to let his fellow soldiers down because of some medical condition that he thought was stress-related. I wish he had his last months with his family. They shipped him right home. But there was a hitch. The guy was in the same unit with his son, so he went right home but they wouldn't let his son go. I was burnt out at nine months and they were there twice as long as me.

Their unit was told they were going to be there three months in the beginning of the war before it got extended to six months, then to "indefinitely." Then their orders changed from "Wait until your replacements are here and you can go home" to "Nope, sorry, we need six more months out of you."

We signed up for this, I understand, but how much can you ask of one person? No one, including a soldier, understands truly what they're about to sacrifice when they sign on for this.

That was a pivotal point in our deployment. After the Easter attacks, the military insisted convoys couldn't travel without a set number of gun trucks, so the gun-truck-to-semi ratio jumped dramatically. Our platoon had three crews dedicated to escorting our convoys. Gun truck companies also were created based on what happened on Easter. At the same time, a gun truck company was formed and their sole responsibility was to escort convoys. Unfortunately, our company had to give up around twelve soldiers to the gun truck company. Between losing soldiers for details like the gun truck company and those going on sick call, it became difficult to find enough soldiers to put in trucks to run our convoys.

We had two 50-caliber machine guns that we never even unpacked because no one thought we would ever need them. We were so inexperienced on these weapons that only the prior active duty soldiers who had used the 50-calibers had an inkling of how to use them. When we finally pulled them out of storage and dusted them off, no one remembered how or was very competent on them. We had a vague idea because some were trained on them once, but that was it. It was the same with the Mark-19 (grenade launcher). We trained ourselves by reading the manuals. We had college kids reading them trying to figure out how to put them together, take them apart and fire them. If there were any questions or troubleshooting that had to be done on the 50-caliber, we had to wait until we went to BIAP. There was a Special Forces unit stationed there and they helped the guys become more familiar with it and also provided us with spare parts. The guys from our platoon who rode in the gun trucks were experts on the weapons in no time. By the end, the military had a special company set up designed to be convoy escorts. They were trained far better than we had been on weaponry and how to run a convoy.

Another thing that changed was how we chose our routes. Before Easter, convoy commanders chose which routes to take. Afterwards, it was extremely structured by movement control so that convoys were on heavily patrolled routes. Another adjustment in the way we operated was that convoys had a clearer picture of which commercial drivers were on the convoys. The company was required to give us a docket of the driver's name, which country he was from and the truck license number. This way we had better command and control during the convoys.

The attack turned out to be a benefit for our platoon in that it pulled us together and gave us confidence, and it also showed us the seriousness of what we were doing. We maintained our equipment and our weapons and tried to be on the ball because we knew shit like that was likely to happen again.

One of the downers of always being on the road together was that we were always in each other's business. It went on and on. This person thought that one was getting special treatment and that one was upset because they picked this one to be their partner instead. It was like workplace gossip, family squabbles and roommate bickering all rolled in together. It was a lot of catty, petty bullshit. But after Easter, all of that went away. No one cared about it anymore. It put everything in perspective for us and we began to realize what was important and what wasn't.

I'm glad the attack happened when it did because most soldiers have stories about it happening right before they were supposed to leave. It worked out for us that the Easter attack happened in the beginning because we didn't have any casualties. We were able to process a lot of it as we went and I was able to keep overcoming my fears and realize nothing was going to happen out on the road most of the time. It showed me that I always had to keep my wits, though. I had nightmares after Easter and I was hypersensitive to loud, banging noises, but I was de-sensitized again by the end of our deployment. Hearing mortars around me was nothing and I just learned to shrug it off again.

After the attack, the military started taking protection more seriously, but we still couldn't get the resources we really needed. Rumor had it that all the protection we needed was sitting in Kuwait, but for whatever reason, we weren't getting it. The gun trucks needed to be up-armored so the guys could have half a chance against roadside bombs. Our trucks had polycarbonate on the doors for protection; we later found out that even if the stuff was three layers thick, it wouldn't stop a bullet. We knew we needed better communication and more escorts for protection, but it was never available to us.

One of the most classic cases I can remember regarding resources was when I went with Schrack to up-armor his gun truck. We went to Camp Arifjan and there were contractors whose sole job was to up-armor Humvees. When we got there, Schrack asked if they could throw some scraps of metal on the doors of his Humvee for a little protection. The contractors snubbed him and said they were way too busy for a walk-in. They said it would take months before they could fit him in.

"Excuse me, but I would really appreciate it if you could just throw a little something on this Humvee. I'm really afraid to go on the road because my truck just blew up last mission and I almost died," I explained in my best damsel-in-distress voice. "We're going to Iraq tomorrow and won't be back down to this camp for a long time. Do you think you can help me out?"

Suddenly, three of the contractors stopped what they were doing and offered to help. It was only because I was a female asking for help and they were more than happy to put whatever armor I wanted on the truck. Schrack pointed to all the spots that needed armor and I would point it out to the contractors. When the head contractor asked me if I had my work order from my unit authorizing them to do the work, I just looked at him with my big, blue puppy-dog eyes and said, "I forgot it." He smiled and told me not to worry about it. They asked if I could pick up the Humvee at five o'clock, but I told him that noon would work better for me. That contractor had everything finished by noon. He also offered the special contractor's Internet and telephones to use while we waited. I thanked them in my sweetest voice as Schrack and I walked away.

"Oh my God, I can't believe they totally disregarded me but fell all over you when you asked," he said shaking his head with a look of disgust.

I told him if guys were going to gawk at me every day and I had to deal with the harassment, I might as well use it to our advantage and the benefit of our squad. It was pathetic that flirting got armor put on a truck, but it did.

That same day, we were heading to Camp Navistar and I pulled out a map to figure out which way to go because we hadn't been there in awhile. I figured out that if we left right then, we'd make it just in time before the chow hall closed. Well, "Wonder Boy" decided he didn't need the map and could tell *me* how to get back to camp. I argued, but only briefly because I didn't feel like taking on Schrack's huge ego that day. We missed a turn and ended up in downtown Kuwait. It was the first time either of us had seen actual buildings and civilization in a while, so we were in awe. It was about five o'clock in downtown rush hour. People were staring at us as if to say, "What the hell are you two doing here?" I told Schrack he'd better get us out of there and back on track so we could make dinner. Food was very important to me and I didn't like to miss a meal, especially when it was going to be a hot one for a change. Every turn we made took us back to the same spot—kind of like "National Lampoon's European Vacation." Instead of seeing Big Ben, we saw the same McDonald's about ten times. We decided if we passed it again we would get some food because we had already missed chow. Naturally, we passed McDonald's again and pulled into the drive-thru. The workers were speaking to us in Arabic over the drive thru speaker.

"English?" I squeaked into the microphone.

Fortunately, someone spoke English and we ordered more burgers and fries than our bodies could handle. In the States, what we ordered would have cost ten bucks. There it was more like thirty, but I didn't care. It was the first McDonald's either of us had eaten in so long and it tasted amazing! We eventually found our way to camp and destroyed the evidence so the others wouldn't get jealous.

Mullen and I were awarded Purple Hearts shortly after the ambush. To qualify for a Purple Heart, we had to get injured in combat and require medical attention. Although Mullen and I qualified because we got shrapnel in our arms, we didn't want them. We didn't think our wounds were serious enough to warrant a Purple Heart. Sure it bled a lot and they had to scrape the tiny pieces of shrapnel out of our arms so the wounds wouldn't get infected, but it didn't seem like enough of a risk to me at the time. Looking back, I realize the potential for what could have happened, because if the RPG would have hit an inch higher, it would have hit the cab instead of the frame and exploded right between us.

Anyway, we were standing in formation one day during an awards ceremony when a two-star general started handing out awards and handing out the Purple Hearts. I quietly started arguing with my first sergeant because I didn't want to walk up to be recognized or receive a Purple Heart, but he insisted I was going up there. We argued back and forth until I lost. Mullen was on leave and I hated him for not being there.

I knew I had to write something about the ambush because it was printed in the newspaper. I had to write about my experience and I didn't even want to think about it. It took me awhile. When I finally processed it enough, I sent a letter. I didn't want to glorify my experience or write things that weren't true. I just wanted everyone to have the facts. I tried to be as honest as possible within reason. There were things I couldn't say for security reasons, but I had to quell the rumors that I had lost an arm and half of my face was blown off. Someone wrote me a letter saying they heard I killed a bunch of people and that really hurt me. We didn't even see anybody. I fired shots, but it wasn't at anybody as far as I knew. It wasn't like I had a target and took the shot; I was firing blindly out the window.

The pressure my mom put on me to write the letters really helped me process everything. She didn't want me to bottle it up, so she made me talk.

My parents didn't believe my injuries were minor until I sent the medical report home. When I arrived home on leave, I handed my Purple Heart to my dad and told him he deserved it because it hurt him more than it hurt me. I haven't seen it since then.

– 5 –

May

Killed in Action: 820

Wounded in Action: 5,040

I wanted to say hello and let you all know that I'm still doing well in Iraq.

I also wanted to say thank you for all the mail and care packages I've received. I never expected as much love and support as I've gotten since I've been here.

Since there are so many packages, I was able to share with all the soldiers in my platoon. I made a "community" shelf, where soldiers can grab stuff they need or drop off extra stuff for someone else. I cannot tell you how appreciative we all are to have the supplies, candy and toiletry items readily available.

York and Liverpool sixth-grade classes from Medina County wrote me letters with lots of questions. I decided to answer their questions in this e-mail.

Emily: What is the temperature in Iraq?

It has been in the 120s lately, but it has gotten as hot as 140. We laugh at the newspapers because they are telling us it is only 100 degrees Fahrenheit and our thermostats are reaching 120 to 140.

I cannot explain how hot 140 degrees feel except if you were to stand outside on the hottest summer day in Ohio and take blow dryers and blow them on your body. It is really hot.

Nicole: Is it really hot under your gear?

Yes, it is. We have to wear long sleeve tops and a flak vest and it gets really hot. When we get to take off the flak vest, our T-shirts are covered in sweat. I don't mind wearing the long-sleeve top or flak vests because it keeps me safe.

Anna: Is there a lot of sand?

Yes, there is sand everywhere. Every day we sweep all the sand out of our tent and there is still sand everywhere. We get lots of sand in our hair, ears and nose, and we have to use Q-Tips to get all the sand out of our ears!

Caitlyn: Does it ever rain?

Yes, it rains occasionally, like once every couple of weeks. It will rain for 10 minutes and then stop. It usually doesn't rain for long periods of time (yet). They tell me there is a rainy season and it may rain longer than 10 minutes.

Casey and Callie: Do you sleep in tents?

Yes, we sleep in tents. There are 11 of us that share a tent. The tent has a wood floor, air conditioner and lights. We sleep on cots unless we build our own beds. The doors are just flaps of fabric. We have to walk to trailers that have showers and toilets. If it gets too hot, our air conditioner and power shut off and someone has to fix it. When that happens, it gets really hot.

Marisa: Where do people sleep?

If we are out on the road, we sleep on cots next to our truck. It is like camping under the stars and it is usually really nice. Sometimes there are mosquitoes and sand fleas outside so we use lots of bug spray to keep the bugs away while we sleep. If it rains we have ponchos we string up over two vehicles and we sleep under the poncho.

Marah and Nina: Do you ever feel endangered or scared in the night or when you're only with a few guys or girls?

I feel very safe at night because we always stay at military camps to sleep. There are always people guarding us and watching out for danger while we sleep. Also, all of the guys and girls in our unit take care of each other so nothing bad happens to anyone.

Heather and Amber: Do you shower every day?

We shower as much as possible. If we are at Camp Navistar, we shower daily but if we are on the road, we take lots of "baby wipe" showers.

Lindsay: Are there limits on your showers?

Yes, there are limits on the time we can spend in the showers. If we are on the road and can get a shower, we have five minutes to use the water. That is plenty of time because the water is usually freezing cold and you don't want to spend more than five minutes under the cold water. At Camp Navistar they aren't as picky, but you have to be quick on the showers to save the water.

Stacy: Do you have a vehicle you ride in?

Yes, I am assigned to a tractor-trailer semi. It is a big semi that you see on the roads in Ohio. We haul all kinds of supplies to other soldiers in Iraq. Some things we haul are water, ammo and equipment.

Alaina: How long have you been in the Middle East?

I've been here since February 17, 2004.

What time does your day begin?

My day begins anywhere between 5 a.m. to 8 a.m. just depending on what has to be done for the day.

Michelle: What type of reptiles or bugs do you come across in Iraq?

There are all kinds of crazy bugs that I've seen in Iraq. I've seen lizards, geckos, camel spiders and beetles. We've found a few camel spiders in our tent and beetles too. We shake our boots and sleeping bags out every day just in case there are bugs in the shoes and bags.

Corey: What kinds of food do you eat?

We eat pretty good food when we are at Camp Navistar. They serve things like pizza, cheeseburgers, spaghetti and beef. We have fruit every day and salads. If we are out on the road we'll eat MRE's (meals, ready to eat) that the military provides. They are not really good so we usually take snacks, like crackers and peanut butter.

Adrienne: Do you get along with any of the Iraqis?

Yes, most of the people in Iraq are very friendly and kind. The terrorists are the ones we don't get along with. Most of the Iraq people are farmers or builders and wave and say hello to us. The children give us the "thumbs up" symbol or blow kisses at us. Since the recent terrorist activity, we haven't seen many people or children when we drive around.

Kaley: How long have you been with the 1486ᵗʰ Transportation Company?

I've been working with the 1486ᵗʰ since I was 17. I joined the National Guard when I was 17 and still in high school. I have been in the Guard for 10 years now.

Danielle: Do you like your job?

Overall, I must say that I have a very interesting job. I get to see all of Iraq and all the different military camps across the country. I get to see the different people and culture and it is very exciting. It is also very dangerous because of the terrorists and we have to be very careful so we don't get hurt.

Chelsie: Have you made any new friends out there?

Yes, I have. I've met people from all over the United States and also from all over the world. I've met people from Poland, Britain, Korea, Spain and Denmark. It is cool to meet people from all over the world.

I would just like to thank Mr. Wimer's and Mrs. Slepecky's sixth grade class for all the letters and the questions. I hope I've answered all of your questions. If you have more questions, I'd be happy to answer them. If you send me an email address, I'll send you pictures online of Iraq.

Take care and thank you all for your support! – MZ, May 14, 2004

On our first mission after the attack, we had a delivery to Camp Cuervo. The camp was outside the Green Zone, in the town of Sader City. There were three trucks full of equipment that needed to be delivered. The larger part of the convoy had already delivered at BIAP. An MP escort volunteered to take us to where we were trying to go and he swore he knew how to get there. He took us through the center of Baghdad through shopping centers, people, cars, a soccer field and skyscrapers. There was a traffic jam at a circle in the middle of the city and there were hundreds of people and vehicles jammed together. I was getting nervous because I knew we were sitting ducks. Mullen told me to lock my door. I wasn't about to get out of the vehicle to pull security because any one of us could be kidnapped. A soldier called on the radio to point out we didn't have enough bullets if something happened. My stomach did cartwheels. All I could do was laugh and pick out which bridge I'd be hanging from when I was killed. It was the first time I felt completely out of control in a situation. We were in deep shit if something went wrong, but thankfully, nothing did. The MPs escorted us to Cuervo near the Green Zone.

When we got to Cuervo, the guard ushered us through the entrance gate and we didn't take that as a good sign. Normally it takes about twenty minutes to tell security who we were and why we were there and this guy was screaming, "Go, go, go!" Just as the last truck entered, there was an explosion just outside the gate.

The delivery we made turned out to be the other part of the load that was supposed to be delivered on Easter, but couldn't get through because of all the chaos. We handed over the postal equipment and wished them luck because the connex where the equipment was stored was all shot up from the ambush. The soldier who met us to accept the delivery was so thankful it finally reached their camp. The postmaster said he would have invited us to the chow hall, but it had just been mortared earlier that morning, so he invited us to stay the night instead. We politely declined before we bolted out of there. He brought us Gatorade before we left, which in our world was like a cold beer had just landed in our laps.

– 6 –

June

Killed in Action: 862
Wounded in Action: 5,629

I just wanted to write to say hello. We are back on the road and pretty much into a routine.

There isn't much to say because we aren't really doing anything new and exciting. I think we are all just trying to stay cool in the heat and keep busy so we don't get bored.

I love going on the road because it beats sitting around at the base camp. Time seems to go by faster when we are out on missions.

Even though I love being on the road, I think my parents feel better when I am at Camp Navistar.

Trying to keep my parents from worrying has been the most difficult task from this whole deployment. I try so hard to convince them I'm safe, fed, not too hot, safe, rested and safe.

They never seem to believe me that we are really doing the best we can to stay safe. Maybe it isn't that they don't believe me, but they are so concerned with the current state of Iraq and the violence toward U.S. soldiers that nothing I can say will keep them from worrying.

I let them know that we take so many precautionary measures, rely on excellent Intel and have so many types of support that they shouldn't worry as much as they do.

I try to call home every few days so they know I'm safe and sound, so hopefully that will alleviate some of their stress.

I feel like a teenager again with a curfew. But instead of yelling to their room that I'm home by curfew, I have to call and tell them I'm OK. Either way, they get to keep tabs on me. Yes, I'm 27 years old and my parents are keeping tabs on me.

It hasn't been all work, though, here. After about three months of working seven days a week with only a few hours off here and there, we finally got a day of R&R.

Our platoon got to go to a camp in Kuwait and go swimming in a real pool. The whole day was ours, no uniforms and no orders, just fun in the sun. I cannot describe how relaxing and enjoyable the day at the pool was. It was a much-deserved break that we all needed.

And if we have free time in the future, we'll all be at the pool.

I experienced homesickness for the first time in four months of being in Iraq. I talked to my dad and I found out that my uncle, my godfather, was in the hospital and they didn't know what was wrong with him. I was out on the road and had no time to use or find a phone.

It was so stressful because I could not talk to him because he was in a hospital room with no telephone. I couldn't stop worrying.

I finally got to talk to him a few days later and he sounded so sick. The doctor still did not know what was wrong with him. It was such a helpless feeling to not be able to do anything and not to be able to be there with my family. It was awful.

During this whole time, my sister was getting ready to get married. I was supposed to be her maid of honor. I had helped her plan the wedding before I got activated but I really felt like I was abandoning her.

I missed out on all the fun stuff like the shower and the bachelorette party. I had to hear about how fun it was instead of experiencing it firsthand.

The worst was the day of the wedding. I called and got to talk to my sister, Marie, and she told me about everything that was going on. Family and friends were all in town, all the kids were running around wild and my parents were stressing out with last-minute plans.

I wanted to be there so badly, just to be a part of Marie's big day.

She had to get off the phone to go to the church and I felt horrible. It was so hard to hang up and know I was missing such an important event in her life.

I realized how much of a sacrifice soldiers make in order to serve their country. I missed my sister's wedding and there are soldiers missing so much, too. They are missing the birth of their children, children's first steps, high school graduations, family deaths and more.

Now that I've experienced missing an important family event, I see how difficult it is to be here while life goes on back home.

One of the cool things about being a soldier is that you have an excellent support system. We have a military family that takes care of each other.

The night my sister got married and I was pretty down, some of my fellow brothers and sisters got cake from the chow hall and brought it back to our tent. They surprised me and said it was wedding cake from my sister's wedding.

We sat there and ate cake and laughed about what was happening at the reception. Since I couldn't be there, it was the next best thing.

Marie also promised to send me pictures and video of the wedding so I can watch it like I was there. I know I'm probably going to miss a lot more events from back home, but it is more bearable to know that people here understand when you are down and help pick you back up when you need it the most. – MZ, June 15, 2004

During this time we were already in a transition phase because soldiers were coming in-country and others were leaving. After April, we had the surge of troops from the anticipated transition as well as added troops who had to return until things calmed down instead of going home. The troops who were held over were part of a surge we didn't anticipate and it put a terrible strain on our resources at every single camp. The camps were not equipped to handle that many people at one time. There was not enough water for the showers or tents for transients and truck drivers to stay for a night. The camps were so crowded and, on top of that, the poor soldiers who got extended were not in the mood to deal with this shortfall. As truck drivers, we had all of this equipment we were trying to coordinate and it just made it more confusing. There were about 1,000 soldiers in our battalion trying to move as much equipment as quickly as we could, but the stress was mounting for everyone in-country.

It was also a little more nerve-racking right around this time because we were under the impression the government was supposed to change hands on June 30, but we still had a job to do. We were out on the road when all of a sudden we got an instant message that the country had been turned over to Iraq. We didn't know if insurgents were going to cause problems, but it really turned out to be very anti-climactic. It was a smooth transition and it went great for us. We tried to stay off the road at certain times when we were anticipating the changeover, but it turned out we were on the road anyway so it really didn't matter.

My parents were sending me information about all of this violence and U.S. soldiers being killed and I had no clue of any of it going on. When we went on the road, we got our usual instant messages of all of the activity going on in the country in order to detect patterns, but we never heard of soldiers getting killed. The only casualty count we ever saw was in the *Stars and Stripes* and it always came days after the fact. Most of the time, it was on the roads we were driving. We would make it through an area and then the convoy in front of or behind us would get hit. We had a lot of luck on our side, but it was also the way the New Mexican unit taught us how to run. They didn't lose anyone and neither did we. Maybe it was because we had the bigger trucks. Or maybe it was because we were just lucky. Rumor had it that the enemy constantly surveyed us and watched how we reacted, stopped and every other move we made. On our usual routes, we would rarely get attacked. Probably because the enemy just let us go. Other units in our battalion got attacked every time they went down the same roads. Who knows why, it just worked that way. It was the roundabout routes and detours we had to take where we would get attacked. It was just something about our unit and how we ran.

Our unit was assigned three detached soldiers when some of the replacements came in the summer. One guy had just returned home from serving a year in Iraq and found out his wife left him. Since he had nothing else, the poor guy returned to Iraq and did another tour. One girl assigned to our unit was in basic training when we were initially deployed, so she met up with us and finished out her deployment once she completed basic. The last replacement soldier was a young woman who had recently had a baby. She was recouping after the birth of her son when we were sent overseas. She might have had some medical issues, too, I'm not sure, but she was deployed to finish the tour with our unit. It must have been difficult to leave a brand-new baby and go into an environment where she might die. When a female in the military gets pregnant, she is offered the opportunity to be discharged. If she stays, she is subject to deployment with the rest of the unit. I asked her why in the world she would stay in the military after having a child, knowing there was a hundred percent chance of getting sent to Iraq. Her response was that in order to better her life for her son, she needed to stay in so she could receive the educational benefits. Being deployed overseas, away from her son, was just the price she had to pay to give him a better life.

She was one of many with a family at home. There were several men and women who left children and families behind. Dawn was a close friend of mine so I heard in more detail the difficulties of leaving a child and husband behind. Dawn's baby was only four months old when we got deployed. While she was gone, her son said his first words, took his first steps and did all the things a child does in the first year. There were many nights we sat and talked about how much she missed her family. Her husband was an amazing man and he became Mr. Mom for that year and kept Dawn in the loop with

Michelle and SPC John "JD" Delaney

her son's development. They scheduled "dates" to meet online so she could see her husband and son with the help of a web camera. That really helped Dawn make it through that year.

SSG Brown's wife had a baby while he was overseas. It was their second child and it was rough on him. When he went on leave he got to meet his child for the first time. Brown also had a phenomenal wife. She raised their two kids, worked and never complained about how difficult it was. Less stress on the homefront made it easier overseas.

Since we had new soldiers coming in-country, Mullen and I had to split up. We were getting on each other's nerves anyway. Mullen took one of the new soldiers and I took JD.

John Delaney was a twenty-four-year-old college student. He stood 5'10" and had dark eyes and dark hair. They say he's very handsome, although I never realized it because I looked at him all day. But when I sent pictures of him to my friends, they'd ask who the cutie was. I'd say, "Who? Oh, that's just JD. He's not cute; he's my co-driver." Of course, John was flattered when I let him know he had a fan club.

A wretch picks up a connex used for hauling

JD was studying biology and planned on going to medical school. He was one of those freakishly smart kids and it was a breath of fresh air having him in the truck. Really, anybody would have been a breath of fresh air at that point, but JD was awesome to ride with. He reminded me of my baby brother, Mark, because they had the same warped sense of humor, loved music and were very compassionate. JD and I had the same outlook on the war, the Iraqi people and how to treat people, which also made things easier. But JD also had a mean streak, which kept it interesting. He was the hardest, most competent worker in my squad and he never complained about anything.

JD had lost his license back home and the military wouldn't let him drive overseas without it. After some research, I found out he only needed a military license to drive in Iraq, which he had. We needed bodies to ride in the trucks so I made a "drug" deal with our truck master. A drug deal is when someone begs, borrows or steals in very creative ways to get things done. I bullshitted them into allowing JD to ride in my truck by saying that I would drive the whole time and if I got tired, JD would ride with someone else while a licensed driver drove my truck and I rested as co-driver. Somehow it flew and JD was on the road with us. Our platoon was spread so thin by this point due to all the soldiers being put on work details and those on sick call. Plus, leave was beginning for some, where soldiers were able to go home for two weeks and see family.

On our first mission together we had to haul water. Hauling water was the biggest pain in the ass. A forklift put pallets of water on the truck and we would have to put up sideboards and strap the water down. It doesn't sound that difficult, but in 140-degree heat, the time-consuming process of preparing the load was dreadful. The other discouraging factor in hauling water was that only half of it would make it to the destination because the roads were so beat up. In one spot there was an eighty-mile stretch of road that was just sand and potholes where Iraqi's scurried to grab the boxes of water that fell off. We were told the water was for the soldiers stationed in Iraq, so it made hauling it a little more bearable.

106

When we got to Anaconda, the place that distributed water all over Iraq, there were thousands and thousands of boxes of water everywhere. There was enough water for every soldier for eight months! I guess the majority of the water was going to be buried once it reached its expiration date and never even be used. We'd ask the following

Michelle with SPC John "JD" Delaney

questions: Why are we bringing water that you aren't going to use? Why can't the water you are burying be given to the Iraqi people to at least use to do laundry? Why isn't anyone looking at this situation and correcting it? Here soldiers are risking their lives to drive this water through Iraq only to see it get wasted. Again I was frustrated. This was our mission for most of the summer.

JD and I started securing our load and I thought I would give him the easy job since it was our first mission together. He had to climb on top of the water and when I threw the straps to him, all he had to do was take them to the other side of the truck and drop them. I would run around and finish securing the load. It took forever and it was really, really hot. Of course it was the hottest day of the year on a black top and I kept checking to make sure he was all right. He kept insisting he was fine. I soon found out he was afraid of heights. About halfway through tying down the load, JD broke the news to me that he was scared of heights. I asked him why he didn't say anything before climbing up top and he said he didn't really know. I just laughed and made fun of him until the load was secure.

I loved his sick sense of humor. One day, after he got his civilian license back, we had just switched drivers because I was so tired. We had been driving for hours and didn't get much sleep. JD took over and I was going to take a catnap before we hit the "bad area." I was in a deep, deep sleep when out of nowhere, JD starts screaming as loud as he could. I woke up and my heart was beating so fast and I yelled, "What's going on, what's going on!" He looked at me, laughing, and asked if I could hand him his cigarettes. He said they had slid over and he couldn't reach them. I wanted to kill him, but it was pretty funny afterwards.

107

JD and I had such an amazing system that it got to the point where we didn't even have to talk anymore. We had a CD player and some speakers to keep us occupied. There was a set order of which CD we'd listen to and when. It was a routine that we both knew and liked. We also had a designation for where we put stuff in the truck and who did what on the truck. If he ran out of water and was driving, it got to the point where I would climb out of the truck to the catwalk and grab more water and he would do the same. The coolers didn't fit in the cab of the truck so they were strapped on the top of a metal box on the catwalk.

In the morning, I had to go to the bathroom a lot so JD would drive and roll his eyes when I'd climb out to pee. The trucks were zooming at sixty-five miles per hour down the road and all of us felt comfortable climbing out to get stuff and pee. The convoy rarely stopped so we had to figure out how to manage and still roll down the road. If the road was bumpy and one of us was on the back, the one driving would honk the horn to let the other know to hold on tight. It's amazing nobody fell off and got killed. In the beginning when I asked JD for a drink and he had to climb out there, he was really nervous because of his fear of heights. A good co-driver would have stopped asking him to climb outside, but I wasn't one and continued to ask for drinks.

Everyone had little relationships within their own trucks that eventually became heated for one reason or another. We called them lover's quarrels, but it wasn't really like that. JD and I always sat together in the chow hall. One day I couldn't find him so I went by myself. I decided to fix him a plate because I knew he'd be hungry. I thought I was doing such a nice co-driverly thing but when I got to the truck he yelled, "You bitch, why didn't you take me with you?" I then realized we had a permanent date for everything. He was pissy during the whole three-hour ride home. After that, I had to extend a personal invitation every time I went to the chow hall so he wouldn't act like a little bitch. We used to tease each other and say, "Ahh, your work husband is pissed at you." It sucked, too, because we were stuck with each other in that cab and it made time almost stand still when we weren't speaking. Luckily JD and I rarely fought.

To pass the time and entertain each other, the two of us would act silly. JD would sing to me or tell me funny, untrue stories. I would dance and lip-synch to Aretha Franklin's "Respect." One of the PXs had the Bee Gee's greatest hits. JD and I were disco dancing in the cab one day while we were driving and one of our gun trucks in front of us watched the whole thing and thought we had gone crazy. Another time the convoy had stopped on the road to fix a truck and we got bored. There were some local Iraqi people hanging around our trucks so instead of shooing them away, JD and I got out food and handed it out to all of them. The Iraqis gave us what little possessions they had to return the kind gesture. A little boy gave me some old Saddam money and JD got some jewelry. They liked us so they began playing a kazoo and some other instrument and were dancing in a group. Since it would be a while before the convoy began moving, I walked over and danced with their group. JD recorded the whole thing on the digital camera.

Because of all the time we spent together, I know a lot about JD's life and he knows mine. He knew when I was happy, sad or pissed without really asking. It was a platonic bond that very few people can have unless they spend countless days and nights together. JD also was very protective of his big sister. There was an incident one night where a commercial driver groped one of our female soldiers. It was a huge deal and everyone was up in arms. JD returned to the trailer where I was sleeping and watched over me just to make sure nothing would happen. He was always doing things like that. JD became my co-driver for almost the rest of our deployment.

Meanwhile, I was becoming overly conscious about personal hygiene. I needed control over something, so I made sure to brush and floss, use moisturizer and lotion, slather sunscreen and take vitamins. I cleaned under my nails more carefully. I didn't want to worry about finding medical or dental assistance in a foreign country with limited access to medical care that wasn't as good as at home. It was nothing like the way I took care of myself in the States. It was more for self-preservation, so I made sure to eat the right things and cut out caffeine, although I never declined dessert.

In addition, I started pampering myself with gifts I didn't even get to see. I was ordering things online and sending them home. I bought a lot of outfits from Old Navy and Victoria's Secret underwear. My dad scolded and then laughed at me for spending so much money on underwear. He wanted me to save as much money as possible so the deployment would at least have a purpose. But he sure didn't mind getting all the Victoria's Secret catalogues! When I got home, I had fifty pairs of brand new underwear that my poor dad had to pile up in my room. There was also a featherbed top, a down comforter and the softest, most expensive sheets waiting for my return. I wanted to be as comfortable as possible. I even promised myself a pedicure once a week when I got home and massages.

In Iraq, everything in the laundry became the same color because they just threw it all together, so we valued the few things we could keep nice. In a PX in Iraq, I bought a silky shirt for sleeping in that I hand washed so the laundry service wouldn't destroy it. We each had one outfit over there that made us feel like human beings: mine consisted of Capris and a t-shirt.

Michelle surveys a load of water pallets that shifted and fell during a mission. Whenever this happened, Hajis would rush to pick up the water bottles, which were valued more than oil

Since makeup during the deployment was out of the question, I couldn't put eyeliner on when I got home. Scraping the pen across my eyes felt like sandpaper. I grew my hair to one length, no style, no layers. When I got home, I just kept playing with it and cutting it until it was different than I wore it overseas.

But I didn't even feel like trying to look like a girl while we were there. I would look in the mirror long enough in a day to brush my teeth, floss and whip my hair up into the usual bun. There was no reason to primp. Nothing about that place made you feel glamorous and there was nobody there to impress.

There was only one time over there when I felt like an ass and self-conscious about my looks. My glasses broke and I went to one of the vendors at a camp stand and bought a pair of name-brand knock-offs. My hair was a sweaty mass in the afternoon heat and I could feel the drops sliding slowly past my sunglasses down my sunburned cheeks. As we entered the chow hall, I took off the cheap glasses not thinking anything about it. I had this melted black goo all over my nose and eyebrows. I looked like I had a unibrow and I had no idea. I was talking to Willy and he was acting like nothing was out of the ordinary but people were staring and giving me that look like something

110

was not right. I went outside and finally realized I had black shit all over my face. Everyone else was howling, but it was hell scraping that stuff off my face.

"Why didn't you tell me?" I scolded him.

"I needed something to laugh at," he quipped. "Besides, now I know what you look like with a unibrow!"

Although we had basically settled into our routines, I always discovered something new about my environment and the people around me. As each day passed, I began to feel sorry for the Marines. They really had it the worst. They were in the worst parts of the country and they didn't have much to work with either. These guys were stuck in the same place fighting every day to stay alive and they didn't have the right equipment.

We were running a "blue light special" war and we all knew it. I pray to God that things are better and equipment has improved. But after I left I received an email from someone who didn't have a truck with armor yet. I can't imagine why it would take that long.

One thing that surprised me was the air support provided by the Air Force for security. The Air Force always supplied the F-16 for defense. Apparently they were in the sky 24/7 to protect us. None of us knew they were up there until they told us about it one day in the chow hall at Camp Anaconda. Our convoy had finally arrived at Camp Anaconda after a very long day. I was tired and spent and just wanted to eat some food. Sweat had drenched my DCUs (desert camouflage uniform) and I hadn't slept in what seemed like forever. Some pilots sat next to a few of us in the chow hall and they were so friendly and happy. I hadn't seen genuine happiness in such a long time. I was mean and bitter by then and their cheer was just annoying me. How in the hell can they be so happy? Then they told us that they only deploy for three months at a time and go home for three months. How wonderful would that be to go for three months and return home to recoup and then return? Yeah, that didn't happen in the Army. I must have been growling because the flyboys stopped talking to me. I cherished my dessert and ignored their stories of "the better life" that I would never experience. They looked puzzled at my disdain for the war and their cheer puzzled me. We were even. That was the point I realized I didn't smile anymore and that distant look was in my eyes, the same look that the soldiers in Arifjan had when I first arrived in-country.

Michelle (second from left, facing camera) briefs a group before a mission

- 7 -

July

Killed in Action: 916

Wounded in Action: 6,181

I would like to tell you all the good and bad news.

The bad news is another trailer of mine caught on fire, this time due to a brake problem. The good news is nobody was hurt and we were able to put the fire out and save the trailer.

SGT Boron saved the day and put the fire out. Apparently in his past life, he was a firefighter and saved my trailer.

Again, this is just another reason I love the diversity of the National Guard. Everyone has hidden skills and talents that have come in handy since we've been activated.

Our maintenance team has already replaced the axle on my trailer. I seriously will never live this down. I was told the fire was out of my control, but at this point nobody cares and I have been teased more than you'll ever know.

My second home has been the maintenance tent lately. I have had something break every mission for the past month and maintenance has had to fix it.

Our unit has the best maintenance team. They are the hardest workers and they give 110 percent on every vehicle. I am always confident once they've looked at my truck because I know that it will run smoothly. These guys work so hard and get barely any recognition. They work every day, with no time off because our trucks have to be ready for the road and maintenance can't wait.

These men and women will work nonstop until the vehicles can run without any problems. They also send a soldier on each mission to do quick repairs if needed.

As long as I'm on the road, the maintenance soldier who is in our convoy is busy.

So, from the bottom of my heart, thank you 1486ᵗʰ maintenance. And by the way, the maintenance guys tease me more than any group. When they see me coming, they yell to each other, "Oh, boy, Zaremba is coming. What did she break now?"

Even though they tease me, I love them to death because they treat me like their daughter, take care of me and make sure my vehicle is safe and ready to roll.

Our last mission was historic. We were in Iraq when the government was handed back to Iraq. It was a surprise they handed it over early. We were all speculating what was going to happen in Iraq, what danger we were in store for, if we were going to be stuck somewhere for weeks due to problems with the transition. It turned out the trip was uneventful. We were actually on the road when it was getting turned over.

I think we are all unsure of what the future will be in Iraq, so we will continue to be as cautious as possible and not let our guard down.

My parents send me articles online about the violence constantly and tell me to be careful. There is very little information that we are given about the incidents in Iraq unless it pertains to us or we can get a hold of a newspaper.

It is disturbing to hear of all the deaths, kidnappings and destruction going on all around me. I feel bad for everyone back home because you are getting all the news, the whole picture and know all the potential dangers soldiers face.

I think it would be too overwhelming to hear about everything as it's happening around me and try to do my job. We always say, "Old news is good news." If we don't know about it before we read about it, then we are fortunate. If we aren't part of the news, it's even better.

I have to get ready for our next mission. I'll write as soon as I can. – MZ, July 3, 2004

No shit, there we were driving down the road hauling a pretty heavy load of water to the distribution camp when it happened. We were listening to music and enjoying the easy part of the trip where nothing ever happened when JD threw his cigarette out the window. All of a sudden the guy in the truck behind us started screaming on the radio, "Your trailer is on fire! Your trailer is on fire!" I was sure it wasn't our truck and continued to drive until JD saw the smoke coming from under our truck. Oh God, I thought, it was JD's cigarette that he had just thrown out the window. It was actually the trailer that caught fire caused by a bearing that had seized up and started smoking.

The trucks were so old that the grease seeped out from the axle and there was no way for JD and I to know. It was just my luck that another trailer caught on fire! Putting out that fire and the entire situation made me realize the diversity of what the Guard had to offer. We had firefighters stubbing out

Shortly after Michelle's axle caught fire (one of several times). "We chained it up and drove to camp"

the fire while the maintenance people figured out a way to rig the trailer to get it to the camp. It was too dangerous to just leave it sitting there. Of course everyone had to make fun of the fact that it was my trailer that caught fire. I was so frustrated because I felt like all these little incidents were making us look bad. Really there was no way for us to know that it was bad. It was something that maintenance was supposed to check and supposedly it was checked by the unit before us.

When we got back, the maintenance crew was able to take an axle off another trailer and get it going again. Every time I pulled into the bay, I would get the look from every guy in there like, "Now what the hell did you do?" But I always hung out and helped them fix it, so I ended up learning a lot about trucks. I figured if anything happened on the road, I would be able to fix it.

Besides that I really didn't mind hanging out with the maintenance guys since they were the only ones who stuck up for us. Our platoon got such a bad rap from the rest of our unit because we were the partiers and not very "military." But our platoon always made sure each vehicle was ready to go before we did anything else. I guess the other platoons didn't do that and maintenance would be sure to point that out when anyone was badmouthing us. Those guys worked insane hours for us, too. At one point, they were a twenty-four hour operation. For my axle, we had a crane lift it off the trailer and it was ready to go the next day. They had three shifts and they always managed to fix whatever we needed them to by the next day. They had a ninety-five percent ready rate, which was incredible for a combat zone. The only barrier they had was getting supplies. Some people have been criticized for cannibalizing other trucks, but we did the same thing to survive.

Our big excitement for the Fourth of July holiday was getting a hold of some star clusters, the pyrotechnics that we were supposed to launch into the air to make the night look like midday for a few seconds. It was as bright as daylight and then it just fizzled—like our holiday.

"Oooh, happy Fourth of July," we teased.

That was our big celebration, but I really didn't care. It was a million degrees outside and it didn't really feel like a holiday. There was no beer and we sure as hell weren't celebrating our independence. Despite our efforts to remain optimistic, the hands of the military continued to strangle our spirits and our pride.

We started getting all kinds of "new rules" around camp that were supposed to make us safer, but all it did was piss us off.

One of the new rules said we couldn't fly the American flag in our trucks or on our tents. Our battalion headquarters was the only place that was allowed to have a flag, so most of the soldiers had Ohio State, Kent State University and Notre Dame flags just to personalize their little area. But when they decided we weren't allowed to have American flags, our tolerance for their ignorance disintegrated. Whether they claimed it was for security or not, it really killed the morale for us. Besides, it wasn't like the enemy didn't know where our camp was, but we couldn't have a flag in or on our truck. It was always comforting to see that big American flag roll up on the other side of the street because it was like we weren't alone in a country where people were trying to kill us. We had pride in what we were doing there. Then all of a sudden, the flag that was supposed to unite us now divided us.

Eventually it was decided all of the flags on the outside of the tents had to come down, too. It looked so drab. Our spirits just plummeted to the ground. We asked what we *were* allowed to do and never got an answer. We just wanted to identify with a piece of home and where we came from.

One of the most ridiculous rules was that there would be no wood in the tents anymore because it was a fire hazard. This was obviously dreamed up by someone in the military stationed far away from the war. It became an issue after an air-conditioning unit started a fire in the female bathroom in the middle of the night and we all woke up to a soldier screaming, "Fire, fire, fire!" It was a pretty big deal and had to be put out quickly because our whole camp could have burned down in a matter of minutes. Military firefighters and some of our soldiers who were firefighters in their civilian lives used every fire extinguisher in the camp to control it. After the infamous bathroom fire, the fire marshal was pretty strict about what we could do in our tents. All of the walls had to come down. We weren't supposed to daisy chain power cords from our two outlets anymore, but we did it anyway. When inspection came, word spread through camp and we would scramble to hide anything that might look like a fire hazard. Whoever heard the fire inspector was coming first was like Paul Revere yelling down the rows of tents, "The fire inspector is coming!"

But when they said we couldn't have wood anymore, we were stunned. We had wood everywhere. Our shelves and our beds were the top two things we were going to fight to the death to keep, but pretty much everything was wood. We were living in kerosene-soaked tents and they didn't see the logic in our argument. Surely a canvas tent would go up quicker than wood. The people making these decisions were living in trailers and were exempt from the order. Our sergeant major didn't think that was fair and, doing as he was told, immediately started tearing all the wood out of the joint trailer he shared with his boss.

"What the hell are you doing?" the Battalion Commander demanded to know.

"You told us to take all of the wood out, we gotta get rid of the wood," he explained.

After the sergeant major's performance, we were allowed to have wood in the tents again. It was petty bullshit like that that disgusted us, but it rejuvenated us to find out someone in a decision-making position was on our side.

When our new battalion came in, they decided no more civilian clothing would be allowed. Then they changed it to say that we could wear them on the weekends, but we didn't know what our weekends were because we didn't have office jobs. Then we were allowed to wear civilian clothes on days off. Of course, every day at camp became everyone's day off. They gave up on that one pretty quickly.

A basic rule of combat is that we do not salute officers in the field because they can be targeted and killed. But then they changed their minds. I can't even describe how impossible it is to salute officers in our tiny camp because everywhere we went, we had to salute. The officers hated it as much as we did. Then we went up north and we tried to salute and they hollered at us. Then we'd walk by an officer at another camp and he'd yell at us for not salut-

117

ing. We were truck drivers for God's sake. The rules were different in every camp and we didn't care to learn them.

At camp we were now supposed to do physical fitness on the two mornings we were there, but we didn't need structured PT. Most of us had passed our PT test so it was clear we were doing enough on our own. Besides that, we got enough PT climbing up and down on the trucks and walking miles to get to chow and showers. I wondered if we were in Camp Garrison, a full-time Army base where soldiers wore immaculate uniforms and always responded with an enthusiastic "Yes, sir," and "No, sir," or if we were going to face the facts that we were in a combat zone struggling to survive. I really wanted clarification on that and no one ever could offer a good explanation, but they wanted us to fight a war and play perfect soldier at the same time. I think we did one PT session before we ignored that rule.

They tried to put speed limits on our convoys, which was one of the only things we had to keep us safe. We told them to go ahead and write us tickets and they threatened to take away our licenses, but we were not slowing down. We had to laugh because we knew we were the lifelines for soldiers across the country.

Every time they came up with a new policy, morale dipped just a little lower. We never knew coming back into camp how angry we were going to get over their unrealistic restrictions.

I called my mom to tell her that I couldn't wait to get back on the road and she just laughed while I rattled off the most recent rule changes.

"Well, at least you're safe at camp and out of harm's way," she'd say. "I'd rather hear you bitching about that stuff." She always put things into perspective for me.

As leaders, we never knew what rules to implement. We never knew if it was one of the rules that would vanish or the one they would start counseling people over because we didn't follow it. We would watch twenty people do the same thing and then the twenty-first person would do it and we would be questioned on why we let it happen. We just figured all of those rules would eventually slip away.

By the time they told me to take down the piece of wood that was my only barrier for privacy, I'd had enough. We had to rearrange the beds a certain way because of it, which created another new stipulation. We were told no females in the male tents and vice-versa before it was allowed again with time restrictions. There were ten women in our platoon and they were trying to segregate us from our fellow male soldiers with whom we had formed a real sense of camaraderie. The Army's key phrase was "Train like you fight," so if we all slept by each other on the road we couldn't fathom why it was a big deal to stay with our teams in our camp. I was in charge of people and I was being told I couldn't do my job because I wasn't allowed to walk in a tent and check on them.

That was when I quit. I told them if I was going to be treated differently for being a woman, then I didn't want to do it anymore. Since access to my guys was limited, I didn't feel like I could do my job effectively, so I told them to get one of the guys to do it. By identifying me as a female instead of a soldier, I was pushed out of the loop once again. I was promised it would change and it would all work out, but it never happened because at some point, the higher ups decided females and males could not live together. It made me so angry because I wanted to be with my guys and work with them like we did on the road. It seemed so stupid to us because six out of seven days of the week, we were living together on the road. But then one or two days, we were segregated in a camp. Then they put restrictions on the hours we were allowed in tents of the opposite sex. We women were stuck in a tent by ourselves. They expected us to stay away from the people with whom we had strong connections and bonds. That was one of those rules that lasted about a week and I ended up not quitting. All of the rules they created along with way eventually did fade away.

Out on the road we knew we had only one rule and it was to take care of ourselves. It didn't matter if the lowest private came up with an idea; we did whatever made the most sense. As leaders in the platoon, our egos were in check enough to listen to all ideas and then make a decision based on common sense. It wasn't very hierarchical at all. We all shared the work and responsibility of certain jobs. The staff sergeants ran the convoy and acted as convoy commanders, but we trained all of the sergeants—the soldiers a rank just below us—who we supervised to run the convoys once we got into a routine and felt comfortable letting them take the reigns. Funny enough, everything ran smoothly and we never had any problem with our one rule, which was the only one that meant anything to us.

We just got back to camp a few days ago and I must say the air-conditioned tents are nice.

It is getting really hot outside and they say the worst isn't even here yet. I think we are all going to melt before the summer is over!

One of the places we have to deliver to does not have any type of shade or tent for us to use while we wait for our trucks to get unloaded, and we are miserable. Sometimes we sit in 120- to 140-degree weather and wait for eight to ten hours to download and it gets unbearable.

Some ways we've found to deal with the wait is to sit or sleep under the trucks. Even if we are just sitting, the sweat pours from our bodies and drenches our clothes. It looks like we took water and dumped it on each other, but that isn't the case.

The drenched clothes aren't even the worst part. You should smell us!

Most places have some type of shower facility for us to use now. That is the one thing that we all look forward to at the end of a long day.

Some of the shower facilities are pretty rustic. One place has an outdoor shower and it looks like the shower from the TV show "M*A*S*H." There are two sheets of plywood made into a "T" and four pipes coming out from above, and a basin of water on top of this structure, which creates four showers.

It was a little strange at first showering outside in this thing, but once the heat hit I was looking forward to the "M*A*S*H" showers more and more.

There was some excitement on our last mission. One of our trucks got hit with a roadside bomb but it did not do too much damage. When it hit, it all seemed routine to us and nobody overreacted.

Maintenance did a great job of recovering the vehicle so we could continue with the mission.

There was a hole in the fuel tank and to stop the leak maintenance found an "interesting" way to plug it: a tampon and a stick.

When our convoy got off the road and to a parking area, I saw the hit truck. I also saw a tampon and busted out laughing.

Oh, well, it worked.

We've had a few days off to relax and it has been so nice. Some people took an R&R trip to the pool, others stayed back to write letters and watch movies. Some just caught up on sleep.

I, of course, had to have maintenance fix a few things on my truck.

Maintenance said I'm not allowed to give my truck to anyone else because it is almost "Zaremba-proof."

Jeez, you have a few maintenance issues and you get a reputation.

Having a few days off really gave us a chance to refocus and re-energize. It helps us get mentally ready for another mission and keeps us from burning out.

Nancy and I were getting ready for bed the other night and a mouse ran across our floor. Now we've both been shot at, mortared, etc., and you've never seen two people jump and scream as fast as we did.

I think we both were more scared of the mouse than anything else we've been through over here. I could not sleep that night because I kept thinking that mouse was going to climb in bed with me.

120

I thought the females were bad with bugs. Well, some of the males are twice as bad. If they see a bug, they'll scream, run out of the tent, and the brave one goes back in and stomps on it.

The bugs are much bigger here than in Ohio. – MZ, July 15, 2004

My friend, Dawn, had been working as the commander's driver while we were deployed. Dawn was twenty-four years old, married and had one child. Everyone said she looked like Drew Barrymore and she had the personality to match it. She was always positive and could talk to anyone. When she wasn't driving the commander around, she was stuck working in the administration section office. The job became a little more permanent when the admin guy got shot the first time he went on the road during all the Easter attacks and she was forced to do his job until he returned. But she was a truck driver and begged repeatedly to go on the road to get out of camp. Finally, she was able to go on the road with our platoon. As we were heading through the most dangerous part of our trip, Dawn's truck was hit with a grenade or something. I remember someone calling into the radio that they had seen a flash and the truck in front was hit. Dawn was like my daughter because I had mentored her over the years, so when I heard it was her truck my stomach dropped. As soon as we made sure everyone was moving we found a safe place to stop and assess the damage. We called the sheriff station on the radio and they had two tanks protecting us while we were stopped.

As we assessed the damage on Dawn's vehicle, someone noticed a hole in the fuel tank. The maintenance guy was thinking out loud wondering what he had to plug the leak when Dawn heard him and jumped into the truck to grab a tampon. Everyone agreed and the leak was temporarily repaired with a tampon and a stick. That night it took forever to get to our destination. There was activity farther up the route and the convoy had to detour into another camp for the night. We had been awake almost twenty-four hours so it was time to stop. I had to give one guy an IV because he was dehydrated from the heat. Dawn and her co-driver had to get assessed from the medics because both of their ears were ringing from the blast and they needed to make sure there wasn't any permanent hearing loss.

Schrack used his Humvee to haul the soldiers to the medical tent. He had two coolers sitting on either side of a piece of wood, which was used for a bench/cooler. A lieutenant jumped into the Humvee not knowing it was a loose piece of wood and it catapulted him inside. It was one of the best moments because he was acting like such an idiot. They had to take him to be looked at too, but I didn't feel sorry for him. I had to walk away because I was laughing. If the lieutenant had listened to us, which he never did, it would have never happened.

We ended up getting to bed around 2:00 a.m. and had to be up around six or seven to get back on the road. We finally made it to our destination, but now we wouldn't get our day off in Kuwait because the convoy was delayed. We tried to keep on schedule but the attack threw us off. To boot, the lieutenant that was running the mission had never been on the road with us and didn't know our system. He wouldn't listen to any suggestions, so the mission didn't exactly run very smoothly. After that mission, he was not allowed to be in charge again while we were on the road.

We were in Anaconda, the camp we nicknamed "Motarville." It was the absolute dead of summer but we had to wear our full battle rattle because the camp got mortared at least once a day if not more. There was water on our truck that had to be unloaded and it took a long time because we needed the forklifts and the forklift operators were busy, so we sat next to our trucks melting in the heat. Talk about angry, bitchy people. There was a big parking lot where everyone parked their trucks. The lot was full of us and our commercial drivers. There was no protection from the elements and there were just herds of us hanging out in the 140-degree heat. We were dirty and miserable with no way to feel comfortable or think about cooling off. All the truck drivers wanted was an air-conditioned tent to cool off in. There were none at this point in the deployment. By the end of the deployment there were tents set up for the truck drivers. But in the meantime, we baked in the afternoon sun.

I wanted to tell anyone who would listen how awful it was and that we weren't being taken care of, but who would listen? One soldier had sun blisters all over his mouth and the sun had bleach his eyebrows bright white. Most of us were losing a ton of weight because we didn't want to eat and we were just sweating out the water we were drinking. Our uniforms were covered with salt rings from the constant sweating. Willy and I wondered if it was healthy to lose that much salt and tried to put extra salt on our food, but we didn't think it really mattered. On some days the vicious heat paralyzed us by mid-afternoon and we couldn't do anything but pile into the few trucks we had with air conditioning.

One of the things the Army started rationing was a case of Gatorade per trip. They sold them at the PX for five bucks a bottle, so getting free Gatorade was a bonus. Sugar was the only thing I really enjoyed eating anymore. People sent hard candy, like Sprees and sour candies, and I loved it. Someone sent me a care package with gummy bears. We were broken down on the side of the road one day and I decided to share my gummy bears with everyone to lighten the mood. I was the hero for the day when I announced I had them. When I opened the extra-large package, it was one big gummy bear because they had melted together in the heat. Half laughing and half pissed, I heaved the bag into the desert. It was the one thing we wanted to eat and it had melted. There was no chocolate in-country at this point because it didn't keep. It would just melt. I don't know how people live in those conditions, but I remember saying I would be a suicide bomber if I had to live in that heat.

Just before we were due to return to Camp Navistar, we found out the Second Platoon, which had been stationed at a different camp in Iraq, was moving back with us and all hell broke loose. We were on the road and helpless to have a say in what was about to happen with the living arrangements at the base. The Second Platoon was moving back to Navistar because their mission was cancelled and so they were at the camp within twenty-four hours of being notified of the cancellation. Our unit had to scramble to provide tents for them in that short time. Each of our platoons originally had four tents and now we would only have three per platoon.

Elaine had returned to Navistar a day before our convoy came in and she grabbed a radio to call me as we pulled into the gate. She cautioned that the move wasn't pretty and that I'd be pretty pissed about it all so start bracing myself before I walked to the tents. Elaine was trying to give everyone in the convoy as much detail as possible since nobody in charge would give us any information. Suddenly a voice came on the radio commanding us not to talk about the move. We had to wait to see it for ourselves.

We wondered what they did with all of our stuff. We knew the soldiers at our camp had to move it all without us being there and our first sergeant had to make a call about how the tents were going to be set up without any input from us, and we knew we weren't going to like it.

My blood was boiling and I kept taking deep breaths as I walked back to the tents. I braced myself for the worst before I realized I had no idea where I lived. Finally, someone who had helped with the move directed me to my new home. All the other females sat and watched my reaction. I think they thought I was going to flip out when I saw it. Thank God Elaine prepared me for the worst because when I saw my new home, it wasn't so bad. It was cramped, but the females had taken the time to make the beds for everyone on the road, which made the transition a little bit smoother. Almost everyone who could go on the road was on the road, so there weren't many people available to move stuff. But they did a fairly decent job and took care of us the best they could. I am so glad to not have been a part of that mess. The horror stories from the people that did the moving were enough to thank my lucky stars I missed it.

It was a messy situation because people's personal belongings were being moved and there were only eight hours to get it done. Many people lost things in the move like clothes, pictures and supplies, which wasn't that big of a deal. Others lost irreplaceable belongings. SGT Boron had hundreds of dollars in cigars that were sent from back home. He had a cooler that he made into a humidor and no one knew what it was so they destroyed it during the move. His son's first written words, "I love you, Daddy," also were thrown out. When he voiced his concern about the missing words and the ruined cigars, nobody seemed to care.

They ended up moving all of the females back together, which was hell. We had females from our platoon and headquarters, which wasn't that bad because we all got along well enough, but we went from eight in a tent to fifteen from all different platoons overnight. The dynamics of our relationships with our guys changed because we had to be segregated again. We felt more like visitors in each others' tents than family. And once again, I had to start knocking to enter a tent that used to be mine.

We were cramped in there. My new tent was older and smaller than the other one and it was filled with bugs. Not only did we have a small amount of time to prepare for the next mission, now we had to unpack again and find everything before the next mission. I would guess Nancy and I shared about six feet of space.

Someone commented prisoners had more space than we did. Those living conditions lasted for months. Tension was high, our space was cut and we were living on top of each other. They were prime conditions for serious conflict. Our attitudes worsened with each passing day. The females felt so neglected and alone. We weren't even with our guys anymore. Luckily the females in my platoon and headquarters got along enough to bear it, but other groups of females were having issues and did not get along very well. I became the housemother again in our tent and I was tired of it. If anything went wrong, they'd come find me. We were at war and struggling to win our own personal battles.

We were now sharing our old, shitty tent with the bugs, scorpions and mice that started coming into our tents to keep cool. We were getting our shit ready for a mission when a mouse ran across the floor one day and Nancy and I screamed like we had been shot. Not only did we get a crappy tent, now we had to deal with rodents. One of the guys put down sticky traps and we didn't think much of it until we returned a few missions later and I couldn't figure out where the god-awful smell was coming from in our tent. There it was, that mouse, dead and decaying behind my desk. I had no idea how long it had been there, but it had to be a least a week judging by the smell. I could wrap up an injured person and wipe blood off them, but I was not touching that mouse. I was such a girl when it came to that. One of the guys had to come in and throw it out for me. After that, there were no more mice in the tent.

Even though the mouse incident disgusted me, it was better than what happened to another one of our soldiers. He was sleeping one night when he was awakened by a scorpion crawling through his area. He captured it with a pair of pliers and a water bottle. Our camp had a "bug" contractor, so if there were any issues with bugs, snakes or mice, we would go to him. Schrack took the scorpion to the bug guy only to find out scorpions travel in pairs. Needless to say, the other scorpion surfaced about a week later in the same area. I teased him by telling him if he kept his area clean, he wouldn't have bugs and stuff. It irked him that I said that because he was such a neat freak.

The living conditions got progressively worse. They took away all of our freedoms and we felt like prisoners. It wasn't like home anymore. They just kept taking everything away from us and we didn't want anything from them but to get out of there. We were bitter. Their ridiculous decisions took away any chance of feeling comfortable and our attitudes steadily decayed.

There was even more pressure for me as the convoy commander. The worst was assigning people to vehicles and positions in the convoy. I always thought to myself, is this the mission when a roadside bomb will go off and hit someone in the convoy? What if the person dies because of where I placed them? I absolutely hated that part of the job. The other part I hated was choosing the time we left camp. I would think, is this the time where we'll get attacked or should we have left earlier or later?

We had all developed little superstitions that we felt were helping us through the whole ordeal and never wavered from them. One guy peed on the front tire of his truck before every mission. I would grab my partner's hand and squeeze it every time we rolled out. We always packed our trucks the same way. We ran through our maintenance checks the same way every time. I had a Saint Michael's necklace that my Marine boyfriend's grandmother had given to him and he gave to me. I never took it off while I was there and I would always touch it on our way out of camp. I felt safer having that with me. I wore the same boots and cap and had my wallet on me the whole time, keeping everything in the same spot. I had a Medevac form in my pocket and another in the truck in case anyone had to call for medical assistance. I kept the cab clear in case I needed to jump out.

We tried to keep everything as consistent as possible so we wouldn't forget anything, but it was more for peace of mind. One of my friends made me a bracelet out of 550 cord in the beginning of the deployment and I never took it off until we left country. It smelled so bad by the time I got home that it made me want to vomit, but I wasn't about to chance taking it off until we were safely home.

– 8 –

August

Killed in Action: 982
Wounded in Action: 7,076

Describe a "typical" day at camp

There is never a typical day at camp. We get off our mission and have to do maintenance on our trucks and then usually some stuff for the company. If we are lucky, we get a day off the next day. A day off usually means we are still doing some work for someone, but we are not on the road. We (senior noncommissioned officers) fight tooth and nail to get time off where the company isn't bothering us. We are getting better at getting days off for our troops. Most of the time, we are back on the road after our maintenance day so there isn't much down time.

There are tons of things that we have to do when we get back to camp. We turn in laundry, repack for the next trip, use the Internet and phones, and get mail. Most of us have a routine for getting our personal stuff done while are back at camp.

Describe the "off time" when you all sit on your beds and watch movies

When it is unbearably hot, we watch a bunch of movies and TV shows. We all share movies because you get really sick of seeing the same things over and over again. Many people have TV show series. They are nice because they are short and you can watch as many as you have time for. We like "M*A*S*H," "Sex and the City," "Friends," "Will and Grace," "The Simpsons," "The Sopranos" and "Oz."

Describe a typical day on the road

A typical day on the road is driving for 10 hours, nonstop. We will take little breaks where we can pee and check our load. We generally drive three hours before we stop unless there is a maintenance issue. Don't tell on me but I'll hop out of the truck *while it's moving to get more water and pee. The convoy can't stop just because some-one has to go to the bathroom. Most of the boys pee in bottles; girls climb out on the catwalk and go.*

Is there anything you miss about camp while you're out?

The only thing we miss is the air-conditioning, the mail and chow.

Describe the writing on the street signs. Are you getting used to it?

Street signs are in Arabic and English. The military writes important stuff in spray paint if we need to know it. I am used to it and I barely notice it anymore. I can recognize some of the signs, but not all.

How hard is it to figure out where you're going? Do you ever get lost?

It isn't too difficult to know where we're going because we do the same routes every time. We rarely get lost, if ever. It is too dangerous to not have someone with you who knows 100 percent where he or she is going. We don't want to end up in some bad neighborhood and not know where we are.

What happens when a truck breaks down?

We take extra vehicles so if trucks break down we can tow them. We also have maintenances support and they can fix anything.

What does it smell like?

Iraq and Kuwait smell different. In Iraq, there are oil towers that burn constantly and there is a distinct smell in that area. It smells like something that is indescribable and I've never experienced a scent quite like it, except that it smells like what burning oil would smell like. It isn't a bad or good smell, it just is. I can tell where we are in the journey based on the smells. The burning oil means we are close to home.

Most of the trip doesn't smell like anything out of the ordinary. It is a very clean and dry smell. The farther north I go, the moister the air is, and breathing is not as dry.

I never thought I could smell humidity until now. I can smell the vegetation, the palm trees and the grass. It makes breathing easier and smoother and gives me a calming feeling. That is my favorite time during our journey.

There are a few dumpsites along the route and those places smell horrible. People bring their trash to a central location and someone burns the trash. There are acres and acres of trash. If you can believe it, people actually live near the dumpsites and cows graze in the trash water. The people and animals look sickly.

128

What do you see?

Sand, lots and lots of sand. Sometimes I can't see because sand is in my eyes. The worst is when I sweat (because it's 130 degrees) and a sandstorm comes. The sand sticks to my body, face and hair.

I'll take a shower and for the first minute, the water is all sand running off my body. My hair holds so much sand, too, along with the corner of my eyes. The sand also changes all our white socks into a beautiful, dull, nasty brown.

What do you think of the sand?

I think I answered that already.

How does the air feel?

The air feels really hot. There are days when the wind blows and it is painfully hot. There is no relief. We aren't very dry because we are sweating all the time but it is dry to breathe, probably because of the sand. It is usually 130 degrees during the day and around 112 degrees during the night. Yes, 112 is the "cool" part of the day.

I have water in my truck in bottles and it gets so hot I can't drink it. Some people cook ramen noodles with the water from their cab for lunch. There is no need for a microwave or stove. The ice melts faster than I can get it.

The sun hurts at times and is very draining. We cope.

What about those bugs?

Most of the bugs that are annoying to us right now are the sand fleas, mosquitoes and crickets. Each mission, I get eaten alive by the sand fleas and mosquitoes. I sleep with a mosquito net and use 100 percent DEET on my gear and use bug spray and nothing helps.

I have seen baby camel spiders. There were two in our tent. We learned they travel in pairs. They look awful and I screamed like a girl and jumped up on something when I saw them. The maintenance guys caught a camel spider and kept it as a pet. It is in an aquarium and sits in maintenance. I can't believe I live somewhere where there are critters that look like that.

What do you eat? Do you eat in the mess hall a lot? How does the food taste?

I generally eat at the mess hall if I am at camp. The mess hall is good. It isn't as good as it used to be because they feed us the same food day in and day out.

I eat the exact same thing for breakfast every morning. It's scrambled eggs with bacon. I hate scrambled eggs with bacon. There are many choices, but I know that eggs and bacon will get me through the day till lunch or dinner, whatever meal I can make.

129

I am afraid to change the breakfast routine and get stuck somewhere and my sugar drops.

Occasionally I'll eat Subway if I'm back at camp. Subway is a nice change and is open 24/7.

If we are out on the road, I'll eat any meal I can and it is always at chow halls. We generally try to make at least one meal in a chow hall while we are out each day. Usually we get two chow hall meals and eat MREs or snacks for the third.

Do you go to fast-food places a lot? Is McDonald's the same over there or different? Do you think of "Pulp Fiction" if you really order a royale with cheese?

There are no drive-throughs in Iraq. I don't trust any food or drinks from the locals. I don't want to get sick.

If we are in Kuwait, there is one McDonald's I've been to. It is nice and it looks like the McDonald's back home. It is super-expensive!

I lied: I've been to two McDonald's. Schrack and I took a wrong turn and ended up in downtown Kuwait. It was around dinner and I was getting very hungry. We saw a McDonald's drive-through and took the Humvee through it. We got many weird looks, but it was awesome getting Mickey D's!

Yes, I always think of "Pulp Fiction" when I see the royale with cheese! I ordered it just to say I ordered it. Ha!

Is there any one meal that you love to eat back in the States that you really miss?

I love Mexican food and there isn't really any around. I also miss Champ's chicken marsala. I miss red wine and eating when I want to. I miss being able to eat. It is so hot here that nobody is in the mood to eat. It is just something you have to do.

I miss Marie's home cookin' (hint, hint, hint). Marie makes the best meatball stroganoff and her sister would love that so very much when she comes home. – MZ, August 8, 2004

T hat was one of the toughest letters to write. Our fuses were short and the tension was unbearable. I had to keep writing, but I didn't have it in me anymore. I knew it helped my mom to hear how I was doing, so I kept writing, but I really didn't have anything to say. I really just wanted to spill my guts, but I knew it would sound like a whole lot of bitching so I just started answering questions people had asked in letters. I had a lot of students writing to me and asking questions, too. I thought if I gave them a piece of Iraq it would make it more interesting when they learned about it in school. I had three different schools writing and I answered every one of their questions. I tried to put the responses in words that kids could understand and it turned out adults understood it better that way as well. Most didn't even realize that there were people whose sole job it was to protect soldiers inside camps, so it was refreshing to offer a little bit of education to everyone at home.

My sister, Marie, came up with a list of questions and told me to answer them. I was due to send another email to the paper anyway, so I told Marie to forward my answers to my mom so she could clean up the language and delete some of the answers that were only for Marie before she sent it to the paper. Of course she "forgot." When my mom told me Marie sent the letter and it was printed as is, I was mortified. I was very honest in it and never thought anyone would see it but my mom and Marie. I talked about peeing off the back of trucks and other candid moments that I didn't really want to broadcast. Whoever read it got to see the real me in Iraq.

After six months the monotony was starting to gnaw away at me. The newness of the deployment had worn off. The only excitement I had was taking new people to watch their reactions to the things that I had become somewhat complacent about. There were no more new sights, no more of Saddam's palaces to explore and no more culture shock. Now it was just a job. We had our routine and nothing changed. We were like robots wandering through a maze with no end.

The bugs were making us even more miserable. Our elbows and necks suffered the majority of the abuse because they were exposed the most, but anywhere was a target for the sand fleas and mosquitoes. They were relentless. The Calamine lotion wasn't working anymore, so my mom started sending prescription spray bottles of anti-itch lotions just so I wouldn't have to touch my skin. I'm so glad I'll never have to deal with that again. I can't believe I was able to stay sane. Just when I healed, I'd go on another mission and get eaten again. We were always freaked out when we heard stories about people being bitten by spiders and scorpions, but it was a whole different emotional experience when we actually came face to face with them. It felt like a hundred of them were running up and down my body whenever I watched one of them scoot away. Other than sand fleas and mosquitoes, no one got bit by anything life threatening. We were sleeping on the highest point we could get to by then because the bugs kept us up all night if we stayed on the ground.

One of the guys told us that he heard a story of someone sleeping on top of a connex and forgot he was up there. He got up to go to the restroom and fell fifteen feet and his teeth landed on a concrete barrier. That thought stayed

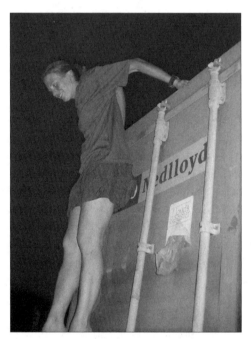
Michelle carefully climbs down off a connex

with me every night I slept on top of a connex. It was like a mental note—remember you are really high off the ground and don't want to fall off.

Meals even became a routine. Breakfast was scrambled eggs, bacon and orange juice. I didn't drink coffee when we were on the road because I was afraid of becoming addicted to it and getting tired without it. I hate scrambled eggs now. I can't even eat an omelet. I don't care much for breakfast at all anymore. The food schedule was different from Kuwait to Iraq, so if we had macaroni and cheese, it seemed like we followed it all the way through one trip. On the first of each month we were given steak and lobster. I can't eat shellfish, but the steak wasn't bad at the beginning. By the end, I didn't even want it anymore. It tasted the same as everything else that was served. In the summer, we ate a lot of vegetables and fruit. We had a Subway and a Pizza Inn at camp and we always made sure to stop at camps with a Burger King just to change it up a little. But even that got old. Elaine commented after a week of eating with me that I had stopped eating. I would take a few bites, push it around my plate and then devour my cookie.

Elaine transferred into my platoon right around her birthday and we went on a mission together for her actual birthday. I was the convoy commander and the plan was to get to our drop-off point as quickly as possible so she could enjoy her birthday at a camp. Unfortunately, there was a change in plans because there was enemy activity on the road we were traveling and our convoy kept getting delayed. There was a firefight between the Marines and some insurgents and we would have been in the middle of it because they were shooting across the road at each other.

While we were sitting on the road waiting for the Marines to finish their firefight, I got a call from Elaine on the radio.

"Z…chomp, chomp, chomp."

"Yes, Elaine."

"I just wanted to thank you for the midnight snack…chomp, chomp, chomp."

"What are you talking about?" I asked, but I already knew that that little bitch was eating my chips and salsa.

"The chips and salsa are really hitting the spot!" she said laughing into the phone.

The PX at each camp had something unique that they sell. It might be a particular food, DVD or sweatshirt that only that particular PX had. Scania, the camp we left before our twenty-hour adventure, had the best chips and cheesy salsa in the country. Every time we stopped there, I would get a bag of chips and salsa and eat them throughout the mission. For some reason I didn't have ice in my cooler and I asked Elaine if she'd put the open salsa and chips in her cooler so it would be edible the next day.

I vowed that if we didn't get killed that night I was going to kill her myself. I knew it would be a while before I could get another bag of chips and they had been on my mind since I put them in her cooler. I was about to explode when a thought came to my head. The first or second mission to Iraq, Willy's co-driver and I were talking in the truck when I got hungry. I asked if their truck had any snacks in it and his co-driver gave me their last pudding snack pack. I ate it and didn't think anything about it. The snack packs were sent from home and there wasn't anywhere in-country to get more. Willy was so angry with me and wouldn't let it go until he got more snack packs in the mail. He still bitches to me about it to this day. At that moment, I totally understood Willy's frustration. When resources are scarce and it's something you really enjoy, you hold onto it and become possessive. Karma got me back!

So our trip that normally only took about four hours took more like nine, so there was no time to rest. We had to deliver the load and be on our way. We were awake for about twenty hours that day and were all exhausted. Poor Elaine got a few birthday wishes, but that was it. Our routine mission turned into a mess and her birthday was ruined. I bought her an outfit from one of the camps and a shirt online from Old Navy, but it sure wasn't like the birthday celebration we would have been having for her at home. Nothing was really worth celebrating and our birthdays over there only reminded us of exactly how long we had been there. It was just another indication that our lives were marching along without us.

When I got back from that mission and called my mom, she broke the news to me about my Uncle Lou.

"Shell, I gotta tell you something," she said.

"OK, what's up?"

I knew before I left that my Uncle Lou, my godfather, had been diagnosed with leukemia. He had his ups and downs the whole time I was gone and he was in and out of the hospital, but this time he was really bad, my mom said.

"Michelle, he's not gonna make it," she said bluntly.

I just lost it. I was so numb the whole time I was over there, but when I heard that I felt nothing but pain. I told her I couldn't deal with it and hung up the phone.

I had just left Schrack's area so he could go through his mail, but I went right back over there and just started bawling. All I could say was Uncle Lou and he knew what was up. He had just found out that his stepfather was undergoing a quadruple bypass surgery so we instantly became support for each other. Schrack had gotten his news on the previous mission.

I pulled myself together enough to call my uncle, who was staying at my Aunt Sandy's house.

I cried so much I wasn't even making any sounds. My body was shaking so hard. I pulled it together long enough to answer a question or ask one and that was it. I was standing in a little phone booth with no privacy and everyone was looking at me wondering what was going on, but I didn't care. I just wanted to talk to my uncle.

I didn't want him to know I was upset so I kept holding it in long enough to speak. This man was about ready to die and he was in so much pain. He only wanted the minimum amount of morphine because he wanted to be coherent enough to communicate with us. He told me that when he died he was going to watch over me in Iraq and he got really excited because he said that he could protect me then. There he was, facing his last days on earth, and he was worried about protecting me. I wanted to hug him and see his face. I wanted to go home.

I told my first sergeant I had to get home before my uncle died. My leave was scheduled for October, but I told him I couldn't wait that long and he scrambled to get me out of there. I wanted to see him one more time. My parents told me not to tell him I was coming home because he was in so much pain and they didn't want him to hold on. I didn't make it in time.

Lou was the first of my parents' siblings to pass away. He and I didn't talk much, but he was always there. We saw each other on holidays and special occasions and always got along, but we didn't talk much on the phone. But he was family. Being gone when he passed away and not attending the funeral, I still can't comprehend that he died. When I was home on leave, there wasn't a gravestone yet, so there was no indication to me that he passed away. Sometimes I have to remind myself that he died and I think it's because I didn't get to grieve with everyone else.

Chad, Elaine and Willy were there for me at that time. I would go out on the road and think I was focusing, but then thoughts of him would slip into my head. At the time, I thought I was doing really well, but I wasn't. I was lucky to have their support.

When I got back from a mission, I went to make my routine phone call to my mom at school. Peggy, the other secretary, answered the phone and she told me my mom was at home. I called my mom at home and she said Lou had a bad day. I asked if he was alright and she said yes. She didn't want to tell me that he had died because they were worried for my safety. They waited a day or two to tell me, but I already knew. My first sergeant told me that he passed away and I cried briefly before calling my parents. I was still numb inside, but now I was pissed.

"How dare you not tell me that he passed away!" I shrieked. "Now I can't even buy flowers because the service is over."

They asked for forgiveness, but I was hurt and angry and I wanted to take it out on them. I had to go home on leave the following week. The family was returning to their normal lives at home and now I was on my way, but I needed to go on leave. I was spent.

We lived vicariously through the first to go on leave until it was our turn. We wanted to know everything about it: what beer tasted like, what they ate, what they did, what was going on with their family life. Every two weeks, we had a new person to ask.

I wanted to look my best when I got home because I knew I would have to see a lot of people, so I was careful to use things like lotion and sunscreen every day. I tried to keep my face as clean as possible and went for a haircut at one of the camps, but the last mission before leave just kicked my ass. I tried to strap something down and got a huge bruise on my foot. JD moved something in the truck that hit my arm and there was a big bruise. I was getting our cots down off the top of the truck and I stepped down into the dip on the catwalk, dropped the cots and fell onto my back. I caught myself between the fuel tanks with my hips. Of course, everyone heard the cots fall and rushed to see what happened and I was lying there. After they realized I was fine, everyone just busted out laughing. So, I had a bruise on my arm, two huge bruises on my hips and a bruise on my foot. Even though I was trying to be extra careful, I wound up with more bruises from one trip than I did during the first six months!

Insurgents had blown up a bridge very far south and very close to Kuwait. I was afraid of getting killed before leave, but I wanted to go on the road to get away from my thoughts. We were taking alternate routes that we'd never gone on before and it turned out to be pretty uneventful.

Privacy was a rare commodity when on the road. Here, Michelle is caught in the act of buttoning up after using the "outdoor facilities"

- 9 -

September

Killed in Action: 1,062

Wounded in Action: 7,782

I am sitting in Atlanta waiting to go back to Iraq. I had such a wonderful time on leave and I'm amazed how fast the two weeks went by. I got to see all my family and friends, eat everything I wanted and just relax before returning to Iraq.

Thank you for all your support. It meant so much to me that I was welcomed back to Medina County and Dayton with open arms. I got to meet and see so many people while I was home and I always felt welcome. I expected to be greeted when I got home, but I never in my wildest dreams thought I would meet and see so many appreciative people. It felt so good to have the support.

I have warm feelings from our community and great memories of the last two weeks to take back and keep me going for the duration of my tour.

It is difficult to think about going back to do my job. I feel refreshed and ready to go, but like any vacation, going back to work is always difficult. I think the worst part of this journey is the many, many hours of waiting in the airports and the 17-hour flight to Kuwait.

I went to the airport in Cleveland at 9 a.m. and my flight will not leave to go to Kuwait until 11 p.m. All I've done is sit around in lines waiting to process to get on the overseas flight. Anytime I fall asleep, someone wakes me up because we have to move to a different line. It is getting very frustrating. Thank goodness I brought my computer and CD player to bide the time.

There are soldiers just like me waiting around for the flight. Some are sleeping, others are talking to friends they haven't seen for two weeks or doing last minute shopping.

137

The one thing we all have in common is that we dread getting back on that crammed plane for the flight.

Even though I am not looking forward to jumping back into the job, I have to admit that I miss all my friends who are still in Iraq. We've spent the past 10 months with each other every day.

During the first few days of leave, I found myself missing the chaos of living on top of 14 other people. I got over that pretty quickly and enjoyed the peace and quiet. But I do miss talking with everyone and just hanging out together.

The one thing that happened on leave that I wasn't expecting was experiencing the war from back home. It is so much easier to be overseas and barely hear about the violence in Iraq and just do my job. I was so upset watching the news and hearing about the growing activity of insurgents that I had to e-mail some of my fellow soldiers and ask if things have gotten crazier since I left.

Their response was that nothing out of the ordinary was happening. I realized right then that hearing about the war on the news sounds much different than living it. I got to see and experience what my family and friends have been going through since I've been activated. It is horrible to sit and watch hopelessly as the war moves on. I have a new understanding of why my parents worry and want me to contact them as much as possible.

I also experienced losing fellow soldier Devin Grella while I was home on leave and seeing how a community grieves the loss of a young man. The war becomes so much more human when you see faces instead of statistics in a newspaper.

I can't even comprehend yet how seeing the pain in the eyes of family and friends affected me. That experience is one that never even crossed my mind as I prepared for leave.

Life is so precious and so much can change in the blink of an eye.

They are calling us to board the plane. Again, thank you for the wonderful trip home. It was so worthwhile and I am so glad I got to see everyone. I now have great memories of my leave to carry me through until the end of my deployment. I promise I will write more soon. – MZ, September 23, 2004

I started my leave process; it was the biggest pain in the ass because there were so many steps to take just to get on the plane, and all I wanted was to go home. I had to go to Camp Doha to be briefed on how to go home on leave. We're talking hours of briefings and then customs. We were crammed into a storage house blocked by chain link fences to keep the men and women separated, as well as separating those going on leave from those leaving for good. Two planes full of people flew out every day. The military had a contract to ship us to Atlanta or Texas and then home from there.

The whole leave area was filthy. There was constant traffic and it reeked because there was no air in the storage house. There were no lights and it had to be quiet because soldiers were leaving at all different times and no sheets on the bunks because no one wanted to haul them home on leave. People from my unit warned me not to take anything but a carry-on so I wouldn't get stuck waiting for bags. I had a sheet to sleep on and I slept in my clothes. I didn't shower because the showers were flooded.

I was there twenty-four hours before they transported us from Doha to the airport with a gun truck escort. They ordered all of us to move quickly on and off the bus because they didn't want us to get killed at the airport. When I hit the top step, I ran onto the plane and started my journey home.

We stopped in Germany for another briefing with a chaplin who was there in case anyone felt like they were stressed and needed to talk.

In Atlanta, people at the airport were thanking me and I was nodding and smiling and trying to be polite, but I was rushing to try to catch an earlier flight. When I got to the counter of the airline heading to Cleveland, I begged them to help me get on an earlier flight because time was ticking. I met a soldier whose family was from my hometown of Valley City and we hung out together in Doha, but unfortunately, we got split up when he was held back getting his bags inspected and I made the early flight to Cleveland. I reserved him a spot on the earlier flight, but he never made it. He was stuck on the original flight.

I called my parents to tell them I was almost home. I used my phone card to call my dad and I just started sobbing when he said, "My little girl's home." It was really crowded in Atlanta because a storm had just come through and flights were delayed. There were tons of people listening to my phone call and everyone around me was crying as they listened to me talk to my dad.

September 11, 2004

I got off the plane, ran through the gate, through the airport, and hurried past everyone in my way. Suddenly, I could hear my dad's loud, gruff voice echoing through the terminal and I could already hear him bragging about me. I felt a wave of relief rush over me just hearing his voice and I was ecstatic to see him. Outside of my mother, he was my number one supporter and I just wanted to hug my daddy.

I saw a lady standing there listening to him and I figured he probably grabbed the first person he saw to brag and explain his daughter was coming home from Iraq.

"This is my daughter," his voice boomed as he wrapped his arms around me.

We burst into tears and just stood there, holding each other and crying. Some stopped to watch us and I could just feel our spectators welling up with tears. I wanted to get away and be alone with him. We had a lot of catching up to do. When I went to grab my bag, he insisted on carrying it. I was so used to being self-sufficient, but I let my dad take care of his little girl.

True to his duties, my dad brought beer to the airport so of course I had to have one. When I met my mom, I was a little tipsy because it had been so long since I'd had a beer. My mom grabbed me and held me for a long time. The whole time I was home on leave she wouldn't let me go. It was the first time I had seen both of them so relieved and happy. All of their kids were safe and that was a weight off their shoulders, at least for the next two weeks.

It was strange to see everyone doing things for me. Sometimes I think it meant more to them than me. My dad took care of all of my bills and he felt that was his contribution to taking care of me. My mom was always sending me things and asking what I needed more of, but there were times that I really didn't need anything. I would tell her this or that would be nice and she would ship it immediately to make me as comfortable as possible.

At last I was home and they were able to do things for themselves. Leave was more for mom and dad because it was their time to relax. Mom said she finally slept the night I got home. She said she hadn't slept through the night the entire time I was overseas. I decided I was going to do anything they wanted because I felt guilty for putting them through so much. I wanted to do what I could to make them happy.

Then the article that I was home came out in the paper and there was a picture of me getting my Purple Heart. I was so embarrassed because I didn't want anyone to know and now it was in the paper. A two-star general gave it to me and I didn't think I earned it because I didn't lose a limb. The people who ruined their bodies for the war were the people I thought really deserved them. Someone had sent my parents the photo and of course, they sent it to everyone they knew.

When I came home, they had a party for me at my hometown church, St. Martins, and the priest invited me up on the altar and prayed over me. Father Dumphy let me thank everyone for taking care of my parents and supporting me and praying for me. After mass, everyone came up to me and told me how pretty and petite I was for a soldier. They were in disbelief. I couldn't understand it. I was getting backhanded compliments that sounded like, "Wow, your picture looks like shit in the paper, but you're actually pretty," or "I knew you in school and I didn't know you could write like that. Who knew you were smart enough to write like that?" I took it all in stride.

One of the first things I did at home was go to the mall and buy shoes, a couple of outfits and things for my hair. I was so excited to do girly things. Everyone treated me like a princess for two weeks. I was constantly on the go and had so many people to thank while I was home. It was so nice to see the relief on my parents' faces and see my whole family together.

One of my first nights at home, a group of us went to a bar down the street from my parents' house and there was karaoke that night. My brother, Mark, wanted free drinks so he started telling everyone I was home on leave from Iraq. Everyone kept walking up to my friend, who was tall and tan, and trying to thank her and she kept telling them, "No this is the girl." They couldn't believe the pale, short girl was the one in the Army. Mark made me do a shot and I ended up puking later that night.

Adjusting to home was a difficult task because so many things were different. There was an eight-hour difference between Iraq and the United States, which made it hard to adjust to the time. I wanted to rest, but I never sat still because there was so much I wanted to do and didn't want to waste time sleeping. The air was harder to breathe, too. The humidity felt different and it took my breath away. I was pretty hopped up on medication because I was having a hard time with my allergies, so I couldn't really sleep at home. I was always cold. My parents couldn't understand why I was shivering wearing a sweater when it was seventy degrees!

Driving in a car was strange and something that I really didn't enjoy. Over there we cut everyone off and ruled the road so I had to remind myself to be extremely cautious when I got back to the States. I was nervous about having to obey laws and drive a car that I cared whether or not it got dented.

The one thing about leave that I wasn't expecting was the countdown that buzzed in my head every day until I headed back. It was a race against time that I would surely lose. My parents reminded me of it every day, too. I was happy, but I couldn't breathe easy because I knew I had to go back. Secretly, all I wanted to do was get back to my guys. I didn't want to answer any more questions about the war. I wanted to answer them all, but it was overwhelming. The letters in the paper did help curb that because most had a basic understanding of what I was going through, but ultimately, it created even more questions.

It was bizarre when people quoted me from the paper. They would spot me on the street and stop me to tell me they were reading my articles. We went to a local restaurant and the manager came out after our meal, thanked me and paid the tab. I got free pizza and booze everywhere I went. It was great, but I just wanted to eat what I wanted to eat and be normal.

It was ironic that the very people that I was sick of being around in Iraq were the first people I called when I got home. Elaine and Schrack's leave overlapped some of mine, so every time I called Elaine we talked for hours because we could relate to each other. She had been home a few days earlier and gave me a heads-up on what to expect. The things we talked about the most were the illusions of coming home. Some things were better than I hoped, others were worse. It was a let down in a way because the reality of going back was always looming. For months all I could think about was the fantasy of going on leave and when I was on leave, I couldn't wait to get back to my guys. Most of us were depressed after leave because we missed our families and there was nothing to look forward to but the end. In the beginning, it was all about making it to leave and the closer we got to the end, we knew it was the only thing that was going to make us happy. I was glad I took my leave later on in the deployment because it was that much closer to the end.

I remember listening to the news while I was at home and being frightened because it sounded like things were escalating. When I talked to people in-country, they said things were the same as when I left and the violence wasn't any better or worse. I sent emails to my guys and they wrote back assuring me everything was just as I had left it. I wanted to be in the loop as much as possible. I craved the news, but in the States the war was a second page story or it wasn't even written about. At that point, I realized the news was reporting only the terrible, rotten things going on. They never showed all of the good things we were doing there. I ended up obsessing about getting back through the rest of my leave because I wanted to get back to my military family. I didn't want to leave my family, but I wanted to be with my other family because I felt guilty being safe and home.

The one thing I'm not sure I should have done was go to Devin Grella's funeral. Devin Grella was the first casualty from Medina County and I had met him in Baghdad only a few months before he was killed. Both of us rode in convoys throughout Iraq. He recognized me from my letters in the paper and thanked me for keeping his parents calm. I told him to give me his email address and to let me know if there was anything he wanted me to put in the paper for his parents. It was a brief interaction because his convoy was heading out on the road and we had just arrived at a camp. But when I found out from a friend that he had been killed, I felt a strange sensation that I'll never be able to explain. I met this kid early in deployment who was only eighteen or nineteen years old and now he was dead. He was killed while I was flying home and his body came home while I was on leave. Another column was

142

written about me while at home comparing me to Devin called "Two Local Soldiers Put a Face on War." I felt so guilty being compared to him in that article, knowing I was alive to read it and he wasn't. I knew his friends and family were reading the same article and I cried just thinking about how much pain they had to be feeling.

My mom really wanted to go to the funeral because she felt connected to his mom, a fellow mother whose child was serving overseas. But my mom would never know how it felt to lose a child over there. I told her I would go with her to the funeral, but I wish I hadn't. The hardest thing I ever had to do was look a mother in the eyes who had just lost her son. I felt so guilty because I made it through my attack and her son didn't. He was a teenager, the same age as my youngest brother. They displayed pictures of him with his friends in Iraq on his computer while two soldiers guarded the casket. That's what we do for each other, I thought as I sat there. We protect each other. I felt another pang of guilt as I thought of my guys still over there, wondering what they were doing and who was protecting them at that moment. Then I started picturing my own funeral and it freaked me out. I gave my mom the look and we left. I wanted to pay my respects and get out before someone recognized me from my picture in the paper and started making a big deal out of it.

I vowed to make it through the war because I couldn't bear putting my family through something like that. I convinced myself I was going to make it, but it didn't make it any easier returning to that environment.

The day I had to get back on the plane, I was full of dread. My mom and dad took me to the airport in Cleveland and I had to wear my uniform. Everyone was staring at me with expressions of sadness because they knew where I was headed. My parents were trying to be supportive and didn't want to cry so we kept cracking jokes to fill the time.

We went to the counter of the airline and I was treated like royalty again. My parents got a special pass to accompany me to the gate and sat on either side of me talking until it was time to go. We ran into my friend from Valley City who got held up waiting for his bags on the way home and he started telling me about how his parents were reading my letters. I was so sick of hearing about it. It was time to get back to the war, the place where I was just like everyone else and not special at all.

When we started boarding the plane both of my parents lost it. I just kept hugging them and crying, and everyone around us was crying as they watched us. It was even worse than saying goodbye the first time because we said goodbye a hundred times the first time around. I said goodbye when we left Mansfield. There were women holding their children up to the windows of the bus so they could say goodbye to their fathers one last time. It was agonizing. I said goodbye when we left Camp Atterbury. It was one goodbye after another and I just wanted to get on with it already. This time we had one shot, though. I mustered everything in me to get on the plane without crying.

Just as with every time I had been on a plane since we left, they announced over the speaker that we soldiers were flying with them and everyone had to thank us. We didn't get special attention overseas for being a soldier because everyone was in the same boat. I appreciated the support, but I just wanted to feel normal again.

The flight headed back to Atlanta where I met up with all the other soldiers returning from leave. While waiting, we saw a unit coming home for good. The entire airport started clapping and screaming and thanking them, and I couldn't wait for that to be me. I was so jealous. I realized they had done their time and deserved to come home, but I could imagine my homecoming just watching them.

The plane ride back to Kuwait seemed like it was over in the blink of an eye and my heart sank as we set our boots on the sandy ground once more. Leave was officially over.

– 10 –

October

Killed in Action: 1,125
Wounded in Action: 8,437

Well, I'm back in the swing of things. I've been out on a few missions since I got back from leave, and to be honest, I enjoyed getting back on the road.

Everything was all fresh and new, sort of like when we first started missions. I missed all my friends and fellow soldiers.

Probably the best thing that happened on my first mission back is that Elaine and I sat on the hood of her truck and talked for hours about our leave, our family and camp gossip that we missed out on when we were at home. It was wonderful.

The newness has worn off since I've gotten back from leave and I'm just doing my job like everyone else, counting the days before I can go home.

The weather is cooling down at night and it is almost bearable throughout the day. Over the summer, I just used my sleeping bag for a cushion and my mosquito netting as a blanket. I actually had to wear a long-sleeve shirt to bed and sleep inside my sleeping bag the past few nights on the road.

The morning drive is cooler than usual but about 10 a.m. it starts getting hot again. It is still a huge improvement from the summer when it was unbearably hot all the time.

The bugs also have started coming out now that the weather is better. The flies are everywhere. I think there are a million flies in our camp alone. They are very persistent, too. Swatting them away does nothing. They won't fly away until you actually make contact with them and fling them off of you.

We've hung up fly tape everywhere and it still hasn't stopped them. I hope fly season doesn't last much longer.

When I got back to camp, there was a big pleasant surprise. Our softball diamond was completed. The camp decided to build us a softball field and had people sign up for teams. Our platoon signed up for a team and while Elaine and I were away, we got signed up to play, too. We are the only girls on our platoon's team.

When we are in between missions, our team plays other groups at our camp. The field looks like a field back in the States. There are lights up around the field, bases and a concession stand. The concession stand gives away free nachos, hot dogs and drinks to everyone there. The camp also donated gloves, bats and balls. It is one of the most fun things we have here. I really feel like I'm back in the States when we are playing softball.

The odd thing about playing people from our camp is that everyone knows everyone. During our first game, Elaine and I sat out and cheered our team. The only problem was that we were cheering for our team and the opposing team because they were also from our company. It was fun and everyone had a blast. It is one of the few "getaways" we have from the war and we love it.

Gearheart is our coach. He is one of my soldiers in the platoon and he was a die-hard softball player before we left for Iraq. Since he lives and breathes softball, we have practices, games and more practices. He wants us to love it as much as he does. Gearheart is the happiest I have seen him since we got in-country. The games give us something to look forward to when we get off the road.

There isn't really anything new going on besides softball. We are all working hard and getting excited because we are down to our last four months. I can't believe we have been here for eight months already. As I live it, it seems to drag, but looking back, time has flown.

The time I've spent here has really made me see how close my family is, how wonderful my friends really are and how great my community is to take such excellent care of me while I'm away. I am so fortunate to have so much in my life. Thank you all for that. — MZ, October 11, 2004

F or birthdays, we always found some kind of cake in the chow hall and we would sing and get loud and obnoxious just to embarrass the lucky birthday boy or girl and make them feel special. We even did it on the road. But I wasn't having it for my birthday. I was bitter and angry because I missed my family and wanted to go home and live my life.

I was twenty-seven years old and had been thinking about finding a husband and settling down before I was called to go to war. Now that I was twenty-eight and there was a good possibility I could die, I was pissed. All my plans were put on hold. Everyone was afraid to sing to me because I threatened to kill them. So the first sergeant, who outranked me, started the whole birthday chant. I couldn't even fake happiness. I had just come off of leave, I was back in hell and it was my birthday. They made me a cake and I was with my friends so it wasn't the worst thing in the world, but it sure wasn't a place I wanted to celebrate

SPC Elaine Knopf and SPC Ryan "Willy" Gearheart

a birthday. I didn't have a problem eating the cake, though. For some reason, the chow halls made the best cake.

Elaine didn't have time to get me a present so she called her husband and told him to buy a bunch of Victoria's Secret stuff. He wrapped it and mailed it over so I could open something on my birthday. I got two gold necklaces from one of the little shops. My parents bought me a front porch swing for my house that they were saving for when I got home. I told them not to send anything over to me because we were trying to downsize our possessions. There were rumors that we could be leaving in December and we convinced ourselves we were leaving, so we told everyone to stop sending things. Rumor had it that our replacements were on their way. They weren't in-country, but rumor also had it the war was looking really good and we might be headed home sooner than planned. Morale was on the upswing by then and we spent the days looking forward to softball games. Every day in between was just another day closer to home.

Sallee and Elaine had just returned from leave and they were jet-lagged. Usually after leave, soldiers got a few days to adjust to the time difference, heat and stuff like that, but unfortunately, Sallee and Elaine didn't get those adjustment days. The truck master was scrounging for people because there was a mission and not enough soldiers to drive the trucks. Elaine and Sallee had both come back from leave and were dead tired. They rode together on the mission and both had to keep the other awake. Both were falling asleep as they were driving down the road when all of a sudden they started getting mortared and the civilian truck driver in front of them stopped. Elaine was

From left: SPC Elaine Knopf, Michelle, SGT Dawn Hostettler (behind Michelle) and SGT Tara Sauer pose at the baseball field at Camp Navistar

honking, trying to get him to go. That was about the extent of their excitement that day and everything turned out okay, but they sure woke up after that.

I was refreshed when I got back on the road. It was a little cooler and it felt kind of new to me again. I didn't mind being out and I was excited to see JD again. We had one mission together before he went on leave. While on our mission, we stopped for the night at Scania. I had a dream and it disturbed me. That next day we were heading into the dangerous part of our mission. I was extra-alert and nervous. JD asked what was wrong because he immediately noticed me acting funny. I said I had a dream that my grandpa told me the end was near. JD blew it off and said, "It was only a dream. We'll call your grandpa when we get to Anaconda and you'll feel better." I looked at him and said, "My grandpa is dead." JD immediately sat up and we both nervously headed to the camp, not saying a word to each other. The trip was uneventful, but the dream scared the shit out of both of us.

Elaine was on my first mission back. We climbed up on a truck, watched the sunset and bullshitted for hours. We talked about leave, the missions, what was going on with the camp and she filled me in on her first mission back from leave.

*   *   *

While I was home on leave, the soldiers in charge of MWR (Morale, Welfare and Recreation) turned a portion of our camp that we weren't using into a softball field and added a concession stand. They even put up big gas lights that ran on diesel to light up the field. It felt like being back in the States, even though the sand was obviously different and there were rocks mixed in. It was humorous watching someone try to field a ground ball because they didn't know which way it was going to go. We received gloves, bats, balls and everything needed to play thanks to a donation from someone. When not playing, I enjoyed being a spectator and screaming at the players. We even came up with silly cheers that made us feel youthful and carefree. Screaming at the players and cheering helped relieve some of our aggression and was much better than yelling at people for no reason.

All we had to do was sign up a team and we could play. It was probably one of the biggest morale boosters. We rushed off our missions to go play ball, usually waiting until it got dark when it was a little cooler. We called the concession stand the "meth lab" because it was so dark and had no windows. But it did have nachos, soda, hot dogs and popcorn—and it was all free! Finally, we had something positive we could all look forward to.

The one thing I did enjoy about Iraq was the job I was doing. At home, I sat at a desk protected from the elements with everything I needed in reach. Over there we were driving trucks through the desert. It was the first actual blue-collar job I'd had since college when I worked summers in a steel mill. It was physically demanding. I had to climb all over things, get dirty and sweaty, and deal with the elements. But I held my own and enjoyed the demand of the physical labors. On good days I used to say that I wouldn't mind losing my job back home and going into more of a manual labor job, but then it would rain and I'd say to hell with that, I'm going back to my office.

My muscles had become more defined and I was in much better shape than I had been back at home. It was also the first time in my life that I spent almost every day and night outside. The only time I spent indoors was in my tent or truck cab. Going into a real building that was made of bricks and had a roof was a real treat. I can count on my hand the number of real buildings that I stepped foot in for that year.

Our camp had a gym. I would occasionally go there to pass the time. Dawn was there a lot because she had just had a baby and wanted to lose the extra weight she had put on. She showed me around, being sarcastic because I was rarely in there. She would say, "Oh welcome Michelle, let me show you the equipment. Here is where you get water and towels." I would laugh at her and she was just pissed that I was so physically fit and hardly did anything, and she had to work her ass off to get in shape.

There was another physical fitness nut who would work out every day for hours. Working out was his life. When we took our PT test, he and I scored the same, a perfect 300. It baffled him that I could sit around and eat cookies and cake, not work out and score the same as him.

We also had a unique perspective on the fear of death over there. Every day, we'd get the death toll. Most of those who died were "babies." They were eighteen and nineteen years old, just out of high school and away from home for the first time. We'd hear about a few in their twenties or thirties, but most were still "wet behind the ears." There were many dying in convoys and we soon became desensitized to it. Our perspective on death changed. We focused more on the important things in life. The petty shit didn't matter anymore. I learned to hold onto my friendships because at any moment, they could be gone. I stopped holding grudges for the ridiculous arguments that meant nothing there but that would have been a big deal back home. Clearing the air was more important because just in case something did happen, there would be no regrets.

When I got home, I was so disgusted by the things people worried about. I couldn't believe these were the issues that consumed them.

Many soldiers began evaluating their lives over there and whether or not they were truly happy back home. Those who realized their lives were unhappy at home made drastic changes for themselves. Some got divorced; some quit their jobs and went back to school. Once we all figured out how we wanted to live our lives, we changed them almost immediately upon returning home.

For me, I realized how much more confidence I had. We didn't have time to let problems fester over there. We had to get it out and move on. I had more patience when I got home. The organization I work for is grant-funded, which means I could lose my job at any time, but I came to terms with the instability of it while I was in Iraq. I was comfortable with the fact I might not have a job to come home to. I was more forward than ever before. I said what was on my mind instead of tiptoeing around issues. It is so much better to be straightforward and it takes much less energy

– 11 –

November

Killed in Action: 1,262
Wounded in Action: 9,854

We continued hearing rumors that we might be leaving in December. We had built it up in our minds because it gave us something to look forward to, but it was just another let down. SGT Brown was really excited about leaving and I asked him what he'd do if we weren't going home then. He said it wouldn't be a big deal because we'd only have a few months left. It sounded like a good plan to me, so I started believing we were going home in December.

The reality of the pain we were causing the Iraqi people started to get to me. It wasn't the days on the road that took a toll, it was watching the destruction all around the innocent Iraqis, who would later come and thank us for what we'd done.

We heard stories about Iraqi men heading for work only to be killed in the crossfire when gunfire broke out on the street. We heard about insurgents taking over towns and our troops fighting back and of course, there were innocent civilians who were shot or killed. But it was war and there was no way around it. We tried to think about it from a cultural point of view and consider the man as the patriarch trying to protect his family only to be stopped at a checkpoint with American soldiers waving guns in his face. And we wonder why they hate us so much. Actually, I don't think they hate only us. I think they hate the insurgents and everyone else trying to take over their country.

151

We were driving down the road once and saw a wedding party stopped at a checkpoint. Since we were never sure if it was a setup, we had to be aggressive. But just imagine your wedding day. It's supposed to be one of the happiest events in life and these soldiers are ruining it. It's supposed to be memorable, but for these people the memory would be tainted by guns being waved in their faces. I don't know if many soldiers looked at it from that perspective. Maybe they realized it, or they will someday, but it was something that always stuck with me.

Morale was hitting an all-time low because most of us had come back from leave and only had going home to look forward to anymore. Even the upcoming holidays looked bleak.

* * *

It started raining at Camp Navistar the night before a mission and our crappy tent flooded. It started as a slow trickle where the water dripped through all the holes in the roof, but the tent was canvas so once the roof was drenched with water it easily seeped inside. It dripped on my face while I was trying to sleep, so I slept with a garbage bag over me. My computer was wet before I could get it into my big Rubbermaid action packer. I couldn't wait to get on the road and get out of there. My guys were in a newer tent that didn't drip. As the females were scurrying to find plastic bags, one of the guys made the comment that his tent was nice and dry. He was quickly run out of our tent because we didn't want to hear it. The tent was replaced before Thanksgiving. I was on the road at the time and someone else had to move all of our shit out of the tent...again.

That's when the rainy season started. We were at Scania, one of the tiny convoy support camps. The majority of the camp was a big parking lot for convoys to spend the night. Generally, we'd sleep out by our trucks because it was too much of a pain to request a tent for the night because it was so far away. It started raining while we were there and it continued raining for several days. They didn't have many port-o-potties around the convoy area, so people just peed outside. Because of the rain, nine months of urine had resurfaced and it smelled awful. There is not a time in my life when I've ever smelled something like that and I probably never will again. I could see the pee in the puddles and it was disgusting. We slept on our trailers that night because it was the highest point above ground. When it finally stopped raining, the place smelled like a big piss pit in a humid hell.

I woke up in the morning after a great night's sleep. I rolled over and as I was climbing out of my cot, my pillow fell into a piss puddle. It was the most disgusting thing that could have happened. I was so pissed. Literally! I rushed to the PX to buy myself another little pillow. I had my sleeping bag and pillow, and that pillow was the only thing to keep me company, so I was pretty upset. Of course, the PX was out of pillows. All I could do was laugh. Up until then, I had never dropped my pillow off the truck and of course it had to fall the one day there was a huge piss puddle under me. The next PX we hit, I bought three pillows so I never had to go through that again.

We're finally home to Camp Navistar. Our four-day trip turned into about 12 days.

Our mission was changed while we were heading into Iraq, and we had to take a more priority load to a different site. That caused us to be on the road a lot longer than we had anticipated and, unfortunately, we all didn't pack for a 12-day trip.

Luckily, some soldiers from our platoon had to meet up with us for our new journey and they brought everyone extra clothes. They had to dig through our tent to find uniforms, socks, shirts and whatever else we were going to need so we wouldn't have to stay dirty after we were through our original four days' worth of clothes.

They were the most popular soldiers when they rolled up with the bags of clothing. We still are training troops from the new unit and they had never been to Iraq until this last mission. They sure got more than expected with this last trip. After the 12 days, they felt like old veterans who had been on the road forever. Maybe that had something to do with the fact our mission got changed to deliver our loads to Fallujah before the major attack on the city.

I felt so bad for the new soldiers. I kept telling them Iraq isn't that bad if you pay attention and are cautious. There was no fooling them when they learned of our new mission. The phrase "baptism by fire" kept coming up throughout the trip. Thank goodness for us all it was an uneventful trip.

It is now the rainy season in Kuwait and Iraq. Before we left, it rained really hard and water came through our tent and soaked my clothes, bed and computer. I finally got everything in dry places and went to sleep. I kept waking up in the middle of the night because water was dripping on me. I was too tired to care, so I just tried to ignore the drops and fall back asleep.

I thought it would be better in Iraq. I was wrong.

The first couple of nights we thought that since the sky was clear and the stars were shining it meant we could sleep without worry of rain. We were wrong.

It poured almost every night, but we got smart and used ponchos to keep the rain out or found someplace indoors to sleep.

I don't know what I like better, hot or rainy weather. But I do know I'm catching onto the rainy season. No matter what, be prepared for rain.

I have to admit there is one major thing I miss since I've been deployed: shopping. I love going to the stores, especially around the holidays. Unfortunately there are few places I can go to fill my shopping urge.

I have found a way to compensate. I go to maintenance's supply area and "shop" for things I need for my truck. I walk in and see things I need and get excited. Last week I found a new light cord, a quart of oil, window cleaner and grease to lube my truck. I haven't been that excited in a long time.

As I walked back to my truck I thought to myself, I have hit a low point: I am excited about a light cord. At least this shopping habit is free and I'm saving lots of money.

Thanksgiving is right around the corner and we are decorating for the holiday. Some people got decorations in the mail, so the tents have things hanging up to remind us of Thanksgiving. Some of the soldiers are getting a Thanksgiving party together so we have some activity to do on the day.

The mess hall staff decorated our eating area with tons of streamers, cardboard cutouts of turkeys and pilgrims. The decorations are all over the place and the taller guys keep hitting their heads on cardboard cutouts when they walk through.

It didn't hit me until today that Thanksgiving is tomorrow. It feels like another day at work and there isn't any holiday spirit looming in the air. I don't think many people are thinking about Thanksgiving because we've been so busy on the road. At this point we've missed all the holidays since January, so it isn't too big of a deal. We'll see if everyone gets excited about Christmas.

Staff SGT Drushel just got back from leave and he brought a huge turkey and the chow hall said they'd cook it for our platoon. We still have no idea how he got it to Navistar from Southern Kuwait without it thawing out.

The chow hall is also going to stay open past the regular hours so we can feast as long as we want.

There is also a pie-eating contest tomorrow. The one thing most soldiers miss is the traditional Thanksgiving dinner and helping make the one thing they are famous for making. I guess it is just the family traditions that will be missed the most this season.

Our little Army family is planning on eating our Thanksgiving meal together since we won't have our families with us. We'll be OK this Thanksgiving because we have each other.

I have some good news to report: The drippy tent was replaced with a brand-new tent. This one passed the test and didn't leak when it rained the other day. Things are looking up. – MZ, November 24, 2004

November 28, 2004

I stopped writing as much. There was nothing new to talk about and we were busy training our replacement unit. As far as I was concerned, I was going home in December or January. The Marines were getting ready to go into Fallujah because of the insurgent activity and attacks, and it was all over the papers back home. It was going to be the first big invasion since the initial attack when the war started.

Our missions did not stop. We were headed to Anaconda on the Iraqi Express. We were starting to train our replacements from Nebraska, the 1075th Transportation Company, and it was only the second or third time they had been on the road.

When the 1075th went on its first mission with us, I just so happened to be convoy commander. They were stunned that a woman was in charge because they only had a few women in their unit and none at my rank. Not only did they have to follow my orders, I was a woman who was about to lead them into a combat zone for the first time. They weren't scared and they never said anything chauvinistic, but they all had a look of confusion because they had never seen anything like it. It was a different kind of culture in their unit, but they were very respectful and listened to everything I said. The guys in my unit made sure everyone in their unit knew I had a Purple Heart because they knew how much I hated to talk about it and that it would make me blush and roll my eyes.

We saw how nervous and alert they were. Immediately, we could all relate to those emotions and the expressions on their faces. That was us nine months ago. Now the tables were turned and I remembered how crazy I thought the New Mexican unit that trained us was and how we swore we would never do the things they did. Now we were just like them: burnt out and knowing what was important to pay attention to and what wasn't.

We needed more radios and armor but the priorities were so screwed up that our battalion bought a plasma television so that they could display a map. That's right—a map. When the new unit arrived, they had double the people on the road and not enough equipment. Instead of buying $100 Motorola radios, however, those in charge bought an expensive television set. Apparently, there was funding set aside for that.

*   *   *

The first time we took the new unit on the road, we got mortared. It was minor and we didn't really get worked up over things like that anymore. Now, when someone called on the radio to say they got hit or there were mortars in the area, the nervousness in their voice was gone. Now it was more of an annoyance, one that would cause us to roll our eyes. We all knew what to do in case of emergency by then, so it was just another routine.

I called on the radio this time with more of a matter-of-fact tone than a panic. Just then, a roadside bomb exploded near a truck with an "old guy" and a "newbie" from the new unit. The old guy was in shock and the new guy was screaming on the radio, "What do I do, what do I do?" The one thing we are taught when there is a roadside bomb is to not go with natural instinct and stop; you have to keep going. And so he continued on. Right where he would have stopped if he hadn't had that radio was right where a second bomb went off. And that one was even bigger than the first! If he had panicked and stopped, he would have been sitting on top of the bomb. If he hadn't had a $100 radio he wouldn't be alive. I can't prove it, but I'm convinced that if the circumstances had been different, odds are he might have stopped.

I can't even describe how many times we would get so upset over things that the higher-ups did but we were powerless to change. But that was war, I was told, and no one seemed to question it. I didn't accept that as an explanation, though.

After the incident, one of the new guys came up to me and said it was soothing to hear a woman's voice come over the radio through the attack. He thanked me for calming him down. It made me blush again. It had been so long since gender had been pointed out and I was taken aback.

We took turns switching people around in trucks to make room to train the new unit, but never touched the gun truck crews. We relied on them to know exactly what they were doing and we needed experience in those trucks. The new unit rode in the trucks to learn, but only one of their guys could ride in the gun truck with the original crew. We were too close to going home to risk getting killed from inexperience.

The new unit had a different perspective than us on the war because they had heard a lot more on the news than we had before we left. Without TV and newspapers, we had no clue what was going on. According to the news in the States, things had gotten worse and these soldiers knew what they were walking into. It was a lot hotter up north and they knew it. In addition, they were a bit more timid than we were when we first arrived in-country, again probably because there wasn't much news about attacks back then.

Once, Schrack was in charge of the mission and I was there to assist him. That was how every convoy ran: one person in charge of the convoy and another person to help with personnel. Schrack and I decided to leave all of our experienced sergeants at camp and take the rookies on the road because we wanted to give our younger, experienced soldiers in our unit a chance to teach

Michelle in front of an Iraqi plane at Camp T.Q. (Taqaddum)

the new troops. Besides that, it was a rare opportunity to give our sergeants a much-deserved break. We had only experienced E4s and us on the mission, which meant the average age of the soldiers was probably twenty-two. It was one of our routine trips that practically ran itself, so we figured nothing could really go wrong.

We were heading down the road on the usual route when we got an instant message to pull into the camp up ahead. Schrack called me to relay the message.

"No, we have to pull over," he urged.

"What for?" I snapped back in my most sarcastic tone.

A general was waiting for us at the gate and I didn't take it as a good sign. I had never seen a general at that camp, let alone one greeting our convoy.

We were instructed to drop the load we were carrying and pick up a load that was a higher priority. I wondered why they were working so fast to get our trucks unloaded and reloaded, when Schrack approached me with a look that I never want to see again. He was definitely concerned and disturbed by something.

"Michelle, we're going to Fallujah," he whispered.

"What do you mean? We can't go to Fallujah. We've got all these kids and new people with us," I started rambling. "We're not equipped to go there."

We were told we had to go to Fallujah to deliver concrete barriers and those were all the instructions we were given. All we could do was guess where these things were going. I wondered if we had to drive through downtown Fallujah to set up the barriers while the Marines were attacking, and I wondered why they needed them so badly. It wasn't looking good for our convoy. We needed our sergeants who we trusted. Word had already spread through the home camp about our mission. The other two gun trucks from our platoon were sitting at our camp listening to what was happening. They were two very competent gun trucks and they knew they were needed, so they fought hard to meet and escort us. Baxter, the sergeant in charge of one of the gun trucks, came up with a story that our convoy needed clothes because there was a good possibility we'd get stuck in Fallujah for as long as three weeks and they needed to bring clothes to us. Somehow that story worked and our gun trucks were on their way to roll with us. The camp where we loaded was trying to kick us out so we could continue with the new mission, but we were dragging our feet so that our gun trucks could catch up. We were getting a little antsy wondering how long we could we stall before they kicked us out of camp.

The guy I was driving with was SSG Greiss. His wife had been deployed a rotation before him and never had to go on the road because of her job. She was stationed up at camp as a supply sergeant. The first time she went on the road, a roadside bomb hit her and she died immediately. Greiss found out about her death while he was mobilizing to go to Iraq. He was preparing for deployment when two soldiers came up to his door and paralyzed him with the news.

"My wife told me she never goes out on the road because she didn't have to," he later told me. "She said she wouldn't go if she didn't have to."

After all that, he was given the choice to go to Iraq or back out. He told me he still had to go to be with his guys and see what his wife had experienced. He didn't tell me this until we were crossing the border to go into Iraq. He asked if I had a husband and I asked about his family. "Do you have a wife?" was really all I said. Based on the look he gave me, I was expecting the usual story that they weren't doing well, were separated and blah, blah, blah. I'd heard it all by then. As we literally crossed into Iraq, he told me the story about the roadside bomb killing his wife. Oh dear God, I thought, and he's driving. He assured me he was fine, but I was going crazy. I didn't want to push, so I didn't ask any questions. I figured he would volunteer the information if he wanted me to know.

So there I was, driving into Fallujah with a guy whose wife was killed in a major combat zone. What are the odds? I was waiting for him to lose control, but he never did. He was an amazing person. He was dealing with the death of his wife and chose to go to war in the place where she was murdered. He told me he needed to see what she did and what she experienced.

Meanwhile, our time had run out while waiting for our extra gun trucks and we couldn't stall any longer. We had a day or two to get out of Fallujah before major pandemonium broke out and we were on a tight schedule, but we needed to meet up with our gun truck crews because we trusted them and they knew what they were doing. We had a plan to get out of the gate and stop for a flat tire, figuring it would buy us the ten minutes we needed for them to catch up. We followed them through the tracking system and knew they were close. We met up with them just in time.

We started into Iraq with the younger kids from our unit, the brand new troops and the gun trucks. When we got to the next camp, we picked up Marine escorts. We never had that much protection yet nothing felt right. We wondered why we needed that much support, but never asked.

We left early in the morning and headed to Fallujah. There had been activity that night and our convoy passed a burning vehicle, but we didn't think much of it. Things were definitely heating up. One of our trucks broke down. I was in a bobtail, which meant I had the cab and no load and so was available to haul broken down vehicles if needed. After maintenance spent some time trying to fix the problem, it was decided that it had to be towed. The Marines were getting restless and it was time to move anyway. We heard gunfire nearby coming from a U.S. security patrol, but we didn't know who they were firing at. We later found out there were some civilian vehicles approaching them and they had to fire warning shots to stop them; but it scared us at the time. Once the truck was hooked up, we were on the move to catch up with the rest of the convoy. As I was driving there were two civilian trucks coming toward me in my lane and I had nowhere to go. I didn't want to upset Greiss, but all I could think was that it was a car bomb. There was a civilian vehicle on each side of me and I hit the gas, figuring one of us had a chance. Car bombs were growing in popularity with the insurgents. Obviously, I'm here to tell the story, so I didn't die. The only thing I could think of was I that I had a guy with me whose wife just died and now he was going to die. I just about crashed into the convoy trying to avoid the potential car bombs and catch up to them in the dark. My co-driver didn't realize what kind of danger we were in and I waited until later to tell him why I was so concerned.

We headed into Fallujah to drop off the barriers to the Iraqi Army whose camp was just outside the Marine base. The Marines had been training them and were about to go into Fallujah to fight side-by-side with them. Once we got there, we were stuck. We were on hold for a couple days, waiting for escorts to get us out of there before the big battle. When they finally gave us the OK to go, we had only hours to get out that night or we would have been stuck for who knows how long. All the roads were closed due to the attack and no one was supposed to be moving around, but since we were with the Marines who had other instructions, we were allowed to travel with them. We let our unit know we were leaving; they wished us luck. We missed the attack by a few hours. The entire time we were there, there was nonstop artillery fire between the enemy and the Marines. It was deafening. The noise, the soldiers preparing for the operation and the medical support standing by waiting to retrieve the injured all made for one intense situation.

I took some video of the Marines getting ready to attack. They were huddled together, psyching each other up. It looked like a bunch of high school football players in a huddle getting ready for the big game; only they were heading into a life or death battle. It sickened me to think that some of them were not going to make it out alive. I was filming the ambulances and everyone gearing up when a tank let off artillery close to me and I hit the roof. All we could hear was the boom-boom-boom behind us as we headed out.

Since it was not a routine mission, Schrack was training the sergeant from the 1075th to be the convoy commander. He took over again instead of having the brand new troops deal with the craziness, and they were grateful. They had done everything right, but that was too much. We whooped and hollered when we got back to camp. We made it back just in time for Thanksgiving.

*   *   *

There was a little feast prepared for us on Thanksgiving Day. The mess hall was decorated and our officers and people in charge served dinner. Missing holidays back home didn't feel like a big deal anymore because we had each other. Also, our deployment was going to be over February 17 at the latest, so we figured we'd be home in no time. We got half a day off to lie around. Most of us just watched movies. It was seventy-eight degrees, we were in Kuwait and it was Thanksgiving. We spent a lot of time that day sharing what we would normally be doing on Thanksgiving back home.

A few days after Thanksgiving, a sergeant returning from leave brought us a turkey that he had won from one of the camps in Kuwait. He ran off the bus towards the tents to put his frozen turkey in a freezer and nobody had a clue what he was up to until he explained it. It was decided that our platoon was going to have another Thanksgiving dinner. He went to the workers in the chow hall and asked if they would prepare it. They were Indian, con-

160

tracted by KBR to cook for us, and they enthusiastically agreed to cook the turkey. The day of the big feast, the cooks had the bird all covered up and we were so excited to eat. The cook uncovered it and the reaction was priceless, a look of "What the hell is that?" It was barbequed and they had torn it all apart. It startled us. We thanked them and it turned out to be pretty good, but it was just another interesting example of culture shock. Everyone got a good laugh out of it and I still can see the look of horror in everyone's eyes when that turkey was uncovered.

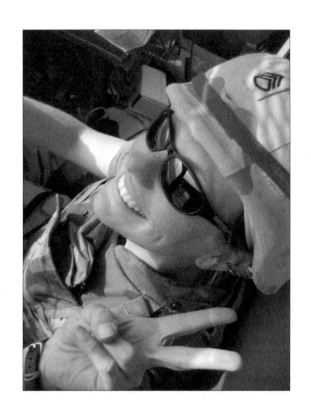

– 12 –

December

Killed in Action: 1,334
Wounded in Action: 10,389

I wanted to let you all know Thanksgiving was wonderful. Our little Army family had a really nice time celebrating together. It wasn't the same as being with our real families, but it was fun. We all went to the chow hall together and our leadership served us dinner.

I asked for ham and turnkey and when I went to eat it, I didn't know which one was the turkey and which was the ham! Oh well, dinner wasn't like Mom's, but it was a fine substitute.

Immediately after dinner, a few of the girls started setting up the Christmas trees and hanging stockings. My family doesn't put the tree up and get in the "holiday" spirit until a few weeks after Thanksgiving, so it was much to my surprise that our tent was all decorated within 15 minutes after turkey dinner.

One of our soldiers, SGT Drushel, won a turkey at a raffle in Kuwait. He brought it to the chow hall and they cooked it for our platoon. At 7 p.m., we piled into the chow hall and sat down for our second Thanksgiving dinner.

SGT Drushel was returning from leave on Thanksgiving, so we celebrated it a few days later for him.

The cooks brought out the turkey and took off the cover. We all gasped as we looked at our turkey. The cooks are from India and aren't used to our American customs and cooked the turkey "different" than the traditional way. They had skinned it and then put red barbecue sauce on it! The turkey took us aback, but it didn't stop us from eating it. It actually tasted pretty good!

Well, the stockings are hung by the bunk bed with care and we are all ready for Christmas. The girls in my platoon picked names for a gift exchange. It gave us an excuse to go to the PX and do some online shopping. All the guys think we are corny for the gift exchange.

The weather has gotten significantly colder in the past few weeks. The lows reach 40 degrees Fahrenheit. Once the sun goes down, it cools off. We've been bundling up and trying to find tents to sleep in when we are out on the road. I didn't realize the weather changed so drastically in the Middle East.

The Army provided us with all types of cold-weather gear when we first got in country and it didn't make sense why we needed it. Now it is getting clear. The one thing I have noticed while driving through Iraq is that the children bundle up with coats and sweaters, but they still are not wearing shoes. I feel so bad for them because we are in trucks, bundled up and they are outside hours at a time and do not have proper footgear. – MZ, December 5, 2004

W e could always tell new soldiers from the old. Old soldiers didn't smile or look at anyone directly. A smiling newbie got the "fuck you" look. We didn't have enough energy left to muster up a smile or even to pretend to be happy. I saw the same energy, passion and fear in the eyes of the newbies that we once had. My spark was gone. I didn't even care if I made it or not. I just wanted to stop doing the job and be done.

I was physically broken, too. My hearing was shot and my back was hurting so badly I couldn't stand it. In the beginning, my back hurt while on the road but after a day off, I could recover and be ready to go again. Progressively it got worse, to the point that I had to go to the medical tent and get a Flexural pill and get realigned by the medic licensed in manipulations. Nothing would make it feel better anymore. JD had to pull me into the truck because it was so bad. I was miserable and in pain. Staying off the road was not an option because if my squad was working and risking their lives, I needed to be there, working too.

With all of the rules, danger and lack of safety, morale was terrible. Our unit tried to throw us a Halloween and Christmas party but nobody was really into it. The unit kept asking us what would make "quality of life" better. The consensus was to get us the hell out of there. People showed up to support the fellow soldier who threw the parties, but I didn't want to be there. They tried to bribe us with phone cards if we showed and we just wanted them to leave us alone. After six months we were fed up; by nine months we were disgusted. And that feeling lasted until we finished our deployment.

Michelle (left) and SPC Elaine Knopf around Christmas

We were so alert in the beginning and so blasé by the end. I remember thinking it might not be so bad getting blown up because they would take me out of Iraq and into Germany or somewhere else. I thought if I died, I wouldn't be tired, in pain or dirty anymore. We lost focus and didn't even care. If there was shooting up ahead, we didn't mind it. But it was interesting how our group started working together. We used each other's strengths and what we excelled in to figure out how to survive. We had a system down to the point that we didn't even have to talk; we just went.

JD and I had nothing left to say to each other. We just pointed and understood what the other one wanted. We didn't even try to make conversation. We just listened to the radio. If JD was driving, I knew what CDs to put in and vice versa. If I was nervous, he knew what to put in to calm me down. If he was in a pissy mood, I did the same for him. I knew how much water he drank and that he liked Mountain Dew in the morning. We had a whole routine down. We were like an old married couple, without the sex.

Tomorrow is our 10-month anniversary of being in the Middle East. We've been deployed for almost a full year, if you count the time we spent at Camp Atterbury. It seems like forever since I've been back to my normal routine. I barely remember what my civilian routine is anymore.

This deployment has been so surreal. Some days I think to myself, "Am I really driving trucks through Iraq and have I been really doing this for almost a year?"

Willy, one of my soldiers, has been putting together a slide show of our deployment from beginning to end. He's shown us what he has completed and it shows every experience we've been through. That is when I realized how much we have actually been through.

The slide show shows the happy, frustrating, upsetting, funny and crazy times each of us have experienced throughout the year. It also shows how close we've become.

There are nine more days until Christmas. Honestly, it doesn't feel like the holidays because our routine hasn't changed at all. There are still missions and we do not get any "vacation" time like most of us get at home, so it doesn't feel any different from any other day.

There is no snow (thank God), no stores with tons of holiday decorations playing Christmas music and no last-minute gift-getting. The main focus of our conversations isn't what people are going to do for the holidays or what they've gotten their friends and family as gifts.

Occasionally, Christmas music is played in the chow hall and I am reminded it is that time of year. It makes it easier because unless we think about it, we don't think about how different this Christmas will be.

I have been asking everyone what they will miss this holiday season. Almost everyone said the thing they will miss the most is spending time with their families. Some will miss opening presents with their children, others will miss making holiday food with their mothers, and others will miss seeing those people you only see during the holidays.

I have noticed that when asking people to think about the special memories they have around Christmas, they become so happy for an instant, like they are reliving the amazing times of holidays past. It is a look of happiness that only comes when you think about the ones you love.

There are little things we've done to get into the holiday spirit. The tents are decorated with little Christmas trees, garlands and stockings.

SPC Sauer plugged lights in because she wanted a little holiday cheer, but she almost burned our tent down. She plugged the lights into the wrong power source, either 220 or 110, and it blew all the lights in the tent! I am so glad the tent didn't burn down. I couldn't bear to lose all my things again to another fire. The other girls were happy there was no fire, too.

We've all done our online shopping for the gift exchange and I'm dying to give my friend the gifts I got for them. I have such a difficult time waiting to give gifts. I want them to open them RIGHT NOW!

I already made Elaine open one of her gifts from me. As for the rest of the gifts, the next big hurdle is finding wrapping paper.

There is a pretty good chance we will be working on Christmas Eve.

The one good thing is that our platoon will all be together. I don't care where we are as long as we are together and safe.

I just hope I'll be able to call my mom, dad and rest of the family so they know I'm OK and can enjoy their celebrations.

I'll be a little bummed that I'll miss our family traditions and not get to see everyone, but I just remind myself there isn't much time left on our deployment after the holidays and I should be back in Ohio soon.

My poor parents are ready for me to come home. My mom has made the comment that I'm grounded when I get home because of all the worrying I've put here through. Can 28-year-olds get grounded?

I was thinking last night how difficult this deployment has been on my mom and dad. I have the easy job; they are the ones watching the news and worrying about me.

It dawned on me last night that they have been worried about my safety for almost one year! One whole year they have spent wondering how I am and if I am safe. They have such little control over the situation and they have to battle so many emotions and fears. I have put my poor family and friends through so much and there is so little I can do to alleviate their fears.

My baby brother Mark has had to call my parents while on vacation to make sure I was still alive because he heard on the news that a convoy got attacked and soldiers were injured. He shouldn't have to take time out of his vacation to worry if I'm OK.

My mom has had to hold back tears to stay strong for me when I talk to her on the phone. She does a good job hiding her emotions, but she can't fool me. I know how heart-wrenching this is for her. I couldn't imagine worrying about my baby the way she and my father have had to.

When I talk to my dad on the phone, I can feel his relief that he knows I'm OK at that moment. He tells me that daddies are supposed to protect their daughters and he is so helpless in this situation.

I can't wait until I'm home and they won't have to worry about me like they are now. I have always been the good child that Mom and Dad never had to deal with too much. (Ha, ha Marie, Mike and Mark! It's my letter and in my letter, I'm the good kid!)

Who am I kidding? I know my parents are rolling their eyes about now.

One of my friends e-mailed and asked me what I am most thankful for this holiday season. I wrote and told her I am so thankful to have the best, most supportive family and friends and community. I never expected to have this sort of support while I was over here. Each and every one of you have made this experience a little easier knowing I have so many prayers coming my way!

I have received so many e-mails, letters and care packages that lift my spirits and let me know I'm loved. Thank you all again for being so wonderful to me and I wish you all happy holidays. — MZ, December 16, 2004

Members of the 1486th Transportation Company, 3rd platoon at Camp Navistar in Kuwait, Christmas 2004. SGT Andrea Motley's family sent Santa hats for everyone and Christmas cards were made out of the photos and sent home to the families

It was our ten-month anniversary and I just couldn't comprehend that I really had been living in a desert carrying a weapon everywhere, driving around a combat zone and living with the uncertainty of whether or not someone was going to die for that long.

Willy started taking pictures and collecting all the digital photos that everyone had from the deployment and putting it to music. We watched it and reminisced about the early days there. It was so nice to look back on everything we had been through together and the craziness of it all. We haven't seen the finished product yet, but it's a compilation of our greatest moments.

The one thing I realized I had going for me was that I was a woman and I started to use it to my advantage. I could get things done quickly just by flashing a sweet little smile. I didn't abuse it, but I used it when it was necessary, like the day we stole clothes for JD.

JD needed some clothing that anyone going into Iraq qualified for, but it seemed like every time we stopped at the camp that had the equipment, JD would somehow miss out. He was so quiet and never complained, that I failed to notice he didn't get the equipment he needed until it started getting cold. We were all wearing the new fleece jackets, but he wasn't.

Eventually, the warehouse moved to Kuwait so soldiers could get the stuff before going into Iraq and it wasn't as easy for us to just walk in and get the clothes issued. He didn't have any of the paperwork we needed to get the supplies. We were issued light, silky underclothes, a fleece hat and jacket, winter waterproof

Michelle and SPC John "JD" Delaney with trucks in the staging area, ready to roll out for a mission

boots and summer tennis-shoe-feeling boots that allowed our feet to breathe. We were given T-shirts and the women were given sports bras. The sports bras were awesome because they breathed nicely in the summer. The only problem was we didn't qualify for the supplies because it was only for people stationed in Iraq and of course, we were stationed in Kuwait. We never understood why we couldn't have it since we spent most of our time in Iraq.

One day JD and I had a delivery to a camp in Kuwait. It just so happened to be the camp that now housed the warehouse with the clothing JD needed. I got all excited and told him it was our chance to get him his issue. We concocted a story for JD to tell the people issuing the clothing and I was going to wait outside so I didn't screw it up. There was a group of guys standing outside the warehouse smoking and I walked up and said hi because I didn't have anything better to do. I started bullshitting with them about the supplies and how nice they were, telling them I wouldn't have gotten through the war without all this awesome equipment. Meanwhile, JD went inside. One of the guys said that JD couldn't start without him because he was in charge of the warehouse. I got really excited because this guy was being so friendly and I knew I could use it to my advantage. I grabbed him and said, "Well, let's get my guy his stuff," while flashing the biggest, most angelic smile. I was nervous because we didn't have any paperwork, just our word, and I'm a bad liar.

We walked in to meet JD and he was just standing there with a blank look on his face while this woman asked him a ton of questions. Before JD could answer, I quickly walked up and gave him the look. JD shut his mouth and watched me work. I turned my attention back to the guy and started bullshitting again, telling a story that sounded somewhat credible and of course, throwing in a whole bunch of flirting. I could see JD rolling his eyes because he had seen the act before and it pissed him off that I could get so much just by flirting. He would say to me, "Why are guys so dumb? They fall for it every time." This time, though, JD was cheering me on so he could get his stuff. The warehouse guy started to give me a suspicious look and decided to quiz JD to see if he had actually been in Iraq. JD answered all of his questions perfectly since we'd seen every camp in the past ten months. It was good enough for the guy and without any paperwork, JD was allowed to get his supplies!

I told JD to hurry before he changed his mind and kicked us out. Just to be sure the guy didn't have second thoughts, I swung around him and hung on his every word while he told me his "war stories." While he was safe in camps writing out a checklist for supplies, we were rolling down dangerous roads. If the circumstances were different, I would have told him that he was pathetic and I had more balls than he did. I gritted my teeth and told him how brave he was and how he was such a war hero. Inside, I was puking. JD rushed around the warehouse and grabbed all he could carry. He had two huge duffel bags full of stuff. We literally ran back to the truck and sped out of there. JD was so happy and I was in disbelief that we had done the impossible. Nobody back at camp could believe it because so many others had tried so many different tactics and got shot down. It was a small victory for us.

December 24, 2004

It wasn't cold and it wasn't snowing, but it was Christmas. There was an occasional bell or a paper snowman, but we weren't inundated with the usual Christmas jingle bells and such. We did get many packages from home and from lots of support groups that wanted to make sure our Christmas was special. Everyone shared the packages and there was so much of it that we had enough candy canes to feed the whole Army. I told my parents not to send me presents because we were still trying to downsize. They felt guilty and sent me little presents so at least I had something to open. It was stuff that I could turn around and give to the kids.

It was a very hard time for my mom and dad. It was a holiday without their whole family together. They couldn't enjoy it because one of their children was in danger.

At Thanksgiving, all of us girls decided we were going to take part in a gift exchange. We still had plenty of time before Christmas to shop online and make sure the gifts arrived in time. We picked names out of a hat and I got SPC Brooks, the soldier who came in-country late because of having the baby.

On Christmas Eve, we had a party with our company and auctioned off people for dates for the New Year where they would go out for pizza together one night. We used the money raised for our homecoming party. I wondered how that would fly for the spouses back home, but it was all in good fun and lifted our spirits. There was so much energy during the auction; some of the guys even came up with crazy costumes and performed dance routines while they were being auctioned off.

Michelle and SPC Elaine Knopf (right) opening stockings on Christmas

Slowly but surely, our platoon left the party one by one. We had our own Third Platoon party later that night, it was a lot livelier and full of spirits...I mean spirit. We all went to bed and the next day all the younger girls woke us up early to open presents in our tents. We had Christmas trees, lights and all the fixings for a Christmas party. Bah-humbug, I thought to myself.

Motley was the artsy one of the group and made us make T-shirts. She gave everyone a red shirt to decorate with puffy paint. Everyone painted Christmas trees, snowmen and snowflakes. I just made a big peace sign on mine. She made us wear them the entire day on Christmas.

The chow hall had a brunch for us. Actually, it felt like we ate all day long while watching movies in between. I couldn't believe how relaxing it was compared to all of the family drama I knew my relatives were creating back home. I was also glad I didn't have to deal with the incredible amount of snow that was hitting Cleveland. Over here, it was all of us hanging out without a care in the world. For every holiday or birthday, or when we wanted to talk, we had to call home. It was like "Hi, happy birthday to me." We all laughed about it but that's how it worked. Unfortunately, the phones went dead on Christmas and nobody could get through to their families. Eventually they started working again but the lines were long so phone conversations were short.

I finally reached my parents and they started telling me all about what they had planned for the day. I told them I wished everyone a Merry Christmas and then retreated into my movie bubble for the rest of the day. It was probably my favorite holiday because we were nearing the end. We knew there was no chance of leaving early, but now there were only two months until deployment would be over.

Our missions had slowed down because now there were too many truckers in-country. All of the replacement truck drivers were now actively running missions on their own. We wondered why we were still there if we weren't needed, but of course, never got an answer. We just sat and waited for the time to tick away.

At the same time, we were getting frustrated with the replacement unit because they were dragging their feet getting validated, which allowed them to go on the road by themselves permanently. We took them on the road for months and were sick of babying them. When we replaced the New Mexican unit, we went on one mission with our veterans where they were in charge, one where we were in charge and another where all we had was a guide from the New Mexican unit who sat back and did nothing. It took a total of three weeks for us to get validated. We figured the New Mexican unit had served their time and we validated as quickly as possible so they could go home. It sure didn't feel like our replacements were doing the same for us. We were still in charge on our sixth mission with them. It was time for them to step up and run the convoys so we could go home.

Our regular rotation was split because we had to ride with the new people, so it was messing up our whole system. We wanted to ride with our people, not theirs. JD had been assigned to a gun truck, and I missed him and our smooth routine. The handholding was getting old for our unit and theirs. They kept telling us it wasn't their fault and that their leadership was stalling because they didn't think they were confident enough to be on the road alone. But we didn't really give a rat's ass; it was time to kick them out of the nest.

Apparently, they were waiting for this fancy, new up-armor package for their trucks that they never received. Seven months after I returned home, they were still waiting for that armor. Good thing we didn't have to stay until they got it.

The administration talked about supporting the troops, but they didn't give us the equipment we needed for protection. We had armor that was makeshift and we referred to it as "hillbilly." The replacements were hemming and hawing about driving these trucks and we told them to suck it up because we had done it for a year and the unit we replaced didn't have any armor at all.

Right around Christmas, there was a general who tried to extend the units heading home for an additional three months, but higher-ups wouldn't approve because there was no reason for us to be there anymore. I was baffled that this guy wanted to keep twice the number of truck drivers when there were no trucks for us to drive. It's amazing no one shot that man. When the New Mexican unit was extended, the brass knew enough to collect all the weapons and ammo before they told them. I see why now.

We didn't have enough trucks, enough equipment or enough space and they kept telling us to be patient. The general did end up getting us extended two weeks, but it was two weeks of just sitting around, waiting to go home. At the end, when we found out we were extended, we got more money for every month we had to stay. I was so pissed off about the extra money at the time, so I took it and donated it to different groups. One of the groups was Women for Women International, which helps women around the world. I specifically donated to the women in Iraq. I was angry about the extension and figured that if I used the money to help them, it would make the time bearable. It was worth it if one woman could benefit from my donation.

We stopped riding with our replacements but unfortunately, we had to give up our trucks. It seemed premature, but we agreed if it was going to get us out of there quicker.

The time at camp seemed to drag. We didn't have any equipment and couldn't go anywhere when an active duty battalion showed up at Camp Navistar. They immediately hated us and dismissed us as incompetent. We had the most miles of any battalion in the country and the best record, but because we were in the National Guard, we were inept. Our suggestions meant nothing even though they were on their way in and we were wrapping up. They thought they had a better way of doing things and every time they tried it, something would go wrong or they would find out that the way we were doing it was the most effective. They started getting yelled at because their delivery numbers were going down. We all had to log what we were delivering and how much, and their numbers were suffering. This did not go unnoticed by those in charge. Before long, they went back to our way of doing things and I wanted to stick my thumbs in my ears and say, "I told you so." That was always the struggle of dealing with a new battalion. Nobody was as good as they were. Our shitty attitudes didn't help, but we weren't trying to impress anyone. We were done.

– 13 –

January 2005

Killed in Action: 1,441
Wounded in Action: 10,890

We had a wonderful Christmas and New Year. Our unit was fortunate to have almost everyone back at camp for both events.

The unit threw a Christmas party on Christmas Eve and the girls from my platoon had a gift exchange at 6 a.m. on Christmas Day. It was really early to be waking up on our day off, but some of the girls were really into the Christmas spirit and wanted to do it as soon as possible. The gift exchange was fun and it was good to see everyone so excited and full of energy.

The chow hall made Christmas dinner and it was really good. We all called our families, exchanged gifts and watched movies for the holiday.

The weather was great, too. It was warm enough on Christmas that I could wear a T-shirt outside. I heard back home there were snowstorms and very cold weather on Christmas, so I was glad to miss out on that kind of weather.

On New Year's Eve, we all hung out and had to guess what time midnight was. We didn't have a TV, so we didn't see the ball drop or anything like that. We just guessed on someone's watch and did our own countdown.

Some of the guys lit cigars at midnight and toasted with root-bear floats.

Overall, we made the best of it. Hopefully that will be the last Christmas and New Year's I have to spend in the desert.

We've been working hard to pack everything up so we can get out of here. A new unit has taken our equipment, so we are riding with other companies in our battalion.

I wish they would send us home early, but no such luck. So pretty much we are all spread out between the different units as fill-ins.

There are rumors flying around about when we actually will get to leave, but nobody has heard officially. I just hope we don't get extended. We've heard that rumor, too.

We were out on the road the other day and we had to stop our convoy for a flat tire. While the driver was changing it, these two kids came up to say hello to the convoy.

I gave them some food and said hi to the little boy and girl. I asked them how old they were. She was 8 and he was 5.

I noticed they didn't have shoes on and they were walking through sand that was filled with rocks and debris. I felt so bad for them and asked them where their shoes were. The little girl just shrugged her shoulders like she didn't know.

They said goodbye and walked to the truck in front of me.

One of the guys was talking to the kids and the look on his face was like he just couldn't take it anymore. He told the kids to wait a minute and he climbed into his Humvee and dug for something. The kids and I wondered what he was doing.

He came out from the Humvee with two pairs of wool socks. He told the kids to sit down and he put the socks on their feet. I guess his fatherly instinct got the best of him. The kids were smiling from ear to ear. The socks were so big on them but they didn't care.

I watched as they ran away, skipping and waving thank you. It was the sweetest thing I've seen in a long time. — MZ, January 7, 2005

There hadn't been any missions for about two weeks right around the New Year and there wasn't a movie in-country that we hadn't watched. We begged other units for any new movies, but it was useless. We were looking for a little variance to our routine when we made friends with the 1487th, our sister company. Sitting around with them was not very productive because a bored soldier was a mischievous soldier. We were so bored and so pathetic that we started playing practical jokes on each other. One guy set up a broken chair and lured people to sit in it. Once they did and fell to the ground, everyone laughed like it was the first time it happened. We spent the rest of the day gathered around watching people fall over, almost hurting themselves. Something had to change!

All of our trucks had been transferred to the new units, so we knew it was only a matter of time before we got whored out to every unit that needed bodies. We were getting pissy because we were still there with nothing to do. It gave us a lot of time to fester about not being with our families, although I have to admit I was a little relieved because it was an opportunity to tend to my back before going back out on the road.

Most of our camp was flooded from the rain. We spent most of our time just trying to stay dry and keep the wet sand out of our tent. We ventured out only to get food. Everything was full of sand and I just wanted to be done with the war. We had to sweep the thick clumps of sand out of the tent whenever anyone entered. It was just one more thing we had to deal with and we prayed the rain would stop. It went on for about two days and then that was it. The path from the tents to the chow hall was completely flooded. One of our guys had on shower shoes and thought he could make it through the puddle instead of walking around, but he came back soaking wet from the hips down. He said the puddle didn't look that deep but the path dipped down until the water was up to his waist. It took forever for all the water to disappear.

It looked bad that we had been extended and were now just sitting around doing nothing, so they decided that we should go back out on the road. The next day, word came down that we were going on the road with another unit. Instead of sticking us with the new units, though, they put us with the old ones. It didn't make any sense. They were putting us with units that already had their own system down instead of letting us teach the new guys. For some reason, they had new units training new units. We assumed those in charge would stick us with new people so they could have more experience on their convoys, but we were wrong. We were assigned to a unit that arrived in country about a week after us. It was total Army logic and it made no sense.

As luck would have it, the unit we were stuck with was the black sheep of their battalion. Throughout the year, this particular unit had a stabbing between two co-drivers, a girl sent to jail for stealing, a date rape and a first sergeant found in bed with a subordinate. They were trouble. Their trucks were not maintained and they were attacked all the time because of their disorganization. I was concerned that someone was going to get killed right before it was time to go home because someone wanted to make it look like our extension was worthwhile. I sincerely did not believe that I was going to make it through that mission. We didn't have the proper gun trucks, the semis had not been maintained properly and had been attacked so often they were falling apart. We were at the mercy of a unit we didn't feel ran as well as ours did. We had an equal number of deaths, none, but they certainly had more casualties. My squad was angry with me because although I fought and fought, we still had to go with them.

I tried to work it out with the other unit's convoy commander that my people ride together in their trucks so their people could ride with people they knew, but the convoy commander wasn't having it. We had to ride with their people and had no control over any aspect of the convoy. Our safety was in someone else's hands. The longer we worked with them the more alarming the situation became. I was sure we were going to die and so was the rest of my squad. I went back to my leadership and pleaded with them to do something about this mission, but they said it was out of their hands.

On the morning we left in the convoy, I had a lump in my throat the whole time and felt helpless as they made one bad decision after another. It didn't take long to figure out why they got attacked so much—they made easy targets. Their trucks were continually breaking down; they told us that it was routine.

The other kicker was that all of our gun truck escorts were brand new, having just arrived in-country. One of their soldiers held a knife up to a commercial truck driver for no reason. SSG Hupp, the most calm, non-complaining soldier, the one nicknamed "The Rock," came up and started yelling at me. He said if we ever had to go out with them again he'd kick my ass.

One of the biggest problems was their speed. We drove as fast as we could because we knew it was our greatest defense. It didn't help to offer suggestions to their convoy commander, who I was riding with, because they were set in their ways. I know I probably wouldn't have taken suggestions from another unit either.

I can remember the point on the return trip home when I just gave up. We were rolling down the most dangerous stretch of the trip, doing about thirty-five miles per hour when we should have been going at least sixty-five. I was done worrying about getting attacked and all their mistakes. I accepted the fact that I was most likely not going to make it and made peace with it. I sat back and relaxed, ready to accept my fate. Because our unit couldn't support us and told us to go along with whatever we were told, we didn't contact them to inform them about where we were. I decided if they wanted to check on us they had to go through the unit to which we were detached.

When the convoy returned to Navistar, my soldiers fled from those trucks and I made a beeline for TOC (Tactical Operations Center). I got my ass reamed for not keeping in contact, but I charged right back at them and told them they weren't taking care of us and had put us in horrible danger by making us risk our lives with that unit. Sam the truck master and I had it out and then calmed down enough to strategize how to ensure we'd never get stuck with that unit again. He was appalled with how badly the trip had gone.

I liked Sam even though he was such a prick and we fought all the time about the convoys. I demanded more gun trucks and days off and he would yell at me about the missions. But when it was all said and done, Sam was the only one we felt supported us. He would actually listen to our concerns and attempt to correct them with the higher-ups. Sam knew his job and was a bulldog. The higher-ups were afraid of him because he was so gruff and mean.

I remember a mission where we had been going for about a month without a day off. Sam promised that we could have one so people could get stuff done, like refill prescriptions and other personal chores. The battalion told Sam that we were needed and couldn't take the day off. I got called into the office where Sam broke the news. After I explained my concerns, he told me to come with him and he stormed the battalion. He took their paperwork and ripped it up right in front of their faces, yelling and "mother fucking" everyone who had anything to do with messing with us. My jaw dropped and I just stood there. Who was this guy? Our day off was reinstated. I had so much respect for Sam and the way he stuck up for us. He really cared about us and was willing to put his neck and career on the line for our unit. I'm glad he was on our side.

Sam promised me that he would do everything in his power to keep us out of that awful unit's trucks, and we never had to ride with them again.

We were assigned to another unit where we felt much safer. They ran their convoys more like we did. The mission ran smoothly and their lieutenant used common sense. I felt better and so did the squad. Their trucks were maintained and they moved faster than we ever could because they were regulated at a different speed. Another benefit of riding with this group was that they understood we wanted to ride with our people and they wanted to ride with theirs. We made sure to tell them to request SSG Zaremba's group and they did.

Elaine and I finally rode together that mission. We wanted to ride together the entire time we were deployed because we didn't think anything could be better than two best friends on a mission together. In addition, we were excited for two women to drive in the same truck.

I was ready to kill that little bitch by the end of that week. I've never wanted to strangle her like that before and we never tried it again. I seriously wanted to punch her in the face. We were tired, frustrated and we were no longer a comfort to each other. She was mean, I was cranky. And it was tense.

Our borrowed truck ran fine the first two days. Just as we were heading to the dangerous part of Iraq and taking a route that none of us had ever been on, our truck died. I looked at Elaine and she started laughing as she told me our truck was dead. We called on the radio to report we needed maintenance. These were different trucks than what we were used to. There was some type of electrical issue and we had to turn the convoy back and head to the nearest camp, which was BIAP. Nobody seemed to mind the delay because both our unit and theirs were trying to drag the missions out until we went home. Everyone was burned out.

It took a day to get replacement parts but instead of trying to guess what the problem was, we switched trucks with another convoy from their unit that was heading to Kuwait. They hauled our truck back home for maintenance to deal with.

Our entire company was spread throughout the battalion and we lacked cohesion once again. It may have been a blessing because we were all sick of each other by that point. The separation probably prevented the fights that were bound to happen if we stayed together any longer.

But as soon as we were separated on the road, we'd always tried to find soldiers from our company. We tried to meet up at the different camps and spend some time together. It worked well because we spent the time catching up instead of fighting. We would all run up to each other and hug as if it were one big reunion.

- 14 -

February 2005

Killed in Action: 1,499
Wounded in Action: 11,310

We were on the road for the elections.

I have to admit we were all unsure of how everything was going to turn out. There were concerns of increased violence before, during and after the elections. I am happy to report everything was pretty much uneventful.

It was strange driving down the roads normally busy with civilian cars, people and busy stores to find them empty and abandoned except for our military forces. Apparently there was a curfew for all civilians.

At the military camps, all places that soldiers normally gather were shut down. For example, the chow halls, Internet and phones were closed to keep from having large numbers of soldiers in one place at one time. This made for a boring mission, but at least it kept us safe.

We had no idea if the elections were successful or if anything catastrophic happened. All we heard were rumors from people who heard from others about what was going on. It took us until the next day after the election to get on the Internet to get any news about the election.

As we headed back to Kuwait, we could see a change in the Iraqi people. There were more Iraqi police and Iraqi National Guard out patrolling and there were more civilians out driving around. People seemed to be waving at us and smiling more than usual.

But the most moving thing I saw were Iraqi flags hanging from every bridge on one of their major highways. There is definitely pride among the Iraqi people and a sense of ownership of the country that I had not seen before. It was really amazing.

Twenty more days until we come home—or so they say. We've already been ex-tended or the "policy" changed for our end of mission. It was only a few weeks' exten-sion, but it was really frustrating because I have been banking on the original 365 days in-country that was promised.

I can see that we are at least moving the direction of going home. We have no more trucks, we drive with other units now. Our equipment is almost all packed up or given to the new unit that replaced us and we've packed up personal gear to be shipped home. Everyone is mailing boxes and boxes of stuff home that we've acquired over the year.

People are selling things like global positioning systems and televisions to the new soldiers who are starting their year in Iraq. There is certainly energy in the camp that feels like we are on our way home. Let's hope we don't get extended!

There are only a few more missions left and we are being extra cautious with these last ones.

I am pretty sure we are all way too close and getting sick of one another. We all know each other's routines, like what time each person goes to eat chow or shower. It is crazy. We also know all there is to know about each other. There are no more secrets, no more mystery to anyone. We've heard every story that every person has, at least twice. I guess that is what happens when you live and work with people for 14 months straight.

We are also getting bored. There are no more movies, games or sports that we can play together. They all have been played to the point of boredom. The latest time-filler was playing practical jokes on one another. It took a few days, but that got old too. For example, one of the guys found a broken chair and set it up like it wasn't broken. He would lure people to sit down and everyone would laugh when the chair broke under them. Yes, that is how pathetic we are now.

I caught Elaine critiquing Willy on how to properly take an aspirin. We have definitely been together way too long!

I started thinking about how long I've actually been deployed and all the events I've missed back home. I've missed everyone's birthday at least once. I didn't get to go to my sister's wedding and I was her maid of honor. A few other friends got married, some got divorced and I couldn't be there for them.

Uncle Lou, who was also my godfather, was very sick and passed away, and I never got to go to the funeral or say goodbye to him, except over the phone.

I've missed every holiday with my family in 2004. My job in Dayton moved to a new building, so I have no idea what my office looks like or where it is. A few of my friends had babies that I've never seen. My Uncle John had twins that I've never seen.

It has been a huge sacrifice to come to the Middle East. It has been a really good experience, but I did have to miss a lot to come here. I think about the 150,000 troops that are in Iraq and Kuwait now and each one of the soldiers can make a list of all they've missed out on too.

Now, don't get me wrong, we all volunteered for this, but it doesn't make it any easier to miss important events that go on while we are away. It feels like everyone's life has moved on and I have just been removed for the past year. I will have to jump back into my life and try to catch up on all I've missed.

I think the closest comparison I can make would be going away to college for a year and then coming back home. There are many changes and it takes some adjustments. It doesn't necessarily mean it is bad, but it will take some time getting back into the swing of things.

It is also like college in the sense that we all live and work so close to one another. There is always someone to talk to whether you like it or not. You don't have to look far or go out of your way to make plans with someone, they are right there all the time.

Unlike the military or college, I will have to make an effort to hang out with family and friends when I get home.

Since there are only 20 days left, I can't stop thinking about all the things I want to do when I get home. We finally have a new topic of discussion in the trucks: What are we going to do when we get home?

I have had many, many hours to think about what I want to do when I get home and here is what I came up with. First I want to see my family and give each of them a big hug. Then I want to drive in a car, where I don't have to wear a flak vest or helmet, to a restaurant where I can order anything I want. I want to go shopping and wear civilian clothes.

Next I want to go to an all-day spa where I can get my hair, nails and toes done. Then maybe I'll feel like a girl again! I also want a full body massage so maybe my back will stop hurting from wearing my flak vest so much.

After I take a bath that I haven't been able to take for 14 months, I want to go out with my family and friends and have a beer. I want to catch up on all the things I've missed and celebrate finally coming home.

This will probably be my last letter since I'll be focusing on my last few missions and packing up to go home. I want to thank everyone once again for all the support I have been given throughout this deployment. I don't know if I would have made it without all the encouraging words and prayers each of you has given me.

Mom, Dad, Marie, Mike and Mark, sorry for putting you all through this, but thank you for being there for me. I know I owe you big time. I feel honored to have such amazing friends, family and community. You have taken care of me throughout this deployment and I will never forget how wonderful you all are.

Thank you all again and I'll see you very soon. — MZ, February 6, 2005

W e were stopped in a camp in southern Iraq called Cedar. It was from there that I called my parents a lot. The Iraqi election was nearing and everyone was nervous about it. There were extra units deployed for the election and everything, including roads, were closed to civilians. No sooner did I hang up with Mom after telling her we'd be locked down for a couple days and not to worry, we were told to pack up and head out. It was eerie driving down the empty roads. I was used to many people and a lot of traffic, even though there was the occasional exception. We always knew something was wrong when there was no one around.

When we arrived at Camp Anaconda, we found the entire place on lockdown. We had to run in and out of the chow hall because they didn't want us gathering anywhere in large numbers. We couldn't use the phone center or the Internet. I told my mom I would call her every day until the elections were over, but I never called her once. There was no news about the elections anyway. We didn't know if they were a success and running smoothly or if all hell was breaking loose. On election day, the day I most wanted to be off the road, our convoy was driving and making deliveries all over the country.

On our final mission we were sent on the "Golden Route." We were with the unit that we liked and on one of those routes off the beaten track. After an uneventful ride, we awoke at the camp the next day to find out a girl from one of the replacement units was killed. Rumor had it that a roadside bomb had cut her truck in half. It was one day off from when we were traveling on it. It was our last mission and we wondered if we would all make it.

The return journey was another night mission. I was driving in the dark with Ken, who was half-blind. At fifty-one years old, he was one of the oldest soldiers in our platoon and always had some comment or story that kept us entertained. Ken was going to retire when we got home and he seemed bitter towards the military.

On the previous mission, Ken was riding with Gearheart and there were issues with Ken driving at night. We had left Tikrit and were heading to Anaconda when the convoy became separated. Apparently, Ken started following a civilian truck and lost the convoy. Gearheart rarely got nervous but not seeing the convoy in front of him made him uneasy. He asked Ken if he could take over driving and Ken said no. So, Gearheart was at the mercy of Ken's driving.

After every mission, we had to clean our weapons and make sure they were in working order and ready to go. To lock a weapon, you shove the magazine inside, release the bolt and it's locked. Just before I started my mission with Ken, I heard a "tink" as I tried to lock the bolt forward on my weapon. I tried to push the forward assist to get the bullet to rise forward but it would not release. I pulled the charging handle back and saw a bullet was bent in the wrong place and had jammed my weapon. Never before had I seen that happen, let alone happen to me. We were on our last mission and I didn't have a weapon. Ken took pliers and ripped the bullet in half. There was gunpowder everywhere and we had about ten minutes to get the thing cleaned up while we waited at the gate. We scrambled around and finally removed the bullet by putting oil on it. Ken was the rock star hero of the day!

Probably right around the spot where the girl was killed, there was another convoy heading in the opposite direction passing us. The commercial driver in front of me was about to get in a head-on collision with a passing truck, so he slammed on his brakes and swerved. His brakes locked up and we wound up stuck on the side of the road in the dark trying to help him fix his truck. We were trying to be quiet, but everything was metal and it made loud clanging noises anytime we touched anything.

I told them we had to back the brakes off. This had happened to us several times, so I knew what I was doing by then, but these weren't our trucks. A maintenance guy came back from the other unit, which was normally a good unit, and I kept telling him he had to unscrew the brakes and back them off, but he wouldn't do it until someone in his unit suggested it. When one of his guys did, suddenly it became the most brilliant idea in the world. I probably would have trusted someone in my unit the same way, but this wasn't the place for a debate. Hupp made sure to point out that they didn't listen to my suggestion.

We got to the camp at about 7:00 a.m. Breakfast was about to close so we rushed to the chow hall. We got to the gate guard, cleared our weapons and were just about to head into the chow hall when the guard yelled at me, "Hey Sergeant. That's not the proper hat!" We had just been there two days before and no one said a word about it. They were just fucking with me but I wasn't in the mood.

Somehow, we made it in time for breakfast and we were ecstatic because it was one of our favorite places. We had thought about it for the last ten hours while on the road and I almost missed it because I was wearing the wrong hat. What's more, the jerk's comment wasn't even really directed at me. With every new person they brought in to a camp, they changed every little thing to show who had more power. It was nauseating watching their little pissing matches.

The next day we were heading out and Ken was driving again. Usually he didn't like to drive that much but he wanted to drive into Kuwait, so I indulged him. I had a little mesh bag filled with goodies to throw to the kids and I told him to move to the right so I could throw the candy. There was a

185

pack of girls that I was trying to throw the food to, but Ken was watching what I was doing instead of the road. We ran over a huge crater and went airborne. I prayed he wouldn't lose control of the truck. He didn't.

We heaved a sigh of relief as we pulled out of Iraq. It was bittersweet. I felt like we were abandoning the Iraqis and the soldiers who were still stuck there, but I was happy to go. It was hard to accept that they had to serve their time just like us. I still checked in with the replacement company when I was home and sent them a few packages just to let them know I was thinking of them. Even though my war was done, I wanted them to know we were still connected.

- *15* -

Homeward Bound

We were told 365 days. It was bullshit. We landed February 18, 2004 and expected to be there until February 18, 2005. They lied. We ended up staying there an extra ten days before being sent home. Ten days doesn't seem that long, but so many promises that had already been broken made the ten days seem like a bigger deal. Each extra day felt like a thousand.

We out-processed at Camp Doha next to the airport around 7:00 p.m. They wanted us to stay up all night to keep us on schedule back in the States, so that's what we did. I had never seen people work so hard to get through something and end it. We wanted to get home. We had to wait for another unit to go through security before being led into a big building where soldiers had to dump all of their belongings onto a cot for inspection. There was shit belonging to 150 people spread out everywhere. It was getting hot and everything we owned was on display for everyone else to see. Then they led the dogs through to make sure we weren't smuggling any drugs. It took two hours to get everyone inspected. The hard part was over.

We stowed our bags in one room while we began briefings. One of the guys in my squad found a full thirty-round magazine of live ammo that he accidentally had in his duffel bag. Throughout the whole deployment, we had so much ammo and so many magazines in our trucks and belongings that it wasn't a big surprise it was there. Luckily, we saw a soldier from a transportation unit and gave him the magazine.

They told us what to expect when we got home, what not to be upset about. The chaplain talked to us and . . . blah, blah, blah. We were there with

187

the 1487th unit and another unit out of Germany that was going home. There were probably 500 of us and not even one was listening to anything they said. We just wanted to get on the plane and make sure we were really going home.

After the briefing, we were shuttled to another area where they inspected us and our carry-ons. It was around 11:00 p.m. and we were getting tired. An amnesty box was offered to dump ammo, knives or any other items we may have second thoughts about trying to take. Around 2:30 a.m., we finally boarded the plane. We were finally getting out of that hellhole. The one thing that felt strange was that we carried our weapons onto the plane with us (on the way to Kuwait we stored our weapons below the plane). I found it odd because of all of the security we had to pass through to board on normal flights in the States. You can't even take a fricking sewing needle on a civilian plane and we were boarding with rifles.

Once I finally sat down in the seat, it felt real. I was going home.

As soon as we took off, the plane exploded with applause and cheers of relief, excitement and disbelief. I took NyQuil to make sure I would sleep until we got to Ireland. I called my parents when we landed and talked to Mark. I told him we were out of Iraq and he said he would tell Mom and Dad because they were at church. When I told him I'd call them there, he was exasperated. "You can't call them at church," he scolded me. I thought this might be an exception.

My mom ran out of the church jumping up and down and I could hear it. She went and grabbed my dad. Meanwhile, the whole church was wondering if everything was OK. At the end of the mass, the priest always asks if there are any questions. When my dad raised his hand and told the congregation I was out of Iraq and in Ireland, the whole place went crazy. My parents told me it was their first good night's sleep in over a year. It felt so good hearing the relief in my mom's voice that first time I talked to her. Finally, they could stop worrying about me.

When we got back on the plane in Ireland I wasn't really that excited. I was pacing myself trying to get through it. We were so fed up with the Army and each other that we just wanted to get it over with. We knew we had another long day before we could even think about a good night's sleep, so by the time we got on the plane again, we were slaphappy. Of course, we had to cheer again when we landed.

We dreaded going back to Camp Atterbury, but we knew it was almost over. As we touched down in Indianapolis, the Ohio Army officers came to greet us and shake our hands. I didn't care to see them. Screw them, I thought. They didn't even go to Iraq and now they wanted to congratulate us? I wasn't impressed with shaking some officer's hand. I wanted to scream, "Get the hell out of our way, let us get debriefed and go home already!"

Getting to Atterbury took forever. I spotted a pay phone while we were waiting. I realized that I could use my calling card and it would be minute-for-minute rather than ten units per minute, which was about fifty cents. We had to drag out dialing numbers in Iraq, but there I dialed that phone so fast. It was such a bizarre feeling. I called my parents again and they were ecstatic. I was finally home.

As we all stood outside in the forty-degree weather, I realized I wasn't *that* cold. I mean I felt it, but I thought I would be shivering head to toe. When I got to Ohio, the temperature was so cold it shocked my system. For a fleeting second, I thought I wanted to be back in the desert, but I shuddered the thought from my mind.

When we got back to our barracks, the "SSG Zaremba game" started again and I refused to play. I told them no, you guys are grown adults, you've been through war, figure it out for yourselves. I was done.

Every class we took became a therapy session. I swear they were pushing us to see how much we could take. We were all frustrated and all we wanted to do was see our families and adjust to the time difference. I hated being there another four days, but in a way it was good to regroup before reuniting with everyone. They did a thorough job processing us and by the second day, everyone was upbeat. By the last day, we were out of control!

We tried to go out to have some fun, but it wasn't very enjoyable. There were too many fights and too much smoke at the NCO Club. The NCO Club was the first place I encountered smoke in a building and I hated it. Everywhere in Iraq was smoke-free and we weren't used to the smell. My clothes, my hair, everything smelled like a bar.

We were allowed to drink at Atterbury too. We collected everyone's spare change—I think that Mullen was our treasurer— and spent it on pizza, food and alcohol. We raised $500 in our platoon alone. For the first time, we were able to enjoy each other without constant chaos all around us. We were happy and closer now.

Elaine and I rented a car because we decided to stay off-post. They were giving us more freedom since coming home. We could do what we wanted in our spare time as long as we attended our classes. Marie got us a room that reminded us of the Bates Motel. It cost about $25 a night, so you can imagine what the room was like. Marie said we had to stay there because she put it on her credit card, so we decided to tough it out. We figured we'd just come from a war for God's sake; we could handle it. We didn't use the shower and hovered over the toilet wearing shoes. We joked that Iraq was cleaner.

The next day we were due for shots, but we had to take mandatory pregnancy tests before anything. I think in that year and a half, I took at least twenty-five pregnancy tests. Anytime we were given medicine or any vaccinations, we had to get a pregnancy test. Since we had to get blood drawn and shots, the females had to be there at o'dark thirty in the morning and start the process. That day was the first time we females benefited. We got there early to start the pregnancy tests, so we were first in line in the game of round robin and were the first to go through the stations. What we thought was going to take until 6:00 p.m. lasted until only 10:30 in the morning.

Elaine and I snuck off-post and went shopping. We were like two junior high girls, giggling and laughing about how we escaped. We shopped for hours. When we found a Gap, I started screaming and Elaine ducked in the seat next to me. She looked up at me like "Oh my God, I thought it was a car bomb!" We kept scaring each other like that. We were a little gun shy trying to readjust and we joked about how screwed up we were going to be for the rest of our lives.

We ran around the Gap, snatching up as much as we could carry and headed for the dressing room. We were so used to showering together and peeing under the trucks together that we just naturally went in the same dressing room together. People were asking if we were all right, and when we told them we just came home from Iraq, everyone just started helping and congratulating us. That was the happiest I had been in a year and a half. We were free, we could drive without a convoy, no flak vests, we ate at Arby's and it was just Elaine and me and nobody else. It was the first time I was truly happy about something in a long, long time.

When we went returned to Atterbury we had to leave our bags in the car. The trunk was stockpiled full of our contraband, but we tried to hide it until we decided to go out that night. We took turns sneaking in our outfits, but everyone noticed immediately. They knew what was up. It wasn't like anyone cared, though. We were done with our day and they were heading out to shop, too.

Atterbury was so much easier the second time around. We set up a routine, did what we had to do and it just flowed. Everyone relaxed a little bit and, though it sounds funny now, we actually returned to our "Guard mentality." When we were in Iraq, some people, even those in authority, took a back seat because they weren't capable of leading us. But when we came back, they were trying to act like they were in charge again and we just laughed in their faces. They went through an entire war and couldn't even do the simple tasks

190

that a young private could. There were people who wouldn't go on the road. We started ostracizing them, trying to make them pull their weight. It wasn't to be mean; it was more of a survival technique for us. Our emotions were running so high over there and we clung to those on whom we could rely to get us through it. If anyone missed going on the road, it was OK, but they were being watched. If they missed going on the road a second time, that was borderline. Three times and they were a shit bag. If they were not helping us, they didn't care about the team and they got pushed out. It sounds bad, but it was a harsh environment and we couldn't be nice. Dealing with life and death, we didn't have time to pussyfoot around; we were brutal. And the ones who didn't cooperate, we didn't talk to. But when we got home, that all went away. We were just in the Guard again.

It was snowing and raining the day we came home and we just kept joking about how we were going to get killed in a bus accident on the way home from war. The busses were split among the three platoons with the fourth bus being used for overflow. The main group of the Third Platoon sat by each other. It was understood that anyone doing the "remember when" thing would be considered a big loser, so no one was really talking.

As we were driving through Ashland, we came up on the Montgomery Elementary School on state Route 250. The whole school was outside waving and we were overwhelmed with emotion. The school next to our armory also turned out to greet us. I watched all of the guys who had been so hard and tough begin to well up with tears. Everyone was moved, no matter how macho they were. We couldn't help but be touched by these kids. I still get tears in my eyes thinking about it.

People lined the streets with welcome home signs. Some people had signs with names and we pointed out Nancy and Chad's families to them. We got off the bus and were overwhelmed to see our families. I was trying to pace my emotions. I was so excited that I wanted to cry and hold my mom and dad. I wanted to see my brothers and hug my sister. As I stood in the line to get into the field house packed with our families, I saw my little brother Mark. I ran toward him and he picked me up off my feet before he led me to where my parents and the rest of my family were waiting.

I got to spend a couple of seconds with Mark and it was so strange. I don't really know what I expected. I thought it would be like the movies with the music in the background. But it wasn't. It was just "What's up, how ya been?" I just fell right back in sync with my little brother like I had been gone a day or two. As I made my way back to my parents, everyone was thanking us. The news crews kept trying to get an interview with me. I figured it was no big deal until a reporter shoved a camera in my face. I started backing away, but Mark explained to me I had to stay there to get the right visual effects, but it felt like an inch from my face. As I walked towards the field house, the reporter kept asking me questions. I just wanted to talk to my brother and cousin, Ryan. I told the guy that I was finished talking to him and he got the hint. I was so determined to get in that building and see my family.

The shit bags who went home were there to greet us and I wanted to spit on them. We didn't care to see the soldiers who didn't go either. We just wanted to be together and see our families. One soldier who went home early because his back was supposedly so bad came up behind me, picked me up off the ground and spun me around. I just looked at him and thought, wow, his back sure healed quickly.

I still wasn't excited until I saw my friend, Gene, a retired Air Force colonel. He's so tall he easily spotted me in the crowd. He then came over, grabbed and hugged me. It was so good to see him because before I was deployed, he was someone I really leaned on to talk to about my fears and excitement. He drove all the way from Dayton just so he could come and say hi to me for ten minutes. I gave him a huge hug back and then he grabbed my arm and pushed through the crowd so I could see my family. We ran to the back of the field house and there I saw my parents. I started sprinting toward them. I had been fantasizing about that day for a month, often wondering who I was going to hug first. My mom tore through the crowd and gave me the biggest hug. All that thinking and fantasizing and my mom made the choice for me!

I was surrounded by the people who had come to see me. My aunt and my godmother brought me flowers. My uncles from Cleveland came. I didn't think it was that big of a deal, but since they had supported each other through this and they had been dealing with it for a whole year, they came to see it through. They were there more for my mom and dad, and I thought it was amazing that they were a part of it.

They shooed us into a room where we get to see our families for fifteen minutes before they whisked us away for a grand ceremony. We wanted to announce that if they really wanted to thank us, they'd get the hell out of the way and let us be with our families.

I sat next to Elaine during the ceremony. We talked through the whole thing, but we clapped when it was necessary. Mark said our company was clapping in unison, but really it was a disrespectful "fuck you" we were giving. Then came the awarding of the Purple Heart and I thought oh, God, not the damn Purple Heart thing. They made the eight or nine of us stand up. Elaine pushed me back up after I sat down and everyone started to stand up and the applause was explosive. I felt like such an ass. Meanwhile, all the people from my platoon were making fun of me.

When we left the field house, I felt a calm excitement. When I was home on leave, it was good to see everyone, but there was so much tension. This time, it was so relaxing to know that we had the rest of our lives to deal with it. My mom didn't feel the same way. She wouldn't let go of my arm. In fact, everyone who loves me had to touch me. Even at work, my boss hugged me and had to hold my hand the first few times he saw me. My co-worker's did it, too. For a while, it was as if everyone had to touch us to make sure we were really there.

The first time I was out in civilization with my family again was at an Applebee's. Everyone started clapping when we walked in. There were other people there from our unit, so it was embarrassing, but they did it for each of us as we filed in. People wanted to come up and thank us and buy us drinks, but I just didn't feel like we deserved it. We did our jobs and we didn't expect people to go out of their way to thank us. It was just an everyday thing that we did, so we were surprised and didn't really know how to act.

When we got back to my parents' house that night I was freezing. I sat shivering with a heating pad. We had family in and out; it was pretty low-key. My parents went to a class on "Reuniting with your Soldier," so they were super-sensitive about making sure they were doing what I wanted. They kept asking me "Are you alright?" and "Do you feel normal?" and I'm thinking why are they being so nice and giving me all of these choices?

The first full day I was home, I went with my mom to get a haircut at Matthews at the square in Medina and to Panara to get coffee. I was worn out. I wanted to make Mom happy, so I was doing a lot for her benefit, but I was exhausted. We ended up going shopping and then I got to take a bath. I was still trying to get over the fact that I was finally a civilian and didn't have to be around all of the same people.

One of the best things I did in my first few days home was go to the grocery store with my dad. Sounds exciting I know, but it's one of my favorite memories. I looked at all of the food and thought about how I could have anything I wanted. I had choices. I could get fresh fruit instead of old fruit that had been sitting around somewhere for a while. I could get vegetables and make my own salad. I could create my own meal and decide what went into my body instead of eating what the military provided. I am a frequent visitor to the grocery store these days. I love food again.

Food seemed to be the best way to re-introduce myself into the social world, too. Everyone wanted to reconnect with me when I got home and food was the best way to do that because everyone always wanted to go out to breakfast, dinner or for drinks. I felt like a mooch, but I ate everything in sight.

Another thing I did right away was set up all the doctors' appointments that I couldn't do over there. I went to the dentist, my doctors, a chiropractor and every one I could think of just to make sure I was healthy. It felt so good to get my teeth cleaned after a year and a half. Finally, I had some control over my own body and how to take care of it. My health was my second or third priority over there, which is sad when I think about it now.

During the first week I was home, the local spa, Trillium, told my mom that they wanted to give me a complementary day at the spa. That included a massage, manicure, pedicure, facial and makeup. I was quiet and skittish. I felt like a beaten dog that was around people for the first time. I wasn't sure how to act and I felt out of place. But they treated me like a princess and I loved every minute of it.

Another culture shock—in more ways than one—was how the music being played on the radio had changed. I didn't know any of it. Music is such a big part of my life and not knowing anything on the radio made me feel like a stranger, as though I didn't fit in again. I will say my taste in music has changed, though. I listen to more Led Zeppelin, Grateful Dead and the Beatles now, thanks in large part to JD. That stuff helped us relax and it was what JD and I both could agree on.

My dad's taste in music changed as well. We were in the car one day and for some reason, he likes rap now. I found that to be a fascinating twist of events since I had been gone. He started singing all of these songs to me and I was wondering who in the hell is this man? My fifty-two-year-old father knew all the rap music and the cool songs, and I had no clue about them. So he began educating me on who was popular and which songs they sang. Within the first month, I knew all of the songs on the radio and they had become old news.

My mom and dad were so much more technically advanced than I was, too. They were texting each other and I had no idea what that meant.

My body went through a big adjustment being home. Going from a dry environment to a normal one made my skin feel strange and I broke out like a teenager. My hair felt so dry and even my hairdresser pointed out my dry scalp. I used dandruff shampoo, but nothing worked. It took about two months to return to normal.

Driving was another experience for me when I got home. When I was home on leave, I was driving my Oldsmobile Alero as though I was still in a big truck, so people got pretty pissed off when I cut them off in traffic and bullied them out of their lane. I got into a screaming match with some guy on the interstate and I was waving my hands all over the place with my mom in the car. She's thinking, what in the hell are you doing? This guy was in this big semi and I was acting like I still was, too.

I have to remind myself that I don't always have the right of way. I try to be more cautious at lights and intersections. My car is a hell of a lot more comfortable than the truck, though. I don't have to wear a flak vest, I'm not in a convoy and I can drive alone. Bumps on the road were so much smoother than in the semi where I'd have to brace myself in anticipation.

People don't understand how nice it is to have personal space. Everyone keeps asking me if I'm lonely, but I am perfectly content being alone. I had been living on top of people for so long that it was nice to have time to myself.

Another unexpected surprise was the cost of gas. Over there, people use it to water down the dust and the sand. Their fuel is like our water. They would kill for a bottle of water and they waste gas like it was nothing. It was strange when I actually had to pay for a tank of gas instead of just pulling up to the stand and going on my way.

After spending four days at home, I snapped. I still didn't feel like I was home because I hadn't been to my house in Dayton, so I packed up the car and hit the road. I felt like a transient for a year and a half and I just wanted to go to my home. My mom said she understood, but I knew she was disappointed. I called my roommate to tell her I was coming home and when I arrived, she helped me carry everything into the house. She didn't hound me with a bunch of questions, which was nice. I barely knew her, but after talking with her, I knew I had left the house in capable hands. She took care of everything for me.

I stayed the night there and then went back to Cleveland for my umpteenth party. My parents were so excited that I was back. For the first two weeks, I kept announcing everything I was about to do because I felt like I needed permission. Anything from taking a bath to running to the store required an explanation. I did the same thing when I got back to Dayton. I didn't really respond well to people. I was emotionless and reserved. I've never been like that. I'm usually joking around and bubbly, but I was afraid to be like that. I felt like a stranger in my family's house.

My dad planned a trip to Daytona Beach, Florida for "Bike Week" when I got home. We termed it our "daddy-daughter week" and it was all he talked about. But unfortunately for me, we had to drive on his motorcycle. From the last month in Iraq until the trip to Daytona, my back was in excruciating pain. I knew my dad had been looking forward to this trip, so I sucked it up and went. It was miserable. We biked all the way to Daytona Beach, which was a good thing because I didn't feel like talking. I was still in a quiet mood. I started to loosen up and my dad didn't push me about what happened over there. We hung out all week, just me and my dad. Once we got to Daytona, we had an amazing time. It was funny because my dad had just spent a winter in Cleveland and all he wanted to do was sit outside in the sunny weather. I had spent a year outside and all I wanted to do was sit inside a building.

My mom and I decided we needed a getaway together, too, and planned a trip to Nashville. She exploited my Iraq-vet status and got us a beautiful room at Opryland. She mentioned the Purple Heart and they treated us like royalty. We were in a suite that normally costs $400 a night for only $99. We drove down to Nashville, too, but my mom was a little more understanding about my back pain. We drove to my house in Dayton for one leg of the trip and then to Nashville so we could drive in shifts.

After the two trips, I felt like my obligations to my parents were finally over. No matter what, I wanted to reserve some time just for them because they were the ones who were so wonderful through the whole deployment.

While I was on vacation with one of my parents, the City of Dayton presented awards to the ten of us who had gone overseas. Marie accepted it on my behalf because I couldn't attend. The mayor had a special ceremony just for us. I couldn't believe all the attention I was getting.

A few weeks after we got home, the Valley City VFW Post 5563 threw us a party and made us lifetime members. It was nice to bring us into the community. Elaine and I were the first women inducted into the VFW in our hometown. They weren't sure how to take us at first because we were females who knew everything about weapons. They adjusted, though. They gave us T-shirts, sweatshirts and anything they could think of to make us feel like a part of their group, which we really appreciated. I finally understand how important the old vets are to us. They know what we've been through and many, like the Vietnam vets, weren't supported when they came home so they were determined to welcome and take care of us.

The one thing I couldn't wait to do when I got home was to prepare a meal. I don't even like to cook, but over there I daydreamed about cooking a real meal from scratch. When I got back to Dayton, I still didn't cook a meal for myself very often because I had a roommate who liked to cook, but I know I eat healthier food now. Over there, food was only as fresh as the latest shipment. It was strange to once again eat salad that wasn't brown. The camps up north got the first choices for food. They got the Cap'n Crunch and the Cocoa Puffs because they were the people who were in more danger. I didn't mind because I thought they should get the more of the comforts of home.

I've decided I have to work out to stay in shape so I don't get fat since my work isn't as physical now. Since I've been home everyone keeps telling me I've lost a significant amount of weight and I really haven't. My clothes fit the same as when I left. I'm probably more fit and I might have an ass now because of all the climbing, but I'm the same. Everyone was convinced that I had changed somehow. My neighbor told me how skinny I am now and how fat I was before. There has to be some dramatic change in me for them, but I haven't changed. So, since I haven't changed physically, people think I must be suffering from post-traumatic stress or that I'm crazy or something. No one seems to understand that I could've gone through the war, dealt with the changes and accepted them. There has to be something wrong with me. It's amazing that I have to convince people that I'm normal.

Here's a big secret: Most people who have been to war don't like to talk about it. Most people think that's because it's too stressful to think about, but the truth is we're sick of talking about it. We just want to be normal again.

I was home for a week in Dayton when my neighbors welcomed me. I knew they didn't want to rush over and hound me. Plus, it was the end of winter and you don't really see much of the neighbors during the winters in Ohio. Just after the last snow of the season, one neighbor saw me and waved. As I waved back, all of my neighbors slowly started to emerge from their cocoons to welcome me back. My roommate laughed because she said she hadn't seen any of them in months.

One of my neighbors is from India and his wife is from America. She invited me over for dinner one night and we got to talking about politics and culture. It was nice to come back and have a conversation about something I had seen and experienced firsthand, as I had worked with people from Egypt, Pakistan, the Philippines and India over there. I had a taste of their culture and I could participate more in the conversation.

My old next-door neighbors took me out to eat when I got home. They have two kids that I love to death. When I saw them for the first time, they each handed me a bouquet of flowers and it was the sweetest thing. They were telling everyone, "She's back from war, she's back from war." My new next-door neighbor has been helpful, power washing the house for me, hanging dry wall and moving wood out of the garage. We took turns working on each other's houses for a while.

For the first time in two years, I finally felt like I was home. With the money I squirreled away while I was over there, I had enough to fix up my house and make repairs. I had two weeks before I had to be back to work so I ripped the house apart. I replaced counter tops, fixed the basement steps, replaced the driveway, built a deck and manicured the yard to look pretty again.

After three months, the mounds of boxes that cluttered my house were finally unpacked. It was weird to live in a house again with walls and running water and fresh towels under the bathroom sink. And I had a real bed! There were so many little things I missed while I was in the desert. I daydreamed a lot about coming home while I was there. I thought a lot about my house and my community, coming back to them and wondering what that would feel like. It was hard to accept that I was really home for good.

After being back for three months, I finally started to kick the cough that followed me home. When I was on leave, I felt like I had a big weight on my chest because I couldn't breathe due to my allergies. I developed a constant cough because I wasn't used to the moist, damp air. I was coughing all the time, especially in the morning, but then it finally started to go away.

Before I went back to work, I went to see my friend Julie at the Bureau of Disabilities in Columbus. She was my college roommate and we emailed each other all the time before I left. I missed her and wanted to see her as soon as possible, but she told me I had to give twenty-four hours notice for clearance. When I got there, Julie had everyone wear construction paper purple hearts and they all made me sign them. They had pictures of me on the camel and some other embarrassing things. I was just so glad to finally see my friend.

My attitude was upbeat when I got home, but within a short time, the shininess began to wear off and reality took hold. I was in a lot of pain from my back and it was catching up with me. I wasn't able to sleep without moving in the middle of the night and waking up. I was tired and tired even more of trying to prove I was normal. I had to put on a show for everyone so they wouldn't worry about me. It was exhausting.

My first day back at work, I wasn't sure if I was allowed to be there because I didn't know if the paperwork went through. I had been into work to see everyone and every time I went in, everyone kept hugging me. We decided we should probably stop all of that when I returned to work.

At work, my coworkers were amazing. I didn't realize how good they were to me until I heard stories from other people. They held my job for me. My supervisor, who is like a father to me, kept asking me if I was all right and if I needed anything. He let me decide when I wanted to go back to work, but I was even more surprised when he asked me what I wanted my job to be. He wanted to tap into my skills from the Guard, like dealing with large groups, planning and organization. So I thought, hmm, what do I want to do? In addition, he needed help with his job because he was always overloaded and short staffed.

Before I went back to work, my co-workers met with the father of one of our interns to determine how to treat me when I was back at work. He's a counselor at the Veteran's Administration and he had a lot of information for returning soldiers, their families and friends. He told them not to make a big deal out of me being home and to treat me as they had before I left. Other than displaying a natural excitement, they didn't ask a lot of questions like everyone else and I didn't feel like part of a freak show. I was allowed to be a regular worker.

I went to one of my first meetings and didn't know whether to talk or not. When I walked into the meeting, they hugged me and we got down to business. I really appreciated that because there are so many different people to whom you have to reintroduce yourself. It was nice when it wasn't a big deal for a change. I just wanted to focus on my job. I don't tell people I was over there anymore unless I need to. If I'm with my dad, he makes sure everyone around us knows I was over there and that I got a Purple Heart. We'll be at dinner and the waitress will ask for the order and he'll say, "I'd like a burger and my daughter got a Purple Heart." My mom does that, too. What can I say? They're parents.

They had already set up my office in the new building and I was so grateful that a part of my life was organized before I arrived. It really made coming back to work a joy. I thought I wouldn't have anything to do, but they threw me right back into the routine.

Regaining my professionalism was a learning curve for me. Instead of "mother effing" everyone, I had to remember where I was and remember how to express myself without swearing. The whole business atmosphere was a lot different from where I had been. I wanted to start hanging out with my co-workers more because I wanted to remember the professional side of myself. I would hate to be sitting in a mediation and swear or say something ridiculous that the civilian world would not tolerate. Also, I couldn't be as blunt or assertive as I was overseas. I had to figure out a way to add some finesse and polish to my requests. Instead of saying, "Do it now because I said so, damn it," I have to ask, "Could you please…"

It was exhausting trying to work with my hands again, figuring out what to do, acting professional, remembering my job and what I was trained to do. It was like learning everything all over again. In the Army, our job was twenty-four hours a day. Here, work is condensed into eight hours a day. I have to focus to finish everything by the end of the workday.

My boss introduced me as the poster child for the war in Iraq for a while. He would introduce me to people, tell them I had been over there and that I earned a Purple Heart. I was embarrassed at first, but I then I realized he was trying to humanize the war experience and let people know that there are problems with safety and resources for the soldiers.

199

Still, there were more changes to adjust to at work. Trisha, who had replaced me, had a baby; another co-worker, Janet, got married; my supervisor had been to Japan and his father died while I was gone; Cherise lost weight and looked so different; and I missed all of it. It was incredible to see all of the changes. Sometimes it was overwhelming to realize how long I had been gone. I had to see Trisha's baby before I would believe she was a mom. She looked like she did before I left and I missed the whole pregnancy. One volunteer in her sixties had plastic surgery while I was gone. She had her eyes done and a tummy tuck and it felt to me like she was under the knife the whole time. I saw her in the grocery store one day and I barely recognized her. She looked like a version of herself that was ten years younger.

I don't know any of the restaurants around work anymore. We used to go to a soup and salad place that a guy named Jim owned. He sold it while I was overseas and now the place I had such a connection to was gone. It was awful because he made these great chicken sandwiches and tortilla soup. It was as though none of the food I craved over there existed anymore.

I forgot people in Dayton read my letters, too. People come up to me out of nowhere and think they know me because of my letters. I have to pretend it's nice to see them again and I don't even know who they are. They feel so close to me that one woman even gave me a kiss on the cheek. Sometimes I get embarrassed because the letters were so personal and revealed an entirely different side of my personality.

I've been getting a lot of free lunches because everyone wants to hear about my experiences. But they're really not free. They want something for it. But I don't think they really get what they're looking for. I tell them about the people over there. I'm so sick of people asking me if I had to fire my gun or kill someone. There's so much more going on over there that people are unaware of, like the conditions and the people we helped over there.

I find it odd that they don't show anything good about the war on the news. All the American public sees are the bombings and the people dying. They don't see what we've done. I have to look on the Internet. Nothing has changed over there. You can see how the news sways things. They're not showing that it's consistent over there. I noticed the same thing on leave. I thought things were getting really bad over there, but it turns out, everything was the same when I got back.

I've also developed a strange connection with Vietnam veterans. A man at my church who I barely knew came up to me and said, "I know"; that's all he had to say. People who have been there understand and you don't have to say anything. When I talk to Desert Storm and Vietnam vets, they tell me they didn't get the support we do. We received counseling, dentist visits and anything we asked for while most veterans before us were just looking for acceptance and a society who cared about them.

Michelle at the city of Ur

- *16* -

Aftermath

S ome things I remember about war and some things I've forgotten. Every now and again something reminds me of something that happened over there. It's good to see my Guard buddies so we can tell each other the stories; they understand so much better than those who didn't go. Some things stayed the same, others changed, and I had to relearn them.

Men surrounded me over there and I think I'm a little gruffer now. Maybe it's the military mentality, but I just feel like I'm more blunt with everyone. I know I have to watch it because society doesn't accept it here, so I try to tone it down. One day at work, a guy said something and I just wanted to shout "motherfucker" at him. I thought the city I worked for might frown on that, so I contained myself, but I'm definitely a lot more assertive at work. I've learned to speak up for myself more. No one really taught me that; I sort of stumbled into it. I knew if I didn't open my mouth over there, people would take advantage of me. I'm more confident now and not because I made it through war, but because I made the unpopular, tough decisions over there and put myself on the line.

Being around guys all the time didn't mean I always talked to them, although it was kind of hard to avoid them. Only about ten percent of our military was female and the guys were starved for female attention. I'm not necessarily talking about sex, although I'm not excluding it. It was just obvious that the softer side of life was missing over there. If you made eye contact with a guy over there, he would instantly run over and start talking or just stare and try to make a connection. When I walked around the camp, it was eyes forward and the bitchiest look I could give so they wouldn't talk to me. If I did that, they left me alone; if I smiled, I was prey. When I got home, I couldn't shake that habit. I walked around town eyes forward with that same look.

In the chow halls, I could feel the eyes on me. There were groups in there that had been six months in the desert with all males and they would come to our chow hall and eat. They would just stare and they couldn't even help it. They weren't trying to be rude or act like pigs; they just hadn't seen a woman in a long time. I would make eye contact and give them the "Hello, you're staring at me look," and they just kept staring. Most of the time, I would just leave.

When I got home, I was at a CVS pharmacy one day when the guy behind the counter said, "Hello, how are you?" It felt so weird to be treated like a human being. He didn't give me that desperate look and the weird vibe that I had experienced for so long. I just smiled at him and thought how I had forgotten civilians were like that. After that, I started to relax and tried to be more friendly to people.

Instead of going to smoky bars and partying all over town, I'd rather have a cookout in my backyard. I don't like big groups anymore. I now prefer a small, intimate get-together rather than going to a noisy restaurant. Of course, part of that is because I've lost some hearing. I have this ringing in my ears that won't go away. When it's quiet, all I hear is this humming noise. I think they call it tinnitus. When I'm in a crowded bar, I can't even hear if someone is talking to me.

My sense of humor is so warped now. I laugh at things that aren't really funny. It freaks my dad out. He always tells me I should feel sad and I don't. Problems aren't as big as they used to be. When you're in a situation for so long where it's life and death, you just don't worry about the small stuff anymore. You just deal with it and move on. Even the tasks I dreaded doing before don't seem so bad. Cleaning behind my nasty steps in the basement or power washing the porch, it's all just so easy now. Knowing I'm working on my house rather than a job some general wants done makes those kinds of chores much easier and they mean a lot more now.

Elaine and Willy were over one day and we were joking around and making fun of each other the same way we did in Iraq. My mom overheard us and she was so upset at how mean they were being to me. I told her, "Mom, you don't understand and you don't understand the environment we were in." My whole family had to get used to it. My friends did, too. People started telling me that I shouldn't be so brutally honest and abrasive. They were telling me to be sensitive to people and I really had to rethink the way I talked to others.

I've been out on a few dates since I've been home. My boyfriend of only about a month moved on while I was away. We knew each other from high school and met up when I was staying with my parents before going to war. He was a Marine and understood being deployed. I didn't expect it to last and one day after my last mission into Iraq I called him. He acted funny on the phone and the next day I got a "Dear Jane" email. I laughed. It wasn't a big surprise getting dumped when I was too busy to call and had an over-the-phone/letter relationship.

Dating now is difficult anyway. I don't give a shit about all the small talk and polite talk. It frustrates me to sit through that kind of conversation and I'd rather talk about something real or important than crap. Guys also want to take care of me. I'm much more independent now and don't want to be taken care of. I want an equal. After a few bad dates, I just got frustrated and stopped. It was also difficult to figure out how to act again on a date. I felt like a Neanderthal after spending time with all my guys. It's amazing I can make complete sentences now.

The focus has become work and school. Every now and again I think I'm ready to date so I'll give a guy my number and when he calls, I don't answer. Or, if he asks me out, I make up excuses as to why I can't go. I think in my head, oh that guy called four times before he gave up; the guy last week called three times. I have a numbing and emotionless attitude. It's just annoying that I've changed so much and wish that part of me remained the same. I'm jealous of those carefree people who just enjoy life. I want to be that person again. I don't care about settling down and having a family anymore. I feel like that ship has sailed. I feel too old and run down to try to bring life into this world. I am numb at this point, a year after the war.

I've noticed I'm really quiet and more guarded. I don't want to share a lot and several people have made the comment that I'm so quiet. I didn't realize I was doing it, but they did. It pisses me off that I've changed in that way because I used to be friendly and outgoing and now I'm not. So many things have changed.

I've become an organization freak. Over there, I had to keep track of everything. I had a bed and I had to pack all of my belongings around that little area. It was the size of a twin bed by about four feet. Now that I'm home, I feel like everything has to be organized. I've sorted boxes and tubs for storage, my toiletries are all in order. My roommate must think I'm crazy. She has a little bit of clutter somewhere and I clean up and organize everything right behind her. But that's just another lasting result of the war.

My attitude toward my friends who didn't go over there with me also took a turn. I was so self-absorbed over there that I was really angry with them for not going. All I could think about was what I was going through and it was hard to have any compassion toward them. One of my friends got married

205

and I was mad at her for not waiting until I came back. I mean I was really mad at her. We talked about being in each other's weddings for so long and when it came down to it, not only did she not go to war, she got married without me. She got out of going to Iraq at the last second and I was angry that I was there and she was home getting married. When I got home, she called to say hi and it took everything in me to call her back after she had called about five times. Then when I thought about it, I realized that must have been a difficult decision for her, too. She had to stay back and take care of her daughter. She could've gone, but I guess I understand it now. She had to leave the military and lost all of her friends along the way. I was a little more mature about the situation when I finally swallowed my pride and called her. She was in Desert Storm, so it's been a relief to talk to her because she can relate to being rigid toward men and the other things I've had to face. I've learned not to be so critical of the people who made the equally hard decision not to go.

I think my experience grounded me and gave me more personal strength, but it's not for the reasons people think. People think I'm that way because I faced "the enemy," but that was the only thing that made sense over there. I had to stand up for myself, especially as a woman. I've always been the type to try to accommodate everyone, but over there, I learned how to say no to people. I remember one time, there were Egyptians loading my truck and of course, they were completely chauvinist against women in the military. They were loading a palette of water. It was a tricky mess because you had to get the best palettes or the water would leak all over. So when they tried to give me the shittiest palette, I put my foot down and told them to stick it. When one of them started telling me he didn't understand English, I jumped down off my truck and yelled, told him to get that fucking palette off there now and caused a scene. I figured I had to deal with my guys; I wasn't about to take his shit.

I still talk to most of the people I went to Iraq with. We use each other to bounce questions off each other like "Do you feel this way?" and "Does this happen to you?" One of the benefits of being a reservist and going to Iraq with 152 people is coming home at the same time and then returning to a normal environment. Some of the military people went from an environment of being an enlistee to suddenly being home and alone with no military structure and no friends to talk to. I'm lucky because we're all home together and we can talk to each other about being over there.

April 11, 2005

It was the one-year anniversary of the ambush in Iraq. Before we left there, I got SGT Huff and SGT Hawk's phone numbers and I felt it important to call

206

them on the one-year anniversary and thank them for saving my life. I called and wished them both a happy April 11th and thanked them for giving me the next April 11th. Some of my friends wanted to go out, but I wanted to stay in. I sat there and processed everything that had happened that day. It had been one year and I was alive and safe. I made it. Short of getting hit by a bus, I am hopeful that I will live a long and full life, but Easter will never be the same for me.

Every year for Easter, I would write obscene messages on the eggs just to shock my mom. But that first year back, I wrote, "Glad to be home" and "Glad to be here" on all of my eggs. Of course, we wrote obscene things on everyone else's eggs just to keep it real.

These days I'm grateful for the training we went through in the Army. I never thought I would use it. It took me months to realize it was real and people were trying to kill us. It's an odd feeling to know someone actually tried to kill me and I couldn't understand why. I had to tell myself we were in their country and they're trying to kill us because that's what they do for whatever reason. We were de-humanized enemies to them and they were the same to us.

About six months after I was home, I started having nightmares. Some nightmares were about the war and others about my family getting hurt. It became a nightly ordeal. I stopped sleeping all the way through the night, partly because of my back and partly because of the nightmares. I finally broke down and told one of my close friends who had gone overseas with me. He admitted that he started having nightmares around the same time. At the next drill, I asked everyone about the nightmares and many people had experienced them around the same time. After knowing I wasn't the only crazy one, I started relaxing and they have stopped for now.

During Easter of 2005, I was on vacation with my mom and we stopped at my house in Dayton on the way back to my parents' house. My mom was standing in the doorway and I had a bag in my hand. I was coming into the kitchen and someone let off fireworks. I dropped to the ground, duck-walked on my hands and feet and went to cover my mom and pull her into safety. When I realized what I was doing, I tried to pretend like she didn't see it, and she just looked at me and pretended not to notice. It sounded just like gunshots and I forgot where I was for a second. It took me back to the place where it was instinct to duck and get behind something.

The Guard

Their new name should be the Army "Everything-We-Tell-You-Is-A- Lie" National Guard. The whole experience was one "change in policy" after another. I'm fed up with the inconsistency and the "I guarantee it" statements that would change midstream. One example was when the Guard was supposed to give us ninety days off when we returned from Iraq. I got a newsletter in the mail shortly after I got home. Any time I get anything from them, my blood just starts to boil and I don't understand how they can continue to do this to us and lie to us. People had vacations and we were supposed to have ninety days off, but we had to go back to drill twenty-one days early because someone who didn't go overseas decided that was way too much time for us and we didn't need it. Motherfuckers! We did need that time. People had families to spend time with, people planned cruises and all sorts of things during their "guaranteed" time off. I told all of my soldiers to go on their trips and to hell with the Guard. I'll probably get in trouble for saying that, but they needed that time and it was taken away once again. Then they sent us this blasé newsletter like it was no big deal, but someone should have seen it as a big deal. That's why there is poor retention, because of everything they did to us. After I got the newsletter, I hopped in the car to find another unit. I figured that as long as I hated the Guard, I might as well hate it two miles from my house rather than two and a half hours away.

I went to a friend of mine in the Guard and asked him to help me, and to keep it quiet so I could transfer. It became a huge ordeal and once I calmed down, I decided to stay with my Guard family. I love my comrades and would miss them too much if I transferred. We look each other in the eyes and there is a bond that is indescribable. These are people that I will have connections to for the rest of my life. As reservists, we are still benefiting from each other. We all went to war together, came home together, live nearby and still support each other. In other branches of the military, they don't have that luxury. They move from base to base, not knowing what everyone around them has really experienced; but we do.

When I signed up for the reserves, it was with the understanding that I, a member of the National Guard, was a last resort if anything went terribly wrong. We were thrown into the regular rotation without a thought. There are so many marriages suffering because of the fifteen months we were gone. When you're an active duty soldier, it's with the understanding there will be a lot of time away. In the reserves, many were full-time spouses. Now these women are coming home from war with this newfound independence and some of their husbands feel inadequate. They're finding it hard to be intimate because there is a distance you create for yourself in the military. For the men, the main problem was that they felt useless. Their wives had taken over the things they were used to handling.

A big problem for me was that I wasn't used to being around children when I got home. I got nervous around their laughing and crying in the beginning. It just stressed me out and I didn't know how to handle it. Now I question whether I will ever be able to handle having my own children because I don't want to have to deal with the responsibility of taking care of them and the worry that someday they might have to go to war.

I understand the need for reservists and a full-time military. We need protection for our nation. But I don't believe in the mismanagement of the situation I was in. There was so much wasted money and misused resources that it's hard to respect and support the people running the war.

Was it worth it?

Weighing the pros and cons, I still can't figure out if it was worth it or not, but it seems like there was a hell of a lot more sacrifice than reward. I'm a positive person so I can find the good in what I went through. For instance, I made some money. But I also got wounded, partially lost my hearing, hurt my back and put my family through hell. I think it's my fault they had to go through that. I'm pretty jaded about the military and what our government is doing over there. My outlook is so different and I just want to yell at the world about what's really going on. I think many people don't know because they are shielded or guarded from the truth and it's not right. Everyone should know what's going on.

But then I think about the kids I used to see walking to school with cute little backpacks. A lot of them learned to speak English. It wasn't just the boys going to school by the time I left either. It was boys and girls. They were finally on an even playing field. Well not quite, but coming from a country where women sit in the back of trucks with the cattle, it was a big step. It was so depressing to see little girls and women being treated in such a demeaning way. Some of the men didn't even care about them. It was almost like slavery. I support any group going there to educate women and hopefully men too. I hope I can use my experience to educate others so they will reach out to those who do not have the benefits that our society takes for granted.

I know more about myself now. Even though I don't ever want to be put in another situation like that, I know I can take care of myself if it does happen. There were things over there that I was able to do that I'm still proud of. I'm proud that I had the decency to take care of our civilian truck drivers and make sure they were fed every night. I'm proud that I gave the kids food and candy and treated them—and all of the Iraqi people—like human beings. Being able to see the Iraqi women from their perspective, I have tried to tell others in the States how they were treated and educate people about the Iraqi culture. As difficult as my experience was over there, I hope I can make something positive out of it.

I was able to use my skills through writing about what the soldiers were going through instead of what the news was reporting. I was able to shine a different light on the situation. I got to explain that we were giving kids shoes and socks and helping people over there.

I feel more alive having been through this. My emotions are clearer. I love being with my family and friends. I want to tell everyone how I feel and make sure they know. Everything for the past year was so depressing and so emotionless, it just takes your soul away. But to come home and be able to rebuild your soul is a blessing and a gift. I still feel that way.

Thoughts after being home for a while

It was rough to adjust back to my civilian life. I tried and tried to "prove" to everyone that I was normal and unfazed by the war and the experience didn't change me. This made adjusting even more difficult. It took so much energy to convince everyone that I was okay. I made light of how hard it was to adjust back to my life. Six months after returning from the deployment, I had lost ten pounds, down from 115 pounds to 105. Nothing fit, my clothes, my jewelry, nothing. I brought each of my immediate family a puzzle ring from Iraq, and one would fall off my finger if I hung my hands to my sides. My brand-new clothes that I bought for work and casual wear did not fit. I looked sickly. I had trouble eating. Sleeping throughout the night was out of the question. At the six-month mark, I began having terrible nightmares and they wouldn't stop. Of course I lied to my mom and told her I was sleeping just fine. I was miserable inside and broken on the outside. My back was not getting better either. I decided to take the Army's suggestions for dealing with "combat stress" and seek counseling, and began exercising, resting and working. Nothing was making me feel normal and I was frustrated. What else could I do? I followed their guidance to the tee and it wasn't helping. I expected results.

It was only after I admitted that it was truly difficult to adjust and not as easy as I made it out to be or tried to believe, did I start to heal. I also learned that the person I was before the war was no longer alive. I've changed and cannot contort myself into that other person. I have to learn to live with the new me. The nightmares stopped, I learned that by being open and honest, more soldiers from my unit opened up and talked about their own personal struggles. One day I broke down and told Schrack that I was losing my mind. I told him everything that was going on and he just laughed. He was struggling with similar things. Finally, someone understood and I could take my first deep breath. It felt good not to be alone and least I had a friend who was as crazy as I was. Joking about how crazy I am has made healing possible. When people ask, I try to be as honest as I can with where I'm at in this adjustment process and that seems to help.

When I got home, I was fed up with the military. I wanted out and fast. My disgust with the military has subsided a little, but not enough to reenlist. In July 2006, I had been in the military twelve years and that was enough for me. I feel I've given enough to my country through military service. Now that the dust has settled, I've been able to sift out the good and the bad from my deployment to Iraq. When I first got home, people would ask me if I had the chance to do it over, would I? My immediate response was NO. Now I have to think about the answer to that question.

There is still so much violence and I have not seen any positive developments in Iraq in such a long time. I hope it wasn't all in vain. I hope the sacrifices that my fallen brothers and sisters have made won't be wasted. I also see that there are people who have exploited this war and are making a fortune from an awful, painful situation. My eyes are now opened and I'm less naïve about what is going on in the world.

But there are so many good things that came from this experience. I am so much closer to my family and friends. I had no idea I would have such amazing support from my community either. I learned that even in a place filled with hate, I had enough personal strength to treat people with compassion and empathy.

I've learned that you have to trust people and you can't do it all on your own. Everybody needs help at times. Now I know that there are so many people I went to war with for whom I have a deep connection and know they are there for me and I'm there for them, one hundred percent. Those people will be friends for life. I wouldn't trade that for the world.

I was also able to see a part of the world that I would have never gotten to see if I was not in the military. I got to see Ur, the cradle of civilization. That is a once-in-a-lifetime experience that will be with me forever. So, there is good that came out of my experience.

My life will be influenced forever by this experience. I see through new eyes. This was by far the most challenging experience I've ever been faced with—physically, mentally, emotionally and morally. I have a newfound respect for soldiers throughout history. I now understand the difficulties and challenges that come from war that every vet faces.

And the most profound change is still unfolding as I learn that I am capable of feeling love. I am expecting my first child, a son. Although my initial reaction to the news reflected my conviction for what I thought I had learned about myself, I am now surprised to learn that it is possible for me not only to have an emotion, but to love. I am hopeful that other veterans will find themselves capable of feeling the tingle of an emotion. It may not be immediate for all of us, but it is reassuring to discover that some of the most disturbing effects of war, while they will always be a part of us, will not consume us.

I have a few goals that I would like to accomplish in my lifetime. I want to support soldiers and vets in some way. I appreciated the way the vets supported me when I returned. I am not sure how to go about this, but I believe it will come to me. My next goal is to talk about my experience in Iraq. I want people to see a different perspective of the war, a more personal, human side. Another goal is to support the women of Iraq in some way. I can't go on with my life knowing that these women are so oppressed and not do something about it. Again, I have not figured out how to accomplish this goal but I'm sure it will come to me.

My last goal is to live life to the fullest. Our time here is too short and life is too precious to take for granted. All I can do is go on one day at a time and see what happens. So for now, I'll take a deep breath and live.

On the road somewhere in Iraq

About the Authors

Michelle Zaremba was born in Brook Park and later moved to Valley City, Ohio, where she attended Buckeye Schools. She served in the Ohio Army National Guard from 1994 to 2006 as a Squad Leader in the 1486th Transportation Company. Michelle received a Bachelor of Arts in Applied Conflict Management from Kent State University and a Master of Public Administration from Wright State University. Since 1999, she has worked for the City of Dayton, Ohio, where she currently lives with Nick and their two children, Cole and Caleb.

Christine Sima was born in Cleveland, Ohio, and received a degree in journalism from Kent State University. She worked as a beat reporter for a local newspaper for five years before moving into an editor's role for two national trade publications. She currently lives close to her home town in North Royalton, Ohio.

DISCARD